# ILLUSTRIOUS AMERICANS:
# SAMUEL GOMPERS

*One of a series of books
about great men and women,
each studied in three ways*
**BIOGRAPHY
PICTURE PORTFOLIO
HIS OWN WORDS**

# ILLUSTRIOUS AMERICANS:
# SAMUEL GOMPERS

By Bernard A. Weisberger
and the Editors of Silver Burdett

Editor in Charge: Sam Welles

**SILVER BURDETT COMPANY**
*A Division of General Learning Corporation*
**Morristown, New Jersey** • Park Ridge, Ill. • Palo Alto • Dallas • Atlanta

# CONTENTS

**BIOGRAPHY**      7

1 First Impressions     8

2 Laboring Man, Family Man, Unionist     18

3 Toward a Workable Federation     31

4 Leadership Takes a Middle Course     46

5 Gompers Becomes the Voice of Labor     61

6 The War, the Victory, and the Decline     75

LIBRARY OF CONGRESS CATALOG CARD NUMBER: 67-15872
© 1967 GENERAL LEARNING CORPORATION
ALL RIGHTS RESERVED
PRINTED IN THE UNITED STATES OF AMERICA
PHILIPPINES COPYRIGHT 1967 BY GENERAL LEARNING CORPORATION
PUBLISHED SIMULTANEOUSLY IN CANADA

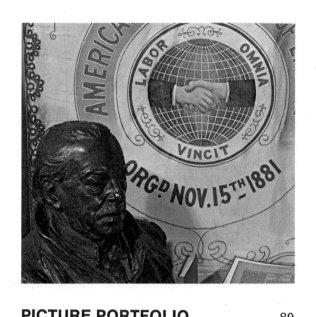

**PICTURE PORTFOLIO** 89

The Industrial Revolution 90

An Anti-Immigration Immigrant 92

The Burgeoning of Industry 96

The New York Gompers Knew 98

Woes of the Workingman 100

The Strife and Striving 104

Symbols of Growing Strength 108

The Varied Relaxations
of a Busy Man 110

Some Rewards of Hard Work 114

Strike and Rift 116

Unionism Now 118

**HIS OWN WORDS** 121

His Youth Remembered 122

Understanding Unionism 130

Politics and Politicians 161

Slow Growth of the AFL 170

The Way He Operated 200

Boycotts and Free Speech 210

The World War and After 220

*Chronology* 230

*Annotated Bibliography* 232

*Index* 235

*Picture Credits* 240

# ACKNOWLEDGMENTS

The biography section of this book was written by Bernard A. Weisberger, Professor of History at the University of Rochester since 1963. Born in Hudson, New York, in 1922, Dr. Weisberger took degrees at Columbia University and the University of Chicago; he has taught at the latter institution as well as at Antioch College and Wayne State University. An authority on American history from the Civil War to the present, his six books dealing with that period include *Reporters for the Union*, *They Gathered at the River*, *The American Newspaperman*, *The Age of Steel and Steam*, and *Reaching for Empire*.

The editors have prepared the boxed observations on Gompers, selected the illustrations, and excerpted about 60,000 words Gompers himself wrote, providing commentary to place each passage in a meaningful context.

Excerpts from the following books have been used with permission: *Samuel Gompers* by Bernard Mandel, Antioch Press, Yellow Springs, Ohio, copyright 1963. *Samuel Gompers—American Statesman* by Florence Calvert Thorne, Philosophical Library, copyright 1957. *Theodore Roosevelt, an Autobiography*, Charles Scribner's Sons, copyright renewed 1941 by Edith K. Carow Roosevelt. Excerpts from *Seventy Years of Life and Labor* by Samuel Gompers are reprinted by arrangement with the publishers, E. P. Dutton & Co., Inc. Copyright 1925 by E. P. Dutton & Co., Inc. Renewal, 1953, by Gertrude Gleaves Gompers.

Mervyn Kaufman was assistant editor for the volume. Henry Moscow wrote the text accompanying the Picture Portfolio. Joan Scafarello did the picture research, while text research was provided by Denise Farrell, Judith Leavitt, and Mara Jayne Klein. Elizabeth Roberts was the copy editor; Venila Drachbar prepared the index.

Designer: Wayne Young

This portrait of Samuel Gompers, painted by Bjorn Egeli, hangs in a position of honor at AFL-CIO headquarters in Washington.

# BIOGRAPHY

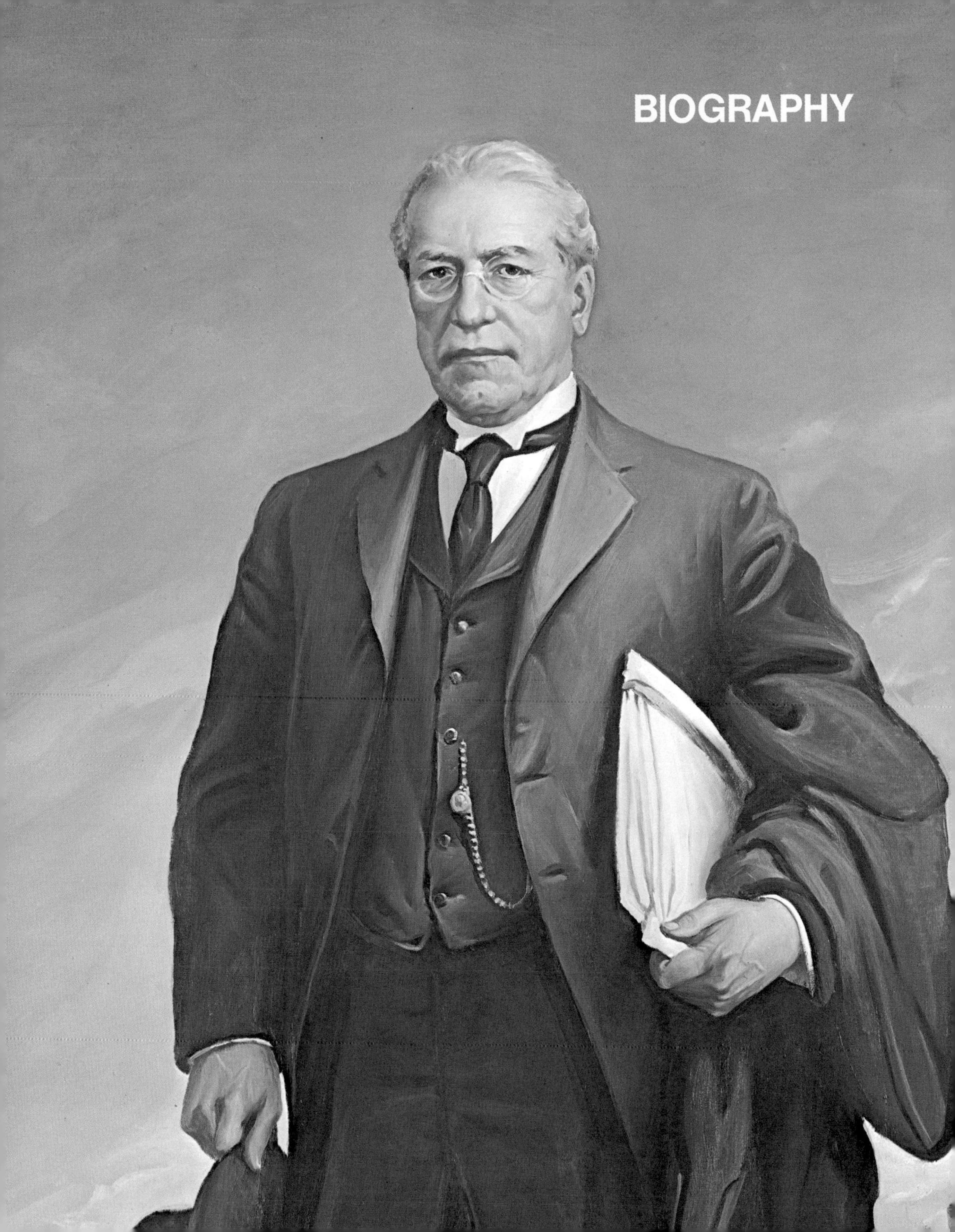

SPITALFIELDS, a rolling meadow dotted with trees and crowned by the ancient priory of St. Mary Spital, lay in the path of England's industrial progress. As London expanded into a center for manufacturing, the pastoral elements of this district receded. The trees were felled one by one, the priory was demolished, and by the mid-nineteenth century not a blade of grass could be seen. Spitalfields, covered now with brick and stone, had become a crazy quilt of factories and tenement houses, alleyways and dark, twisting streets. The first world that Samuel Gompers remembered lay within the confines of this teeming, decaying, poverty-stricken district on the city's east side (see pages 90–91).

It was a memory that did not fade quickly, for Gompers' entire boyhood and youth were shaped by the sights, smells, and sounds of working-class neighborhoods. First he lived in the capital of Victorian England in the 1850's and early 1860's. Then he settled in New York City at the time of the Civil War. Each of these huge cities, grimy and stone-faced, kept its own special sort of school—one that taught hard knocks and heartbreaking realism to the children of the poor. Yet both cities were also living evidence of men's tendency to cluster together. While a quick-witted youngster learned to look out for himself, he also came to realize how much he depended upon other human beings for bread, for shelter, for life itself. The city not only fed its inhabitants on those hard knocks but also bred in them a self-reliance that *could* sour into selfishness. However, it visibly demonstrated, as well, a human interdependence that *could* blossom into brotherhood. Both these aspects of the city, the self-reliance and the brotherhood, had emphatic, permanent meaning for Gompers' life, in New York as well as London.

Samuel Gompers grew up to be a leader of organized labor, a man who never stopped speaking the language of revolutionary idealism—of the brotherhood of all workers every-where. Yet he fought for these ideals on the world's hard terms. He demanded no more than an improvement in labor's material welfare. He was willing to count achievements—often very tiny achievements—day by day, craft by craft, shop by shop. In his own view, and that of his friends, he was a humane visionary. In the eyes of some of his enemies, he was an all-too-cautious conservative. They sharply accused him of being willing to sacrifice dreams of a noble society in the future for a handful of coppers flung to a few skilled workers in the present. Every practical reformer presents history with such contradictory images. In Gompers' case, both images bear a certain resemblance to the truth. He was a man of many loudly conflicting attitudes, all of which could be at least partly explained by the fact that he was raised in the city and destined for the workshop. Quite literally, he was a child of the urban and industrial movements of the nineteenth century.

### A boyhood in London

He began life as an alien, in several senses. He was a Jew and an immigrant's son, born on January 27, 1850, in one of the hundreds of drab brick houses that lined the worn cobblestone streets of Spitalfields (see pages 122–126). The Gompers family had roots in Austria and numbered teachers, rabbis, merchants, and public officials among its forebears. Samuel was a poor relation, however. His branch of the family had settled, years before, at Amsterdam, in Holland. His father's father (also named Samuel), a calico printer by trade, had once quarreled with an employer and thereupon vowed never to work for another man. He went into business for himself as an antique dealer and often visited his son Solomon, who had moved to London in the 1840's and found work as a cigarmaker. Later on, Solomon was joined by his father in the English capital.

Solomon married, and his first son, Samuel, was born. Shortly afterwards, the family moved into a three-story house that young Samuel

This picture of lower Manhattan shows that Gompers' adopted city, unlike his native London, was as yet unscarred by industry.

9

remembered as a building "worn gray with the passing years." There they lived like a biblical household—father Samuel, his wife, and his own five children on the second floor; Solomon, his wife (Sara), and their five (later six) children in two rooms below them; and a Dutchman with his two sons on the third story. The elder Samuel was a patriarch. It was he who had chosen Solomon's bride—that is, he had met her in Amsterdam and brought her to live with London relatives until her marriage to his son. His little grandson and namesake remembered him as a dominating figure, precise in his dress and his accounts, shrewd and informative. He took great delight in gathering his grandchildren together when he returned from business trips to the Continent, and regaling them with stories of his adventures along the way.

Grandfather Gompers could be mellow, and he could also explode into rage when his will was thwarted. For little Samuel, he was very likely an unconscious model for acquiring both self-discipline and leadership of a tempestuous and demanding kind. He was drawn from the pages of the Old Testament in temperament as well as in name.

Little Samuel was exposed to other scriptural elements in his few years of formal education. He attended the Jewish Free School in London's Bell Lane, where the curriculum included such secular subjects as arithmetic and geography. It also contained a good deal of the close-knit legal reasoning of the ancient Hebrew Talmud, a vast work that both comments on, and actually comprises the substance of, traditional Jewish civil and religious law.

Gompers' formal relationship to his Jewish heritage, even in his early years, was slender. His family was "not scrupulously Orthodox," he recalled, though they kept the "important ceremonials." He was not much moved by these rituals, but he appreciated a schooling that offered him, through the study of Hebrew, the key to "a literature of wonderful beauty and wisdom." In later life he neither denied nor practiced his Judaism. Whatever slights he may have known as a Jewish child, he buried within him. Whatever loyalties controlled his life, he insisted on fashioning for himself. His major recollection of his education was simply, and sorrowfully, that there had not been nearly enough of it. Even as a boy, he was beginning to quicken with the characteristic belief of his generation—and his people—that education was the doorway to personal success. But at the age of ten, the door of full-time learning was closed in his face.

From his family's viewpoint, withdrawing him from school was perfectly justifiable. Child labor was the rule then, not the exception, in both Britain and the United States. Solomon Gompers, on his own meager earnings, could not possibly furnish the means for his good Dutch wife to cook her savory meats and thick soups. So he sent his eldest son, Samuel, out to work. The boy was accordingly apprenticed to a shoemaker. As he proved to be unhappy at this work, his father (who seems to have been an amiable, if not a forceful, man) bound him out to a cigarmaker instead, at a wage of sixpence (then about twelve cents) a week. Samuel was left to pick up whatever education he could acquire by his own means, in his scarce free time. Bitter as he was in later life at what he called "the wrong society had done me," Gompers was nonetheless able to learn some lessons in the London streets themselves. For one thing, he had to acquire some skill in brawling, in simple self-defense. For another, there was much to see in the lively, sprawling city of more than two million people.

This was the London of Charles Dickens' novels—*Dombey and Son*, *Bleak House*, *Our Mutual Friend*. It was a town of fashionable residential districts not far either from filthy

Treeless, humorless, and squalid gray was how Gustav Doré depicted the crowded slums in east side London.

Sam's parents, Sara and Solomon Gompers, grew up in Amsterdam, only a few streets apart. But they did not meet until some years later, when each had gone to London to live.

alleys or from narrow, crooked lanes where the sun never shone. A boy could see the glittering carriages of royalty itself roll down the main streets. A boy could also see, as Sam remembered seeing, unemployed workers pacing those same streets, wringing their hands and crying: "I've no work to do. Lord strike me dead—my wife, my kids want bread, and I've no work to do." He could see the technological wonders that were turning London into an international capital. These included the railroads that brought in cloth, machinery, ironware, crockery, and cutlery from England's factories, and the early-model steamers that carried such goods to other realms of the British Empire and to the rest of the world as well. At the same time, a boy could see his neighbors often laid low by many serious illnesses, the result of an abominable, archaic sanitation system.

Smoky by day; gaslit by night; majestic yet pestilent-smelling; its streets crammed with horse-drawn cabs and wagons, with pushcarts of tradesmen, tinkers, and peddlers of every variety, as well as with workmen and vagabonds—London was a schoolroom of life in the raw. And, after working hours, there was another world to sample, one that powerfully appealed to something deep in Sam Gompers'

nature. This was the make-believe world of the theater, to which he went enthusiastically when he could scrape a few pence together. Years later, he stated: "We boys used to pool our pennies and buy matches—fuses, we called them—which we sold on the street for an 'a-penny (halfpenny) a box. If we had good luck and made enough money, we went to the theater for a long evening of delight. If we didn't sell the fuses in time for the play to begin, we would go home and play theater." Sometimes, too, he would go to a concert—a pleasure to which Grandfather Gompers, who loved music, had introduced him as a small child. There, in the concert hall, he could be overwhelmed in a sea of glorious sound—after which he would emerge, able only to gasp, "God! How beautiful!"

### A decision to emigrate

Though the engrossing action and sweet sounds of the stage fed human emotions, they could not quiet physical hunger. The family of Solomon Gompers struggled harder and harder in a losing battle for self-support. Finally, in 1863, when young Sam had just turned thirteen, the family decided to emigrate to America. Every European worker had heard of America's opportunities. The Civil War had put the United States much in the news—with the Union, so far as the British working class was concerned, cast in the role of labor's champion against the slaveholders. Most important, the society of cigarmakers to which Solomon Gompers belonged could furnish emigrants with financial help.

So in 1863 the Gompers family embarked on the *City of London*, a steamship augmented by sail, and endured a seven-week immigrant passage, with all its discomforts (see pages 92–93). Sam's mother and the younger boys spent most of their time belowdecks, seasick, while Solomon, assisted by a friendly Negro seaman, struggled inexpertly to cook the salted meat and the dried and pickled vegetables the family had packed aboard. (Poor immigrants were at that time expected to feed themselves on the long voyage.) The highlight of the trip was a Fourth of July celebration at sea, with fireworks and music. Though no one on the ship knew it, this was the very day that the bloody struggles at Gettysburg and Vicksburg were being decided. Solomon played no instrument but joined the informally assembled ship's band as a fingersnapper.

The promise of America was already beginning to work a spell on Sam. It may well have meant something far beyond the ordinary to him. In London he had been neither a Dutchman nor an Englishman. Nor, apparently, did he feel himself to be very much of a Jew. The United States offered him, an "outsider," the prospect of something to which he could deeply and happily belong. Under the Stars and Stripes, as he and his family sailed into New York, Samuel Gompers began a love affair with America that lasted the rest of his life.

Yet there were puzzling contradictions in the land of the free. The steamer arrived in the tense period soon after New York's draft riots. During these turbulent days, angry mobs, protesting the "abolitionist war" that was compelling them to don uniforms and fight, had lynched and beaten hundreds of black men. Coming off the ship, Solomon Gompers was observed shaking hands with his Negro friend, the sailor who had helped him cook. He suddenly found himself threatened with hanging to a lamppost. His son later recalled that, without compromising his normal dignity, Solomon explained that he had been expressing gratitude for the help the Negro had given him. And he told the crowd, "Any one of you would have done the same." He walked away unharmed—and almost certainly a little puzzled by the first of many paradoxes he would encounter in this new land.

Starting in his early teens, Gompers was an eager and studious reader of New York newspapers, several of which were published in buildings around this Park Row-Nassau Street intersection, then called "Printing-House Square."

## Young man in Manhattan

For America assuredly had its contradictions. Moreover, its advantages had to be earned, starting from the very bottom. The Gompers family moved into the only kind of dwelling they could afford, an East Side tenement situated behind a brewery and opposite a slaughterhouse. "All day long," Sam reported, "we could see the animals being driven into the slaughter pens and could hear the turmoil and the cries of the animals. The neighborhood was filled with the penetrating, sickening odor." Even so, the Gompers' living quarters had four rooms compared to the two in London. The upward trek had begun. Both Solomon and Samuel found work as cigarmakers, first at home. Later, Samuel went on to rolling cigars in various small factories. Thus he eased the crowded conditions in the apartment—three more children were born—and achieved some personal independence (see page 127).

New York City and its blossoming urban culture became the fountain at which Sam eagerly drank in a growing youth's realization of life. Its resources were ample. There was the great city itself—even more polyglot than London, crammed with vitality, full of bright lights and shadows, elegance and poverty. As one observer put it, New York was like a lady in a ball gown with diamonds in her ears and her toes out at her boots. By foot, horsecar, and ferry, Sam's new city was a place to explore with satisfaction. It was just on the verge of the mighty expansion of the post-Civil War years when Gompers arrived. With his own eyes he would see the creation of the first bridge spanning the East River, the first electric streetlights, the first telephones. He would always believe in material progress as a driving force in men's affairs, because he personally had seen so much of it happen—thanks to the rapid technological developments of the Industrial Revolution.

New York slum dwellers defy troops (above) and attack a helpless Negro (right) during the draft riots (page 13) that endangered Gompers' father. Poor people resented a Civil War law that let well-to-do men buy their way out of the army.

Gompers' first New York home was near a brewery like the one above, where the workers lived as well as toiled. Later he wrote: "Conditions were dreadful in the breweries . . . and I became very familiar with them from our back door."

New York, too, had its theaters and concert halls. And more, New York had cheap newspapers. Sam's favorite was the New York *Sun*, edited after 1868 by Charles Dana, a brilliant journalist who held his newspaper rigidly to standards of good writing and probing reportage. For pennies daily, Gompers could read about the growth of the municipality and the corruptions of "Boss Tweed," the grafter on a gigantic scale who was then the chief of New York City's ruling political organization, Tammany Hall. He could follow the gradual collapse of Reconstruction in the South and see what other matters were distracting the nation's attention from the effort to remold Southern society. He could read of the relentless expansion of the railroads into the undefiled West, the mining booms of the Rockies, the beginnings of the steel and petroleum industries. He could follow the steadily increasing pace with which

American factories produced clothing, paper, farm implements, general machinery, furniture, printing equipment, firearms, rails, telegraph wire, flour, and hundreds of other necessities and luxuries of modern civilization. He could sense the eventual plenitude of American life—and just possibly wonder what share in it there might be for him, as well as for all the others who toiled for the lamentably low wages that were then being paid. Very few workers of that period received as much as $10 a week for their long, hard labors.

There were also more formal means of education. One of New York's great institutions was—and is—Cooper Union, a virtual university for workingmen. It had been founded by Peter Cooper, a philanthropic inventor and manufacturer who stipulated that its classes should forever be free of tuition charges. An excellent library was available there. So were

The colorful Bowery is viewed above from the vantage point of Cooper Union, whose founder, Peter Cooper, was the easy-money Greenback party's presidential nominee in 1876. Below, in a Thomas Nast cartoon, Cooper crowns the party's 1884 nominee, General Benjamin Butler, with the air cushion he always carried to ease his discomfort on hard seats.

evening lectures, and courses that the young cigarmaker took hungrily after his long workday. He enrolled for classes in history, biography, economics, geography, debating, mechanics, and electricity. Memories of what the millionaire Peter Cooper's vision had done for him and others may have played a part in making him impatient when, later, he heard orators preaching the "inevitable" enmity between all "capitalists" and workers. He believed that, under the right conditions, the two groups could constructively cooperate.

But work, entertainment, and education alone did not fill all the needs of the man that Sam Gompers was becoming. He was sensitive and independent, yet he needed companionship and the warmth of belonging. He was a natural joiner. He became part of such organizations as the Arion Base Ball and Social Club (later picturesquely renamed Rising Star Social and Debating Club), the Independent Order of Odd Fellows, the Ancient Order of Foresters. He later recalled that "I always wanted a friend with whom to share." These club activities trained him in ways of debate, organization, and management of others. And they opened up in him a deeper need for companionship.

In 1866 he began seeing Sophia Julian, a fellow cigarmaker six months his junior. She was, like Sam, a London-born Jew whose family had emigrated some years before. From summer to winter that year, the two of them were together often—at picnics and parties, on long walks, and at the theater. Impulsively, on Sam's seventeenth birthday, they decided to get married. The next day they exchanged vows before a justice of the peace. For a while the newlyweds lived with the Gompers family. Then, wanting and needing a home of his own, Sam willingly paid the price of responsibility as one baby followed another, even before he had left his teens. His marriage to Sophia was happy and long-lasting, largely because of her patience, understanding, and complete willingness to share Sam with the labor movement (see pages 140–141).

By the age of twenty-one, Samuel Gompers had developed an adult personality of many

16

elements. One part of his heritage drove him to night classes in a passion for self-improvement worthy of any young American dreaming of becoming a success—and a self-made success at that. He was clearly influenced by the patriarchal ways of his grandfather, who had ruled the Gompers household and Sam himself with love and rigor. Perhaps Sam's early marriage was traceable to a desire to be master of his own hearthside. There was a strong will in him to lead and control. Yet there was also in him a streak of good-natured gregariousness, which barred long hours of solitary study. There were also characteristic strains of emotional impulsiveness and of sensitivity to the arts. A proper young man on the make did not spend hours drinking beer and smoking cigars with shopmates, as Sam did. Nor would a youthful John D. Rockefeller or Andrew Carnegie have taken twenty-five dollars of precious household money earmarked for dress goods for his wife, in order to buy a fiddle. Sam did just that, and scraped away happily for over a year before giving up lessons.

He also indulged an idealistic bent that made him thrill to knowledge of American history with its underlying theme of freedom. Even as a fifteen-year-old, his zest for liberty and its champions had thrown him into a depression that lasted for days when Lincoln, the living example of American opportunity, was murdered. Beneath Gompers' idealism there was also a hard core of practical sense that simply had to develop in a young man who had learned to take care of himself in the tough streets and factories of London and New York.

In Gompers, ambition would lead him to pull all these varied traits together and use them with great effectiveness, when he found the opportunity. Ambition would bind his life to working with others in the pursuit of some goal that clasped ideals and reality in a single, eager embrace. Later on, explaining his lack of formal religion, he observed: "I have never been able to separate an act of worship or service, as I prefer to call it, from some concrete human need." But he would always keep for himself

---

**THE SPREAD OF A SYMBOL**

For most of Gompers' adult life he belonged to a Hebrew society formed for the mutual benefit of poor workingmen. He served for a time as its secretary and as its president, but had to relinquish his membership when he remarried late in life, since his second wife was a Gentile.

Lucy Robins, in an interview, described the group and the broad, however indirect, extent of its influence: "When Gompers was eighteen years old, his first son was born. Since there was not enough income to support his family, he joined a beneficial society organized by his father and a group of English, Dutch, and Portuguese Jewish friends. This beneficial society was named . . . Hand-in-Hand and was created to provide medical and burial services for its members. The name . . . was also given to the cemetery where they were to be buried. The emblem of the society upon the gates of the burial grounds is that of two clasped hands. Much later, after the American Federation of Labor was formed, the non-Jewish labor leaders honored Gompers by accepting this emblem of the Jewish society as their own, symbolizing trade union brotherhood. It is this Hebrew emblem . . . Hand-in-Hand, that decorates all of the stationery, books, buildings, and flags of the American Federation of Labor. [See page 89.]

"Gompers fought for admission into the United States of the Territory of Oklahoma. After the admission was granted—all documents and papers had been signed—Gompers was presented with a pen. To reward him even more, the new state of Oklahoma adopted Gompers' Jewish symbol of . . . the clasped hands as the official emblem of the state of Oklahoma."

Over the image of a handshake on the state seal is the phrase *"Labor Omnia Vincit"* ("Labor Conquers All"), the official motto Oklahoma shares with the American Federation of Labor.

---

the decision as to what concrete human needs should be served first—and how they could be served best. As he stepped into his twenties, fully Americanized, he finally encountered a cause that would furnish a lasting challenge to all his numerous drives for leadership, for fellowship, for service to ideals as he saw them, and for practical work. This was America's infant labor movement. At the workbench to which he had first gone when he was barely ten years old, Samuel Gompers began to discover both his lifelong calling and himself.

# *Chapter 2*

# LABORING MAN, FAMILY MAN, UNIONIST

THE TUMULTS of a growing New York were the school books of Gompers' "general" education. The classrooms of his "professional" training were the cigarmaking shops of the city, largely filled by Armenian, English, Dutch, and German workers in the 1860's. They were not the places to inspire hallowed memories. "Any kind of an old loft served as a cigar shop," Gompers recollected. Whether or not it had windows was left to chance.

The workers twisted themselves in various postures over tables of assorted sizes bought as cheaply as possible and without regard for the comfort of men who would cut and roll tobacco leaves on them, hour after hour. The air was thick with tobacco dust and shreds. Sanitary facilities consisted of a primitive toilet, a cold-water tap, and a piece of tobacco sacking for a towel. Yet in these unlikely surroundings Gompers found things that were, to him, fulfilling—for one thing, pride of craftsmanship. "I loved the touch of soft velvety tobacco," he wrote later, "and gloried in the deft sureness with which I could make cigars grow in my fingers." For another, he found one more group to join—Local Cigar Makers' Union No. 15. It was anything but a powerful guild, though it had ambitions; it met in a room over a saloon owned by the father of a member. There were few plans, little organization, and no money.

Local 15 was affiliated with a national association, the Cigar Makers' International Union

of America, but despite the impressive scope of the title, this "international union" was, like the American labor movement itself, in an embryonic stage. Gompers had joined primarily on fraternal grounds, and, as a practical matter, to be part of a "more or less definite group of people employed in the same trade who might help each other out in special difficulties with the employer." Those "special difficulties" were often sudden in appearing: a surprise cut in wages, a curt announcement of longer hours, or an employer's outburst of anger that resulted in an employee's discharge. And they were met by impulsive reactions: a workman slamming his tools down on the bench, scraping back his chair, and announcing, "I am going on strike" —at the same time challenging others to follow, or allow themselves to be labeled "scabs" if they remained.

Sometimes the threat had an immediate effect, and the boss backed down. But other times a long and bitter strike resulted, in which the cigarmakers, without a union strike fund from which to draw benefits, pitted their will against the employer's. They had to gamble that they could hold out against starvation longer than he could stand the sight of his workbenches empty, his orders unfilled, and his customers drifting away to competitors. The odds always ran heavily against the workers, however. Hunger and cold hurt a laborer's family sooner and with more devastation than a declining bank balance hurt an employer. What was more, strikebreakers were not hard to come by, especially when times were bad and sales slow—the very times, in fact, when an employer was apt to cut wages or slash his work force on short notice. The wildcat strike was almost certain to end in failure, and a union without widespread organization, systematic planning, or a carefully accumulated war chest could at best give the proceedings a touch of formality, and pass the hat among more solvent members to help out those whose need was most desperate. Such were the hard facts of the labor situation.

*Only an onlooker*

Gompers saw all this as he moved from job to job—through one little shop after another. All were members of an industry still scattered among small producers competing wildly. In spite of insecurity and the pinch of low wages, Gompers still enjoyed life. As a worker, as a union member, as a gregarious and energetic shopmate, he took an interest in the conditions of labor that was more than merely personal. Yet as he himself said later, he was still only an onlooker. What he saw in that role, however, drew him more and more toward the center of things—toward a total commitment to the labor movement. But it took eleven years from the time of his youthful marriage to a climactic decision that sealed his career. Those years— from 1867 to 1878—were years of change, struggle, and search for those who labored in America and for those who wished to lead the workers—or claimed to.

In many industries, new machinery developed in the nineteenth century gave mass production a jump over craftsmanship. These women cigar workers use suction machines to roll cigars, a job that had once demanded skilled handwork.

19

Sam Gompers was in an excellent position to see that harsh struggle for growth: to watch, to weigh, and to think matters out according to his lights. The cigarmaking trade occupied the hands but left the mind free, nor was it conducted amid the roar of machinery. There was plenty of opportunity for shop discussion on the job, and since many cigarmakers were active in working-class movements and organizations in America (while many more were veterans of Europe's social conflicts), almost every viewpoint had a hearing—in a variety of tones and accents—as the hours of work passed. In addition, it was a custom in some shops to choose one man to read aloud from various newspapers and magazines throughout the day—an indication of the seriousness and intellectual curiosity of cigarmakers as a group. Gompers, who had a good voice, was often picked for this job. Reading through the popular journals of the day as well as a few newspapers especially devoted to economic and labor questions (such as the *Workingmen's Advocate*, or the *National Labor Tribune*), pausing to listen to some workman's comment, objection, or shouted endorsement, he began to sense the complexities of the "labor problem" and its various proposed solutions.

First of all, Gompers read a story of the remarkable shift from skilled handwork to machine production in industrial life. Engines of plenty—tireless and infinitely strong—fashioned the goods of a new way of life based on mass consumption. These varied new engines turned out cheap goods in thousands of units a day—from paper to paraffin lamps, hatpins to hardware, shirt buttons to sugar tongs. The machines could be tended by a girl fresh from the farm, or an immigrant child, or a newcomer who had never so much as seen the finished product. And with the machines' help, these unskilled workers could produce, in seconds, an article that would once have taken hours of devoted attention by an experienced craftsman. For the workingman, the situation created by the new technology was both promising and dangerous: promising, because even a limited income could now buy goods that were once the privileges of aristocrats—the rugs, furniture, and china of an average home, for example—yet dangerous, because the almighty machine devalued the skill that had given the laborer both his pride and his ability to command a good price for his work.

These dangerous implications quickly made themselves felt in the era of President Grant, a Republican—for whom Gompers cast his first presidential vote in 1872. When a crushing depression hit the nation in 1873, wages in all trades were cut again and again, yet strikes of protest failed. Even when the railroad workers, the cream of the skilled labor force, went out on line after line in 1877, owners were able (with the help of government troops) to force them to go back to work. The ordinary worker was helpless in the face of declining pay levels that brought his income down to as little as a dollar or less per day in many trades. Even in those

A cigarmaker reads aloud to his colleagues—a popular practice noted here and in Gompers' memoirs (see page 136).

times of comparatively modest prices, this was an impossible wage for the average laborer with five, six, or eight children to support.

Still more disastrous was a national frame of mind, which—in the normal course of human events—adjusted very slowly to the new kind of society the machine was shaping. Orators in the era of Andrew Jackson or Abraham Lincoln had given plenty of praise to "the man who toiled." But they had in mind the farmer who sweated to plow his own acres, or the craftsman whose hands showed the calluses of his own tools: a printer, a millwright, a hatter. Until about 1870, men worked for others to learn a trade in order to accumulate, dollar by dollar, the means to buy their own shops—and, in turn, to begin to employ other men. The lifelong hired laborer, the perennial sailor or clerk, handyman or porter, was simply not respected much. He was not a witness to the fruitful influence of American liberty on man's potential!

But in the midst of industrial marvels, one remorseless fact became ever more clear: Only a favored few could possibly own the tremendously complex engines of a modern factory— or even *share* in that ownership. The man who took wages from another for his entire life was not necessarily unambitious or unlucky or characterless, as early Americans would have thought him. He was an indispensable fixture of modern economic life. Somehow, a place in the sun had to be found for him; a million dollars' worth of machines run by eight-dollar-a-week men added up to social conflict that American political thought was not yet prepared to handle. What good were the marvels of steam and electricity, the popular press and cheap comforts, if the work force that made them was condemned to social inferiority and intermittent starvation? In 1879 a writer in California, Henry George, brought out the first edition of a book whose title summed up the paradox of what modernity was bringing to America—*Progress and Poverty*.

Gompers read his way steadily into the heart of this problem, and his theoretical learning was reinforced by hard daily experience. In

During the bitter railroad strike of 1877, workers and their wives try to keep a fireman from going to his engine.

cigarmaking itself, the challenge to skill was posed in the early 1870's by the introduction of a mold that enabled untrained workers to manufacture what Gompers called "cheaper grades of cigars." In addition, some manufacturers rented tenement houses, installed whole families (often of recent immigrants), and set them to work. Such families used molds and were paid on a piecework basis—cigar by cigar— at a rate so low it barely kept body and soul together.

The mold and the tenement system together threatened to demoralize the industry. The first reaction of the Cigar Makers' International Union was to adopt rules forbidding members to work with mold-users. Some shops were struck when the devices were introduced. Yet such strikes failed, and presently Gompers, among others, perceived a hard, new truth: The mold had come to stay. A strong union depended upon numbers, and the policy of excluding mold-users only weakened the union in the long run. So Gompers and other members of Local 15 began a campaign to permit the enrollment of all cigarmaking workers regardless of method of manufacture or sex (for women, too, were included among the unskilled cigar workers), and eventually they carried their point. Perhaps Gompers had consciously thought out the implications of this fight—that labor's best policy might be not to resist technological change, but rather to build strong unions and then cope with the reality of mechanization. Perhaps he had not. Certainly, however, the fight over the issue of the molds underscored his awareness of what painful problems the craftsman was up against.

## The eight-hour day

There were other lessons, too, in those early years—lessons demonstrating the hostility of both the public and the authorities to workingmen's demands. In 1871, when Gompers was twenty-one, he took part in an enormous parade of 25,000 workmen through the streets of Manhattan, demanding an eight-hour workday. Members of trade unions stood on the muddied cobblestones holding placards that proclaimed "Eight Hours for Work, Eight Hours for Rest, Eight Hours for What We Will." Meanwhile, speakers at a rally after the parade expounded their concept of a world of improved moral character, higher consumption, and more jobs— if employers, either voluntarily or under legal compulsion, limited the workday to eight hours. Yet such demonstrations bore almost no fruit. While the federal government and a few states legally prescribed (but did not necessarily enforce) the eight-hour day for their employees, observance of this law did not become common in private industry for at least forty years after that parade. In general, public opinion was overwhelmingly indignant at the mere idea of tampering with the "natural forces" that determined the employer's rightful decision as to the length of a day's work.

Three years after the parade, early in 1874, there was another mass meeting and another,

more dramatic, confrontation. This time, the depression was at its worst, and the crowd consisted in good part of unemployed men petitioning for direly needed help—public works, relief funds for foodless families, and the suspension of evictions of the jobless from their tenements. The gathering was in Tompkins Square, a small park in the heart of New York's Lower East Side. The mayor at first agreed to address the group. Then, frightened, he changed his mind; what was more, he allowed the police commissioner to revoke the permit for the demonstration. The news of the revoked permit was not, however, passed along to the thousands who pushed their way downtown on the morning of January 13. Suddenly, mounted police on the rim of this now "illegal" crowd charged, swinging their clubs remorselessly—"right and left indiscriminately on the heads of all they could reach." Samuel Gompers was there; he heard the thunder of hooves behind him; he struggled with a knot of people on the sidewalk to break free and run, and he stumbled into a cellar doorway barely in time to escape a cracked head. Gompers had taken no part in planning the rally. Nor did he entirely approve of its sponsors, many of them radicals and intellectual catchall reformers whom he was coming to dislike. But the brutality he saw that day sickened him. Not only were workingmen's cries unheard, as the eight-hour-day demand had been, but in times of greatest stress society had shown it was likely to retaliate against whatever pressure was being exerted, simply by battering the workingmen's defenseless skulls. A man did not have to read many pamphlets to see that. In hot anger, Gompers gauged the reality of labor's needs and the iron resistance of the general public to their fulfillment.

If the problems of America's workingmen stood out with a stark clarity, the answers were lost in a fog of slogans, programs, and promises. It was not hard to see that laborers across the nation needed organization and leadership, but in what form and for what purposes? The building blocks of the future were at hand in two legal rights that could not be denied—to form

A New York newspaper reported that the Tompkins Square meeting (opposite page) had been broken up by acts of "reasonable but not excessive severity," but Gompers never forgot the panic inflicted by club-swinging mounted police.

unions and to vote. But which of these could or would be most effective? Did they help or hinder each other?

There had been local craft unions in America long before the Civil War. In some cities, like Philadelphia and New York, local unions occasionally leagued themselves together in so-called "trades assemblies" to consider mutual problems. In addition, during the 1850's and 1860's, craft locals in a few industries had joined together to form national unions of their workers—the iron molders, the blacksmiths and machinists, the boot and shoe makers, the typographers, and Gompers' own cigarmakers among them. The preamble to the constitution of the Cigar Makers' International, adopted in 1864, spelled out the advantages of such mergers: "Organization and united action are the only means by which the laboring classes can gain any advantage for themselves."

The question was what step in organization should follow the creation of such national bodies. One early answer was a kind of "union of unions," the National Labor Union, founded

at Baltimore in 1866, under the aegis of the Iron Molders' president, William H. Sylvis. A Pennsylvania-born wagonmaker's son, Sylvis was self-educated and politically alert; he was an editor, a writer, and an orator as well as a worker in iron. The NLU was ambitious enough, but its internal structure was a logjam, each log representing a different approach to society's ills. While it did enlist the national unions— including those with such orotund titles as the Knights of Saint Crispin, who were in prosaic fact the boot and shoe makers—it also embraced such diverse factions as leagues of workers who favored the eight-hour day; advocates of cur-rency inflation through a greater issue of "greenbacks" (paper money used during the Civil War); opponents of gigantic giveaways of public land to private corporations; suffrag-ettes; and battlers for Negro rights. The National Labor Union's answer to the central question— what the future of the wage-earning class would actually be—was to try to undermine the wage system itself through cooperative ownership of factories by workers' organizations. This was

Sylvis' favorite scheme. "By cooperation," he said, "we will become a nation of employers—the employers of our own labor. The wealth of the land will pass into the hands of those who produce it."

## The Knights of Labor

Gompers—smoking, reading, talking shop at meetings of the cigarmakers' local, attending lectures, and going out later to thrash things out over a bite of supper—could follow the story of what happened. The craft workers of the unions were not interested in the lofty rhetoric of the NLU. Free land for farmers, cheap money for investors, rights for minorities—all might be admirable goals. Each of these objectives, however, was far removed from the biting reality of low wages, deplorable conditions, dragging hours.

"Cooperation" may have sounded sweet to the ears of labor reformers who spent so many hours making speeches that they forgot how to use their tools. But the prospect of small union-owned factories taking on mighty national combines—in a contest for credit, markets, skilled management, and transportation facilities—was too wild a dream for realization, even in America. Attendance at NLU conventions—especially by union representatives—dwindled annually, until in 1872 the organization died. Other groups tried to take its place, such as the short-lived Industrial Brotherhood, which was equally embellished with idealistic slogans but equally unable to do more than propose legislative reforms for which there was no support.

One such high-minded fraternity was to have a slightly different career, however. This was the Knights of Labor, founded in 1869 by Uriah Stephens, a Philadelphia garment-cutter with a minister's training and a talent for devising rituals. Known as a "noble and holy order," the Knights operated in secrecy at first, inducting workmen into "assemblies" with secret handclasps, seals, titles ("Worthy Foreman" and "Venerable Sage," to name two). The order offered other encouragements to workers for adopting its lofty official viewpoint, which held "industrial and moral worth, not wealth, the true standard of individual and national greatness." One night a fellow worker of Sam Gompers at Hirsch's cigar factory took him to a meeting held by one of the Knights' local assemblies. What Gompers thought of it at the time is not clear. Writing about it many years later, he recalled disdainfully that "I was conducted into a room and [joined the Knights] and a great lecture ensued . . . the sum total . . . apart from certain philosophical or theoretical declarations, was hostile to trade unions."

The judgment of Gompers' old age may have been a bit harsh. The manifestos of the Knights and the National Labor Union had three basic and significant intentions. One was to restore the worker's self-respect. A second was to float him on the mainstream of America's striving for progress toward perfection on earth, which went back to Puritan days. The third was to hail him as a prince of the production process that made the earth blossom like the rose. The trouble was that both the Knights and the National Labor Union were so enamored of production that they deplored strikes, the workman's one effective and immediate weapon. Further, they were both so dedicated to cooperation that they sometimes forgot the genuine gap that separated the self-employed farmer and businessman from the tenement-house worker. Yet, in time, the Knights were to come close to setting the American labor movement afire with hope, and though they would eventually vanish, a certain visionary quality that a materially prospering America needed very much would vanish with them, and with others like them.

### The Socialist ferment

The aims of a W. H. Sylvis for ending the wage system by giving every wageworker the chance to grow into the role of owner might be described as embodying "middle-class idealism." Another kind of idealism with which Gompers came into almost daily contact was the radical ferment of socialism, which dedicated itself to a kind of justice to be achieved by putting an end to private ownership of the means of production. However, the Socialists, like the middle-class reformers, were not single-minded. Given the fact that the worker had the ballot and the union, they disagreed as to how each should be used. One leading Socialist group, the International Workingmen's Association, was created in Europe in 1864, under the leadership of Karl Marx. It attracted many American reformers by its stated objectives: the creation of a brotherhood of workers that would cut across national boundaries—plus the formation of a society in which workers would directly own the basic machinery of production, so that no man would live by the exploitation of another.

The National Labor Union sent representatives to early meetings of the "International," and, in turn, European veterans of Socialist struggles found their way to the United States to spread the gospel to fellow workers in shops

While usually loath to embrace socialism, American workers definitely wanted the "fair compensation" demanded on the banner carried before 800 women in this parade of striking shoe-factory workers at Lynn, Massachusetts, in 1860.

25

and mills. An American affiliate of the International, the United Workers of America, was founded in 1874, and the same year saw the creation of the Social Democratic Party of North America, later to become the Socialist Labor Party. However, there was no firm understanding among these early American Socialists concerning the role of the trade union in bringing the brave new world to birth. Followers of Ferdinand Lassalle, a German thinker, believed that workingmen should organize a political party of their own, take over the government by strength of numbers, and then use the government's power to establish and support cooperative producers' associations (not unlike those envisioned by the NLU in some respects). Unions had little place in such a plan.

More "orthodox" Marxists, believing that a class struggle was inevitable, regarded unions as agencies to train and discipline workers for the coming struggle. Meanwhile, they argued hotly over exactly how the unions should themselves be organized; what they should demand of employers; whether they should make any demands on existing political parties through agitation and boycott; whether they should cooperate at all with "bourgeois" officials. These questions were debated with theological subtlety and violent passion by men and factions. Many of the participants were European refugees who had taken their battles into the streets of their native lands and had known the insides of prisons.

Gompers was fortunate in being able to follow these struggles, not only through the printed word but through discussions with some new-found friends. The latter were part of this primitive American socialism, yet they were all, in one way or another, tutoring themselves to stand back and view it with some detachment. There was Ferdinand Laurrell, for example— Karl Malcolm Ferdinand Laurrell—born in Sweden, sent to sea as a youth, then taught cigarmaking in Copenhagen. Laurrell had thrown himself into the revolutionary ferment that stirred young Europeans in the mid-nineteenth century. These were the days that

## A "GREASY TOOL OF WALL STREET"

Gompers' opposition to the Socialists within organized labor was bitter and irreconcilable. His colleague Florence Thorne credits this antisocialism to the teachings of Ferdinand Laurrell, through whose influence Gompers developed political awareness during his early years as a union cigarmaker, as is noted on these pages.

Miss Thorne wrote: "Laurrell safeguarded Gompers from Socialism by teaching him the paramount importance of developing economic power through the trade union, using that power to gain higher wages and shorter hours—the two most vital, most revolutionizing forces that come into the lives of workers and their families. Laurrell drilled Gompers in the principles and theory necessary to make trade unions practical, stabilized agencies for service to workingmen. . . . Socialists proposed political action and legislative procedure where [Gompers] proposed economic power and procedures, voluntary agencies resting upon individual responsibility and freedom. Socialists would substitute political party government with police enforcement [in place of] voluntarily associated agencies regulating relationships through contracts and maintaining order by mutual consent."

Throughout his long running battle with the Socialists, Gompers sought a gradual, material improvement in the worker's lot, while the Socialists, more impatient, favored immediate class warfare. "The capitalists own the tools they do not use, and the workers use the tools they do not own," declared Eugene V. Debs, socialism's most eloquent American expositor in Gompers' time. Debs added: "Gompers believes that the interests of labor and capital are identical or mutual. We do not. He believes that these interests can be harmonized and justice done to both. We do not. We believe that labor is entitled to all it produces and that labor must organize politically as well as economically to abolish the existing order." That Debs considered Gompers' labor leadership no less an evil than capitalism itself was undisguised: "Gompers . . . and other pure and simple union leaders are in economic tune with the master class and are held up as model labor leaders by capitalist newspapers."

Daniel De Leon, Debs's avowed rival in the Socialist camp, shared similar views, but being a fanatic and lacking Debs's rhetorical ability, he stated his feelings bluntly and with less discretion.

To De Leon, Gompers was merely a "labor fakir" and a "greasy tool of Wall Street."

Whether they allied themselves with Debs or De Leon, the Socialists in the labor movement had a long list of grievances against Gompers. They criticized his role in the National Civic Federation, his somewhat cautious attitude toward strikes, and his disdain for the concept of industrial unionism. They disagreed not only with his methods of improving the well-being of the workingman but also with his own basic philosophy. He was a reformer, not a revolutionary, and though he advocated a policy of achieving "more, more, more, now" for the workers, this emphasis on material progress was not enough to satisfy the Socialists.

Eugene Victor Debs in 1897

They reproached him for his steadfast insistence that labor should stand apart from politics—and then scorned his 1908 endorsement of William Jennings Bryan, running for President for the third time. They found his restrictive attitude toward immigrant and unskilled workers appalling, and they scorned his apathy toward the plight of minorities. "The Socialist party is the party of the working class, regardless of color," Debs stated, and then to drive home the point, he also declared, "The voice of Socialism must be as inspiring music to the ears of those in bondage, especially the weak black brethren, doubly enslaved, who are bowed to the earth and groan in despair beneath the burden of the centuries."

John P. Frey, an AFL colleague of Gompers, traced the breach between traditional trade unionists and the Socialists (together with their sympathizers) to events in nineteenth-century Europe: "The wave of immigration . . . brought millions of immigrant workmen to our shores. A large number of these had suffered in Europe because of the special privileges enjoyed by employers in industry, the large landowners, and the nobility. The wealth which labor produced had returned little more to them than a bare living, while the privileged individuals had accumulated the balance. . . . Many of the immigrants . . . believed that the wage earners' hope lay in the success of socialism. Many of them, particularly those from Continental Europe, knew but little concerning trade unionism as practiced by the American Federation of Labor. To them Samuel Gompers was an ultraconservative, an obstacle to progress. They were sympathetic with the constant attack which the leaders of socialism in the United States were persistently making against Mr. Gompers and his associates. These conditions helped to sharpen the criticism which Mr. Gompers made against socialist philosophy and socialist tactics, in particular as these were being advocated by the leaders of the Socialist party."

The Socialists' main bid for power occurred at the 1912 AFL convention when, for the first time in a decade, Gompers and his fellow labor officers were faced with an opposition slate. Max Hayes, a Cleveland labor leader and editor of the Cleveland *Citizen*, was nominated for president of the AFL under the Socialist banner. He was somewhat more moderate than Debs, for despite his opposition to Gompers, he regarded the AFL as a useful federation whose activities substantially furthered the workers' cause. Hayes lost, however, by better than 2 to 1.

Rowland H. Harvey, in his biography of Gompers, described Hayes as a man who "has done a fine service for labor. His opposition to Gompers was always of the constructive sort. His aim was to make the Federation a liberal institution with a forward-looking program. His socialism has been parliamentary. . . . He often proved quite disconcerting to Gompers, however, especially when the latter was in the midst of an oratorical attack on the Socialists. Upon these occasions, Hayes would call out from the floor, 'Give 'em hell, Sam; give 'em hell.' "

saw a new Germany created; national minorities such as the Poles and Hungarians proudly demanding voices in the declining Austrian and Russian empires; and workingmen chanting the old cries of the French Revolution. Laurrell himself took part in a Copenhagen street demonstration, was hunted by police, fled to Hamburg, and then eventually came to New York. In the shop of David Hirsch & Company he met Sam Gompers, and passed on to him, in "a thick Teutonic accent," what he knew from his experience as a revolutionist.

He put a German edition of the *Communist Manifesto* in Gompers' hands, translated it, and set Sam to studying German in order to read other important Socialist literature. He told the youthful ex-Londoner to attend Socialist meetings but not to join the ranks, for Laurrell himself was coming around to a new viewpoint, which held that the union, not the political party, was the worker's best friend. He gave Sam some never-to-be-forgotten advice, for use when a new idea seemed overwhelmingly appealing: "Study your union card, Sam, and if the idea doesn't square with that, it ain't true."

Other strong-willed workingmen had an influence on Gompers. There was, first of all, red-haired J. P. McDonnell, an Irish rebel who had worked with Marx in the International Workingmen's Association office in London, and whom Gompers met at meetings of the International to which Laurrell had directed him. McDonnell was "brainy and very gentle, had a beautiful speaking voice and courage for any venture." There was Peter J. McGuire, two years younger than Gompers, a New York-born Irishman who was later to become a master organizer of carpenters. In those salad days of the 1870's, however, he was a hot-tongued Socialist orator with a predilection for slogans like "bread or blood" that brought out the deepest fears of middle-class conservatives. They tended to lump Marxism, socialism, "communism," strikes, and revolution indiscriminately together. Most of America's middle class then had shuddery visions of torch and knife when workers' mass meetings were held.

Gompers also met a lifelong co-worker of his later years, Adolph Strasser, a Hungarian-born cigarmaker of cultivated tastes, refined appearance, and great talent, who acted as counselor, gadfly, and mentor to him. Years later, Gompers remembered having given a maiden speech into which he confidently thought he had poured his all. Strasser came over to him and smiled: "That was all right, Sam. You will yet a good speaker be." There were also Louis and Henry Baer, Fred Bloete, Karl Speyer—members of an informal group Gompers joined, dubbed "The Ten Philosophers." They met in the Tenth Ward Hotel for long and earnest discussions of plans, policies, and theories. Samuel Gompers, over the years, came to know and love these men who, in a babel of accents, fought their way with him toward an understanding of the social forces that gripped them. "In our hearts was courage for any effort," he reminisced. "We were groping and crusading like the knights of old" (see pages 132–134).

He listened to the friends he was coming to love, and to some he distrusted: anarchists like Johann Most, Justus Schwab, and John Swinton; and wild, reforming eccentrics like Victoria Woodhull and George Francis Train. Ideas whirled in his brain, along with headlines describing day-to-day struggles. Life was a round of work, classes, meetings, discussions, brief hours at home with a growing family, even briefer hours of sleep, and then a fresh day. He welcomed it all with the energy of a young man who was in love with life, and who was finding, almost unawares, a goal that challenged his simultaneous yearnings for ideals, useful practical action, and brotherhood. His union card was becoming his gospel.

### A bitter strike

Gompers began to spend more and more time in the actual affairs of the cigarmakers. After a fight with the union leadership in 1872 over the issue of admitting mold-users, Local 15 had been reorganized; three years later it was re-accepted into the Cigar Makers' International Union as Local 144. More and more often,

Sam's poise, knowledge, articulateness, and mature appearance led to his being chosen as a shop spokesman or as an officer of the local at election time. The union was reality to him. The theoretical concepts that he debated only seemed to have meaning for him as they related to union affairs. To a greater and greater degree, he was growing irritated with any ideas and programs that seemed to have no imminent chance of application. There was a streak of pugnacity in him—the old London street boy again—which wanted to do battle. He scorned words in favor of whatever action in the present would gain an immediate, tangible objective—something a workman could feel at once, such as a cleaner shop or a fatter pay envelope.

Union affairs took more and more of his time. But the extent of his involvement did not fully dawn upon Gompers until the bitter year of 1877. Hard times had ravaged all the unions, and the Cigar Makers' International had shrunk to seventeen locals and just about a thousand members. Yet in October, tenement-house workers, pushed to the limit, went on strike. The union had no choice but to support them (see pages 136–141).

For four savage winter months the strike went on. The manufacturers evicted families from their home workshops, fired other workers who sympathized with the strikers, and replaced them with new hands. The union framed demands for recognition—a reduction in tenement rents, and a minimum scale of six dollars per thousand cigars. Every union member tightened his belt. Those who remained employed were assessed again and again, but the war chest shrank under alarming demands. The union had to feed hundreds of families, and in many cases had to rent rooms for them. An attempt was made to set up a union-run cigar factory with Gompers in charge. He worked fourteen, sixteen, eighteen hours a day—making cigars, supervising mass meetings, collecting and distributing funds, donating his own meager earnings to those whose needs were greater, skipping meals and walking miles to and from work to save carfare. At home,

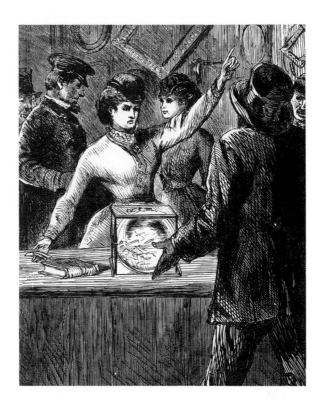

Victoria Woodhull, seen here trying to vote, was backed by Gompers in her fight for woman suffrage, but he considered her one of the reformers who "were not working people and treated . . . the labor movement as a means to a 'career'."

Sophia and the children bravely subsisted on soup made from flour, water, and seasonings.

In the end, however, the strike was broken; there was a limit to how long the depression-weakened union could hold out. Sam himself, blacklisted by employers, remained out of work for weeks afterward. Every stick of furniture he owned had been pawned; his family was in rags; and, worse, another child was expected soon. Right up to the time the baby was born, Sophia was still without a doctor or medicines. In desperation Gompers stormed into a neighborhood physician's office and, with fire in his eyes, threatened to kill the man if he refused to come at once to Sophia's bedside. Gompers must have looked desperate indeed. The doctor came without protest, and Gompers managed to scrape up the two-dollar fee from friends.

The low point had been reached, and Gompers realized now that he owed something to his family. When an election in Local 144 was held, he declined to run again for president, the office he had held for four terms. Instead, he moved to Brooklyn early in 1878, to remove himself from the temptation of remaining in the city at night to attend to union business. Within a few weeks he discovered that it was not the time to turn back. He might give up his official position in the union, but he could not bear to stay away from its meetings. He skipped one week, and was never more uncomfortable. His own words best describe what followed:

"The second week I went to the union meeting. I could not go home to supper and so I had to buy some sort of a meal in New York. I went to the meeting, a discussion arose, an important committee was to be appointed and the president appointed me as chairman of the committee. I could not refuse. I reached home about two o'clock in the morning and a few hours later I went to work. In the evening I met with my associates on the committee, had a bite instead of supper, reached home about one o'clock in the morning, and then it was necessary to attend the meeting on the following Monday night and make report. And so it continued until nearly every evening kept me away from home, involving the expense of eating in restaurants and unfitting me for the work in the factory. I saw that the situation was hopeless, went home one Sunday morning and concluded it was no use; we moved back to New York, and, if possible, with more zest and energy reentered the struggle which has continued ever since. That, in my opinion, was the turning point of my life."

And so it was. At twenty-eight, the education and the groping were over. Gompers was now going to bring into final form and action what he had learned from his reflections, companionships, studies, and deeds. He was ready to impress his philosophy upon the cigarmakers and, eventually, upon all of American labor.

A national figure by the early 1900's, Gompers posed proudly but a trifle stiffly for a family portrait between his wife, Sophia, and daughter Sadie, a professional singer. Standing, from left, are sons Alexander, Samuel, and Henry.

# Chapter 3

# TOWARD A WORKABLE FEDERATION

GOMPERS' LIFE found its focus in those early months of 1878 when, hurrying through the dark and cold streets after late meetings, he realized that he could not separate himself from the cause of labor. His tough constitution could withstand sleeplessness, irregular meals, hasty trips, and isolation from normal family life—so long as his inner hunger for meaningful work was satisfied. And for the rest of his days the union movement fed this appetite bountifully. In the eight years that followed this self-discovery, Gompers would move from youth into maturity, and from service to leadership. In action and conference he began to frame his own ideas of the proper tools for forging industrial peace. What was more, there hardened inside him those stubborn characteristics that would generally keep him in the thick of a fight—and wherever he was, there was sure to be one. As he himself once observed of his stocky, five-foot-four stature, "My legs are so short I can never run away from a fight." The same characteristics would also mold the American labor movement largely in his image.

The outlines of what men would later call "Gompersism" slowly became visible. His emerging program involved experiments and advances in some areas. Elsewhere, however, it meant a departure from the highroad to utopia. Under his aegis, unions were to be put on a solid financial and organizational basis, sacrificing some of the spontaneous benevolence and fraternity they had enjoyed in the era of informality, manifestos, and poverty. But they would also spare themselves their frequent quixotic and unprepared (and self-destructive) strikes at the wrong time and place. The government was to be approached cautiously for such reforms in working conditions as lay within its power. But there would be no futile demands upon either national or local government to legislate a wage-earners' paradise—not to mention a paradise without wage earners. Lastly, Gompers believed that a nationwide labor organization should be created, and that its building blocks should be craft unions. In them and through them the workman could press for day-by-day improvements in his shop conditions. Thus he would achieve his own version of the good life in piecemeal fashion, bit by slow bit, as his hours grew shorter, or his conditions of employment gradually less degrading, or his reward a trifle ampler.

The philosophy underlying these plans was given many names. Among them were "business unionism," "bread-and-butter unionism," or, as Gompers rather liked to say, "trade unionism, pure and simple." Gompers was not the only architect. He drew on the ideas of many friends and associates—Peter J. McGuire, Adolph Strasser, Ferdinand Laurrell, to name a few. Similarly, he drew on the experience of unions other than the Cigar Makers, in the United States, in Europe, and especially in Britain.

### Changing times

Moreover, the times were ripe for changes in the dreams of reformers. In industry, free-wheeling competition gave way, during the 1880's, to the creation of giant combines and trusts. Cities replaced easygoing, equalitarian villages. Waves of immigrants flooded the labor market and also tested America's capacity to absorb deep differences in culture and religion (see pages 94–95). In the West, the wide-open spaces were webbed with rails and were giving way to fenced ranches, farms, and mining towns. In the South, Reconstruction had ended, and that harassed era's high visions of economic progress and social justice, never realized, were all but forgotten. The two major political parties both appeared to be more concerned with spoils than with social ills.

Samuel Gompers was certainly not alone in recognizing the manifestations of material progress. He was not the only man to see that the upward road for a group as disadvantaged as labor would be steep, slow, and wearying. Yet he was the man on the scene, the activist, the one who sought and willingly hefted the burdens of leadership. It was he who provided labor its impetus toward unity. He stamped the movement with his restless, pugnacious, and sometimes autocratic personality. He branded it with his distinctive idealism and earthiness, his spirit of cooperation and individualism, and his self-denial and power-hunger.

It was in the Cigar Makers' International that Gompers began to lay solid foundations for the kind of unionism he believed in. As early as 1877, he was chosen as Local 144's delegate to the convention of the entire union, held in Rochester, New York, and thereafter he filled that post almost regularly. At his first convention, he proposed a plan for benefits to be paid to union members who were sick, unemployed, or moving to a new town in search of a job. The idea seemed almost comic on the face of it, since most locals were so poor that they had not even sent delegates to the gathering, which, as Gompers remembered, numbered only seven. This, however, was the precise reason behind Gompers' suggestion. Depression-shattered unions needed to build their strength by devising means to assure the binding loyalty of their members.

Most existing locals had no treasuries, and little appetite for collecting assessments—even in pennies—from workers who were never far from starvation. Strikes were called only in desperation and were financed by hat-passing among trade brothers employed in other shops. When strikes were not imminent because they seemed either needless or hopeless, membership melted away. Gompers wanted cigar workers to have a continuing stake in the union, in good times and bad. He was impressed with the British unions' system of sickness, death, and jobless benefits. At the union conventions of the

Gompers' eager self-education was enhanced by contact with the varied men represented here. Peter J. McGuire, a onetime foe of unionism who had a change of heart, was the first AFL secretary. Henry George's avowal of a single tax on land drew much labor support. Adolph Strasser, once a Socialist, took a strong anti-Socialist line as head of Cigar Makers' Local 144. In founding the Knights of Labor, Uriah Stephens expressed a hope that its membership would include "all branches of honorable toil." Charles Litchman, whose shoemakers' union was among the first to be threatened by "labor-saving" machinery, urged that labels be used to identify union-made goods.

Peter J. McGuire

Henry George

late seventies and early eighties, he pushed his ideas implacably, and finally saw most of them adopted, as resistance melted away.

Benefits cost something, to be sure; belonging to a union was not cheap. An initiation fee of a dollar and weekly dues of a dime were imposed; later these sums were doubled. But the worker who grumbled at parting with his weekly dime or two had the eventual satisfaction of knowing that when unemployed he could draw on the union for fifty cents a day, up to a total of seventy-two dollars. This amount might seem small indeed, but it was enough to carry a man through a tight spot. More important, it gave him a feeling that his union was worth something to him. More was to follow, for with Gompers' vigorous advocacy the International also adopted an equalization plan. It distributed the funds of all locals throughout the entire union on the basis of membership and need. Each shop was thus bound in a common financial network, as well as a common cause, with the others. A strike fund was also set aside. To those who objected to the relatively high cost of making all these benefits possible, Gompers retorted: "There is not a dollar which the working man and woman pays into an organization of labor which does not come back a hundredfold."

But with financial security went control. A series of changes in the International's constitution (with Gompers on the committee of re-vision) created a policy that bore down hard on what would nowadays be called wildcat strikes. Cigarmakers with a grievance had to submit it to the local. If they simply dropped their tools and walked away from a job, the union made it clear that union men would fill the empty benches. Strike calls had to be submitted to a vote by the locals. And two thirds of the workers involved had to approve a proposed walkout in order for the strikers to be supported by payments of several dollars weekly apiece. If a strike was dragged out for any length of time, a representative of the International sat in with the local's leadership. He reported to headquarters whether or not continued financial help was justifiable. Thus no militant local could involve the entire union in an exhausting battle.

### Immediate objectives

It was a businesslike arrangement. To some members it seemed to put too much power in the hands of the International's leaders. But it paid. The International's president, Adolph Strasser, happily reported in 1883 that in the preceding two years, authorized strikes had been supported to the tune of $77,000, but had brought about wage increases totaling nearly $2,000,000. When most of the national unions in the country agreed in 1886 to make a simultaneous push for the eight-hour day, the cigarmakers persuaded manufacturers to accept the

Adolph Strasser

Uriah S. Stephens

Charles H. Litchman

33

new standard without even resorting to a strike. This was a unique triumph in a general labor effort that had been mostly a failure up to that time in all parts of the United States.

Gompers and Strasser had good reason to feel satisfied with the plans they had worked out. They were compatible men who enjoyed each other's company when the International's headquarters were in New York. Later Gompers recalled evenings of philosophizing in cafés; he invariably drank stein after stein of beer, while Strasser had red wine. Gompers called Strasser the "Bismarck of cigarmakers" after that able but autocratic German statesman. It was Strasser who announced to a congressional committee in 1883 the policy with which Gompers would later become identified. Asked about the union's "ultimate ends," Strasser replied: "We have no ultimate ends. We are going on from day to day. We are fighting only for immediate objects—objects that can be realized in

a few years." Asked what such objects might be, he declared: "We want to dress better and to live better, and become better off and better citizens generally. . . . We are opposed to theorists. . . . We are all practical men."

Strasser had come a long way from his days as an organizer of the Social Democratic Party. Although Gompers' journey was shorter, once he had reached his conclusions about the correctness of trade unionism as the key to labor advance, he evangelized with a zest that soon was drawing national attention. For Gompers, at this time, the union's best weapon was economic pressure—far more useful than action at the ballot box. One discouraging experience in the political arena went far to confirm this belief. In 1881, the union decided to launch a push for a state law forbidding tenement-house manufacture of cigars. It involved the theater-loving Gompers in what was probably his only fling at playacting.

Workmen march through Manhattan's Union Square on September 5, 1882. Labor Day became a national holiday in 1894.

A first and vital step toward passing the desired law was to get eyewitness confirmation of the filthy conditions under which men, women, and children struggled to make a living. Tenement cigarmakers worked in airless rooms choked with tobacco litter, dust, the normal dirt of large and unwashed families; such quarters often harbored one or more victims of tuberculosis, smallpox, or other communicable diseases. Gompers wanted to make an investigation. He knew, however, that immigrant workers in particular were wary of admitting inspectors whose well-meant efforts at cleaning up conditions might cost them their apartments or their jobs. Accordingly, Gompers provided himself with a set of Dickens and came calling as a book salesman. He noted wryly that, knowing the financial and cultural conditions of tenement life, he did not expect to be embarrassed by making any sales. Once inside, he made his survey. The results were published in a New York German-language newspaper and were then used to persuade legislators.

### Pressure on politicians

During 1881 Gompers and Strasser began a long campaign of lobbying in Albany, traveling to and from New York City by Hudson River boat. (The voyage used up eight hours each way but cost only a dollar for the 150-mile trip.) A bill to outlaw tenement work was introduced in the state legislature, but it got nowhere. That autumn, the Cigar Makers carried the campaign to the voters by means of petitions, letters, public meetings and speeches designed to elect legislators who would support the union's position on the question. It was the beginning of a new approach to politics by workingmen: not to organize a new party, but to reward friends and punish enemies in the two major parties. Predictably, the new approach was opposed by a number of Socialists in the union who were determined to have no truck with bourgeois politics. In Gompers' bitter words, they "were willing to see the cigar industry absorbed by tenement-house production unless that fate could be averted by Socialism."

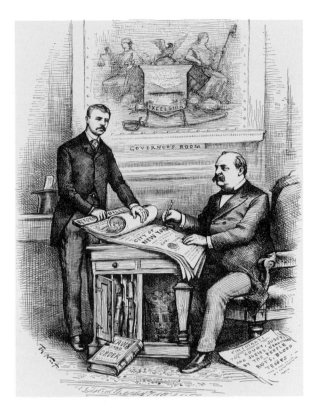

Theodore Roosevelt, a tweedy young reformer in this Nast drawing, presents bills for Governor Cleveland to sign.

Nevertheless, the innovation at first appeared to work. For the Assembly of New York State did pass a "tenement bill" in 1882. Among the law's supporters in that session was a dudish, nearsighted young Republican assemblyman from a New York silk-stocking family. His name was Theodore Roosevelt. Like most proper Harvard graduates and members of gentlemen's clubs at that time, Roosevelt disliked unions. He seriously doubted that workingmen had any problems that the practice of cleanliness, godliness, and Americanism would not solve; he was thoroughly distrustful of any "socialistic" interference by the state in economic affairs. Yet as a member of an investigating committee, Roosevelt allowed Sam Gompers and other union officials to take him through some of the tenements (apparently unarmed with a set of Dickens this time). What he saw and smelled led "T. R." to support his first "progressive" legislation.

"Mr. Gompers has always opposed me," Theodore Roosevelt wrote a friend in 1912, but at that moment T. R. was more angry than accurate. For though Gompers and T. R. differed in many ways, they were alike in being stubborn and in sharing an abiding concern for the cause of the worker.

Roosevelt's awareness of acute labor problems dates specifically from 1882, when a bill to prohibit tenement-house cigarmaking was introduced in the New York State Legislature. At that time Assemblyman Roosevelt, accompanied by Gompers and other "battered, undersized foreigners" of the Cigar Makers' Union, visited tenements to see if legislation was really necessary. T. R. recalled the experience vividly in his autobiography: "I had supposed I would be against the legislation, and I rather think that I was put on the committee with that idea, for the respectable people I knew were against it; it was contrary to the principles of political economy of the *laissez-faire* kind. . . . However, my first visits to the tenement-house districts in question made me feel that, whatever the theories might be, as a matter of practical common sense I could not conscientiously vote for the continuance of the conditions which I saw. . . .

"I have always remembered one room in which two families were living. On my inquiry as to who the third adult male was, I was told that he was a boarder with one of the families. There were several children, three men, and two women in this room. The tobacco was stowed about everywhere, alongside the foul bedding, and in a corner where there were scraps of food. The men, women, and children in this room worked by day and far on into the evening, and they slept and ate there. . . . Instead of opposing the bill I ardently championed it. It was a poorly drawn measure, and the Governor, Grover Cleveland, was at first doubtful about signing it. The Cigar Makers' Union then asked me to appear before the Governor and argue for it. I accordingly did so, acting as spokesman for the battered, undersized foreigners who represented the Union and the workers. The Governor signed the bill. Afterward this tenement-house cigar legislation was declared invalid by the Court of Appeals . . . and in their decision the judges reprobated the law as an assault upon the 'hallowed' influences of 'home.'

"It was this case which first waked me to a dim and partial understanding of the fact that the courts were not necessarily the best judges of what should be done to better social and industrial conditions. The judges who rendered this decision were well-meaning men. They knew nothing whatever of tenement-house conditions; they knew nothing whatever of the needs, or of the life and labor, of three fourths of their fellow citizens. . . . They knew legalism, but not life."

Unfortunately for the union, the state senate allowed the bill to die in 1882, so the battle had to be refought. In the spring of 1883, a bill was finally passed by both houses, and it received the signature of Governor Grover Cleveland. Although no friend to regulatory legislation, Cleveland had been persuaded at last that the law was a sound public-health measure directed mainly against germ-carrying cigars. But before the bill could go into effect, cigar manufacturers appealed it in court. They employed no one less than a former Secretary of State, William M. Evarts, who had also defended President Andrew Johnson in his impeachment trial of 1868. Evarts argued that the law was an unconstitutional violation of the privacy of the home. He stressed the right of men and women to labor as they chose on their own hearth, and to educate their young in the elevating habit of profitable work. The judges agreed and nullified the law on the grounds Evarts proposed.

Back to Albany went the struggle, and in 1884 a new act was passed, modified to meet the constitutional hurdles. But once again it was challenged in court, and once again declared an inadmissible assault on the "hallowed" influences of the home. Four years of work appeared to have been useless. By then, however, the Cigar Makers' International was strong enough to keep up a steady harassment of the tenement manufacturers by strikes and agitation. The manufacturers eventually were convinced that it was cheaper in the long run to operate in decently run factories. "Thus," Gompers concluded, "we accomplish through economic power what we had failed to achieve through legislation" (see pages 100–101, 142–143).

The fight within Local 144 over the propriety of these political tactics had some important long-range results. In the 1882 election of officers, a group of men hostile to Gompers gathered enough votes to elect their slate from local president on down. Gompers claimed that they were Socialists and that this was the reason they opposed him. Some of them acknowledged the charge. But it is also possible that there was a certain resentment over what seemed to be a high-handed policy on the part of Strasser and Gompers. Both men tended to ride opponents down mercilessly, despite the union's having a paper constitution that appeared quite democratic. And Gompers' actions in 1882 would seem to have justified some resentment. First of all, he seized on a technicality to challenge Samuel Schimkowitz's election as the new president. Strasser proceeded to sustain the objection and suspend the new officers.

A bitter wrangle, lasting over a year and involving the International's governing executive board, followed. It ended in various compromise proposals. But, during the struggle, the enemies of the alleged "Gompers-Strasser faction" seceded and set up a new organization, the Cigar Makers' Progressive Union. Gompers denounced this move as Socialist malevolence. Whoever was primarily at fault, the fact was that the cigar trade in New York had become a victim of what Gompers detested: "dual unionism." Two unions competing for workers in the same trade wasted time, energy, and money in battling each other. Moreover, employers could and did play them off against each other. For nearly four years the "International" and "Progressive" cigarmakers struggled. And they scabbed on each other: When either group struck a factory, the other group provided workers to serve as strikebreakers. (The short and intentionally ugly name of "scab" for a man who took a striker's place in this way was a vigorous labor contribution to American speech.) The two cigarmaking unions joined in temporary alliances now and then, but always fought anew—until in 1886 their feud moved onto a new plane.

At that time, a sizable number of "Progressives" were enrolled as members of a local assembly under District Assembly 49 of the Knights of Labor. That development brought to Gompers' very doorstep a battle that by then had already been raging five years—a battle with an enemy other than socialism. The needs of the fight had spurred a fresh effort to federate "pure and simple" trade unions nationally. The stakes were control of the entire American labor movement. And matters had begun moving toward a climax in 1886.

### Terence V. Powderly

Originally, the Knights had met as more or less independent secret lodges. By 1879, however, the organization had become a single national body. Local assemblies were linked

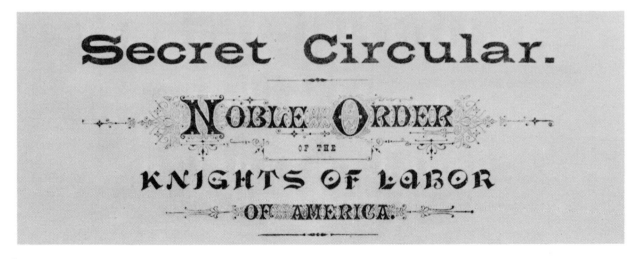

Emphasis on secrecy was not limited to the Knights' internal circulars. Five stars replaced its name in public announcements.

through district assemblies, which began to meet in an annual general assembly. At its very root, this form of organization compromised trade-union principles. For, with few exceptions, the district assemblies were "mixed," comprising locals of various trades. Because of this mixture, specialized craft needs tended to be forsaken. In the framing of policy, there was an emphasis in favor of broad objectives on which everyone could agree. And for the Knights, "everyone" was a highly inclusive term. The original constitution barred lawyers, bankers, gamblers, and liquor dealers from membership. Otherwise anyone was welcome, including reformers of every ilk—and employers, too, if they felt inclined to join.

The breadth of the Knights' objectives was underscored by the personality and attitudes of the man who, in the 1880's, became their national chief, or Grand Master Workman: Terence V. Powderly. In his own way he was as interesting as Gompers, and in many respects Gompers' complete opposite. Strictly speaking, Powderly had been a workingman (a machinist), born to working-class Irish parents in Carbondale, Pennsylvania, in 1849—the year before Gompers' birth. But in actuality he was the epitome of the middle-class reformer. He sympathized with oppressed laborers but heartily disliked strikes as a means of improving conditions. Powderly hoped for the universal adoption of arbitration throughout the industrial world, and he still cherished the old National Labor Union notion of cooperative workshops as an alternative to the wage system. Far from distrusting politicians, he had entered that game himself as a Greenbacker and had served three terms as mayor of Scranton, Pennsylvania. He was attracted to Henry George's proposed single tax on increased land values as a panacea for society's ills.

Despite the early uneasiness of the Knights about admitting lawyers—regarded as the employers' allies—to the Order, Powderly himself privately studied law. Eventually he was admitted to the bar. He tended to view the Knights not so much as a union but as an educational undertaking geared to the work of social uplift. He was a neat and dignified man, and a teetotaler. He disliked Gompers as a person and also as a rival labor leader. For Gompers enjoyed carrying the flavor of the workshop with him, and was willing and able to win friends and influence people in saloons. Indeed, Gompers was prone to play the part of an only slightly polished roughneck, and in the 1880's he sported a fierce black moustache that gave him an extra flourish in this role. In 1886, during negotiations between the Knights and the Cigar Makers over control of cigarmaking, a Knights of Labor circular bearing Powderly's signature stated that the general executive board of that organization had "never had the pleasure of meeting with Mr. Gompers when he was sober." Gompers hotly denied the charge and accused the Knights of "the grossest slanders, false and malicious." Some time later, however, he learned the statement had been added to the circular without Powderly's knowledge.

Between Gompers and Powderly, both of them strong-willed and opinionated, there were differences magnified by a genuine clash of personalities. In a sense Gompers' inborn love of a good fight was reflected in his developing philosophy. He shared neither Powderly's optimistic hope of reconciling the capital-labor conflict by cooperation, nor the Socialists' dream of eventually eliminating the conflict by working-class capture of the state. Gompers preferred to see labor organized to fight a continuing battle. He thought unions could flourish in a permanent, though basically peaceful, state of tension. Workers, he believed, would find dignity and an identity in the struggle. He also felt that if workingmen and their employers competed for a larger share of the fruits of industry, both groups would perhaps be stimulated to greater productive efforts.

### A new federation

Yet Powderly, an articulate man and a good organizer, was attracting attention to the Knights. While they had only 19,000 members

Powderly's refusal to strike, even when the "irons" were hot (above), put him on a powder keg. One explosion came after a newspaper report (below) that a Knights' document cited on this page had impugned the sobriety of Powderly's rivals.

## THEY ARE NOT DRUNKARDS

### MESSRS. STRASSER AND GOM-PERS VERY ANGRY.

**POWDERLY'S PECULIAR METHODS—AN-OTHER "SECRET CIRCULAR" BROUGHT TO LIGHT.**

COLUMBUS, Ohio, Dec. 10.—A story explanatory of the deadly antagonism that exists between Mr. Powderly and certain leaders of trades unions was discovered by THE TIMES's correspondent to-day. Of course there

in 1881, it seemed quite possible that once the clearly imminent organization of labor on a nationwide scale was under way, the Knights would be able to lead it. Those trade unionists in the existing craft organizations who feared such leadership moved to set up their own national network instead. In August of 1881, officials of the International Typographical

Union, the Amalgamated Association of Iron and Steel Workers, and several other unions, sponsored a meeting in Indiana. This meeting, in turn, called for a "national labor congress" to meet in Pittsburgh in November, for the purpose of setting up an organization to "secure that justice which isolated and separated trade and labor unions can never fully command."

When this Pittsburgh gathering convened, it numbered 108, including delegates from various city federations of labor organizations—and from the Knights of Labor as well. But most significantly, the assembly included a large block of representatives from trade unions themselves. Among the latter was Samuel Gompers, representing the Cigar Makers' International. By now he was well known among labor spokesmen everywhere. He was nominated for chairman of the convention, but he lost. However, he did get the more important job of chairman of the committee on organization. The plan that emerged from Gompers' committee was for a federation in which national trade unions would have representation proportional to their size. But all other organizations (such as the Knights, unaffiliated locals, and city labor councils—which often included representatives of political parties) would have only one delegate apiece.

This restraint effectively put control in the hands of the "pure and simple" union men, though they were not entirely sure what to do with it. They voted to call themselves the Federation of Organized Trades and Labor Unions of the United States and Canada, and to hold annual meetings. They also urged needed reforms upon the government. (Gompers served as a member of this committee, and eventually was its chairman.) Among the reforms being sought were immigration restriction, enforcement of the eight-hour day for government employees, the limitation of child and convict labor, and the outlawing of wage payments in any form but cash. The latter reform was to eliminate the notorious company stores in some industries where workers were paid in supplies at outrageous markups.

A declaration was approved that spoke in socialist-sounding terms: "Whereas a struggle is going on in the nations of the civilized world between the oppressors and oppressed of all countries, a struggle between capital and labor. . . ." But the roster of participating organizations made it clear that craft-based organizations, dedicated mainly to economic pressure, were in command. The Molders, the Carpenters, the Glass Workers, the Typographers, and the Iron and Steel Workers were represented there. And all were moving towards the kind of businesslike unionism represented by the Cigar Makers' International.

The new Federation of Trades and Labor Unions (FTLU), however, was provided with almost no muscle. It was to have no permanent paid officials. Its funds were to come from union donations, which somehow were always late and small. It had no headquarters, no office, no publication. Even so, efforts were made to breathe life into the FTLU: A per capita tax was voted, and the support of unaffiliated unions was diligently solicited. Yet annual collections never totaled more than a few hundred dollars, and attendance at meetings dwindled year by year. The FTLU seemed to suffer from the same limitations the United States itself had endured in the 1780's under the feeble Articles of Confederation: no functioning central government and no money. The Federation made one bold move in 1884, when it voted to recommend to all the labor organizations in the nation a concerted push for the eight-hour day, effective May 1, 1886. But when the FTLU held its fifth convention, late in 1885—at which Samuel Gompers was elected president—the group appeared to be on its last legs. It might not have survived at all, except that events of the following year made the coalescing of labor forces not only feasible but necessary. What ensued was a series of events somewhat similar to the crises of 1787 that had led to the drafting of the American Constitution.

To begin with, in 1885 the solidarity of the FTLU was weakened further by a sudden, dramatic boom in membership in the Knights.

For two years, ever since the Knights first advocated a shortened workday, that group had been regarded as the leader and champion of the eight-hour campaign. Now thousands of workers were following the Knights' organizers into the fold, even though the Knights' participation in the eight-hour campaign was more through words than actions.

The FTLU was wary of the Knights' growing strength but also mindful that labor unity was a requisite to labor reform. Thus the FTLU held out a prospect for coalition by urging the Knights to join in the drive to achieve a shorter workday—even through strikes, if necessary. Grand Master Workman Powderly's response to the prospect was guarded and noncommittal. He disapproved of strikes—"a relic of barbarism," he called them. Nevertheless, he did not wish to repudiate the eight-hour workday by implication. He began working quietly *behind* the scenes to discourage the Knights' local assemblies from striking even if the eight-hour workday did not come about by the May 1 deadline. Meanwhile, the Knights, whose mem-

bership had climbed dramatically from 19,000 in 1881 to a high of 700,000 in 1886, were boldly stepping up their recruitment drive. They concentrated on skilled workers in the glass, metal, and printing trades—every area in which unions had been hoping and planning for years to operate successfully.

*The Haymarket bomb*

While this rush to the Knights' banner was taking place, a new event heightened the atmosphere of crisis. As May of 1886 approached, 190,000 workers in various industries followed the FTLU's suggestion and struck for the eight-hour day. Many of the Knights' members joined in the drive, unaware of Powderly's hostility to it. As it turned out, only a few of these strikes were successful. But in Chicago, the eight-hour-day campaign ran into a tragic pitfall. During a labor demonstration on May 3, a number of workers were meeting near the McCormick harvester plant, the scene of a lengthy strike then in progress. As some strikebreakers were leaving the works, they were

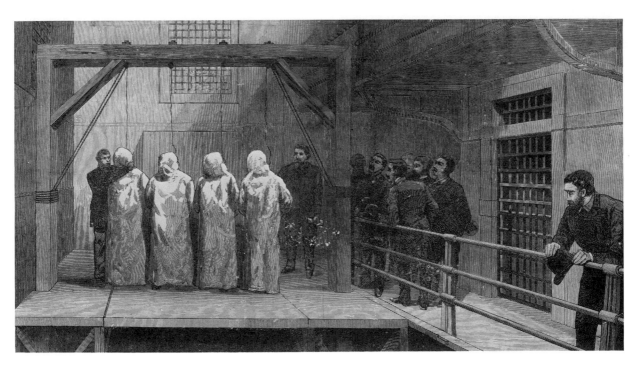

In this sketch, made by an eyewitness, four men accused of the Haymarket bomb tragedy have caps drawn over their faces just before execution. Here on the gallows, one of them defiantly shouted: "This is the happiest moment of my life."

attacked by an angry crowd of about five hundred. Police were called, and there were six casualties in the ensuing battle.

A group of Chicago anarchists—who preached, in theory at least, that all government is evil and that justice can prevail in the world only by the total overthrow of government, through force if need be—called a protest meeting in Haymarket Square for the next evening. The meeting led by the anarchists was peaceful enough. Nevertheless, near its close, a detachment of police appeared on the scene. Then, from out of nowhere, a bomb was thrown—a shattering blast that killed one policeman outright, and wounded several others along with scores of spectators. A wave of shock and panic over the Haymarket bomb swept the city and the nation. Though the identity of the person who threw the bomb was never clearly established, eight anarchists were arrested and tried in a passionately partisan atmosphere. Seven were condemned to die, on thoroughly inconclusive evidence. Labor spokesmen tried frantically to make it clear that the explosion was in no way connected with the eight-hour push. But their actual defense of the convicted men, when offered, was stammering and frightened. A violent wave of public reaction threatened to engulf and destroy the whole movement to organize the working class.

Clearly, a critical period in the history of labor had begun. If the trade unions were to challenge the Knights, the signal had been sounded for action. If a new kind of leadership was to emerge, the strategic moment was at hand. And as if to emphasize this fact, the warfare between Knights and trade unionists flared up anew in Gompers' very front yard. The Powderly organization chose this time to enroll several thousand members of the Cigar Makers' Progressive Union in its fold. It opened negotiations with the manufacturers and granted those who met its terms the use of the union label—an important means of economic pressure, since labor supporters were supposed to buy only goods bearing such a label. The Cigar Makers' International, issuing its own label,

struck back. So the battle of the labels opened up a new front in the general war between the forces of "pure and simple" and of "general reform" in the labor field.

The fight was a passionate and sometimes violent one. A single episode early in 1887 lit up its potential violence and almost ended the career of Samuel Gompers. At a statewide labor meeting held in Albany, New York, a fracas broke out over the seating of rival delegations of trade unionists and Knights. Gompers, who was presiding, ordered the excited, shouting galleries cleared. Suddenly a man rushed up to the platform and pointed a gun straight at the black-moustached cigarmaker. Gompers reacted swiftly and calmly, both to save his life and to avoid a riot. Wearing a fixed smile, he threw his arms around the would-be assassin, pinned the man's arms to his body, and wrested the gun away. Slipping it into one of his own pockets, he advised, "Now beat it, while the going is good."

Meanwhile, the leaders of the national unions rose to the situation by counterattack. P. J. McGuire, Gompers' old friend from labor struggles in the 1870's, was now president of the Brotherhood of Carpenters and Joiners. Like Strasser, he had been converted from militant socialism to craft unionism. McGuire and several other union leaders issued a call for a conference to meet in Philadelphia on May 17, 1886. Twenty unions sent delegates, who proceeded to draw up a "treaty" for presentation to the general assembly of the Knights, due to meet in Cleveland the following week. The proposal did not reflect any Philadelphian spirit of brotherly love. It was, in fact, an ultimatum. The Knights were to refrain from organizing workers in trades that already possessed unions. They were to forbid their members from working below wage scales set by existing unions, and from serving as strikebreakers. They were to issue no union labels and undertake no negotiations with employers regarding working conditions. In short, if the Knights of Labor withdrew from the economic battlefield altogether, the trade unions would in turn recognize the Knights' right to conduct whatever education and propaganda activities they deemed suitable.

The Knights, rather predictably, refused this proposal. In the battle among cigarmakers, in fact, they reacted vigorously by issuing a new order that *all* the Progressive cigarmakers must now join the Knights or be replaced at their jobs. As it turned out, the Knights overreached themselves, for most of the Progressives chose, instead, to rejoin the International. In a short time the Knights were driven out of the cigar trade altogether. The union forces now decided that the time had come to regroup. They made plans for a December 1886 gathering to be held in Columbus, Ohio, to launch a new alliance of trade unions. The FTLU obligingly agreed to meet there at the same time to sign its own death warrant and merge with the new group.

In due course at Columbus, President Gompers dutifully called the twenty delegates to order. Next he went through the formality of proposing amalgamation with the new organization that would be created. The following day he took twelve FTLU delegates, nominated by their unions to serve at the organizing meeting of the new Federation, and led them to another hall to join twenty-eight unionists already on hand. These forty men, plus two who showed up later, represented twenty-five organizations with a total membership of approximately 317,000. Now, as a climax to nearly a decade of struggling to build strong national unions out of the wreckage caused by the depression of the 1870's—and as a culmination to the stormy year of the Haymarket bomb—they ordained and established the American Federation of Labor.

### Movement meets man

In one way, the new Federation did not seem to differ much from the defunct FTLU; AFL official historians, in fact, have often considered the two federations as one, and dated the history of the modern body from 1881. Like the FTLU, the AFL also began with an outburst of rhetoric, repeating verbatim the outcry con-

cerning the worldwide struggle of oppressors and oppressed. It also presented proposals for legislation. It even offered "generous support to the independent political movement of the workingmen," a support which never materialized. But more significantly, the AFL provided for an executive and for funds. Participating unions were to pay the central organization a tax of one-half cent per member per month. An executive council was to be created, consisting of a treasurer, secretary, two vice-presidents—and finally, a full-time, salaried president.

The council was, to be sure, not given any broad powers over the constituent unions. The convention proceedings clearly spelled out the intention of "leaving to each body or affiliated organization the complete management of its own affairs." The AFL's leadership could only mediate conflicts over jurisdiction, encourage the formation of local unions and the consolida-

Gompers hoped AFL solidarity would diminish such strike violence as the overturn of a Chicago streetcar in 1885.

43

tion of such locals into national and international bodies, stimulate the growth of city and state labor federations, and appeal to member organizations for funds to support strikes whenever considered desirable. In short, the organization was to remain a federation, and not a central government of labor. It could not even "charter" new member unions, but merely issue "certificates of affiliation." The assembled delegates from strong-minded craft unions—the Iron Molders, Miners, Typographers, Journeymen Tailors, Furniture Workers, Granite Cutters, and others—would have it no other way. And yet there was to be a full-time leader, with an office, some expense money, and at least a potentiality of mobilizing the power of organized craftsmen for economic betterment. The future of the new organization would depend to a large extent on that leader. The convention turned unanimously to Samuel Gompers. The movement and the man had found each other.

For Gompers this was a second turning point, and the end of a hard road traveled from the night schools and shop discussions of his New York youth. He had thrown himself increasingly into the work of organizing the Cigar Makers on the practical, nontheoretical principles he embraced. He had become a recognized leader in that union. (In 1886 he was also elected the Cigar Makers' first vice-president, an office he held for the rest of his life.) In five years with the FTLU, he had emerged with national stature among trade unionists. Gompers had achieved this by incredible effort. While working at his trade to support his family, he had corresponded with existing unions, written pamphlets, and testified before public bodies. He had also negotiated with cigar manufacturers, engaged in newspaper controversies, and traveled thousands of miles by the cheapest and often the most uncomfortable means. His wife and children knew and endured the worst kind of poverty, compounded by his almost perpetual absence. Even so, his family gave him unswerving loyalty, which kept the edge on his keen enjoyment of life and gave him ever-renewed zest for his mission.

His tough body ("built of oak," he proudly wrote) thrived on its prodigal expenditure of energy. But it was more than mere activity that made him the choice of labor's legions. Gompers was a fighter—hot in argument, passionate in appeal. As his faith in a purely economic approach to the labor problem hardened, he had less and less patience with alternatives he thought would weaken the movement. Yet he was always willing to bring his viewpoints into the arena of combat, whether in union hall or beer hall. And he always met his enemies face to face, man to man. What was more, he prepared diligently for every meeting. When he grew loud and red-faced in a debate, it was not to cover up a lack of information. Gompers knew what he wanted, knew what he was doing, knew his opponents and treated them as men and not abstractions. He could be intolerant but not aloof, high-handed but not sly. As a result, he was able to convert some opponents into allies, and to make innumerable friends of his many fellow workers.

If anyone could pull together the threads of one or two or three dozen half-formed and still discordant unions, *he* was the man. If anyone could represent the world of labor to those Americans whose knowledge of it was only hearsay, *he* could do it. The delegates to the 1886 convention were fully aware of his capacities when they elected him president. With one exception, the thirty-eight annual AFL conventions that followed came to the same decision.

Yet for Gompers it was not so easy. He hesitated momentarily, and at first withdrew his name when it was presented. In his memoirs he declared that he had not wished to accept a salary for Federation office because he felt such services should be a matter of faith and duty. His motives were probably less idealistic, however. It was not at all certain that the promised salary of $1,000 a year would be forthcoming, in view of the FTLU's poor record as a collection agency. The funds it finally turned over to the AFL in 1886, after five years of life, amounted to less than $300. Last but not least, Gompers would have to quit his own trade, his personal lifeline to the workingman's domain. His future would be tied to the future of an organization that was heir to a bankruptcy and could furnish him little except a title.

In point of fact, the AFL *did* rent an office in New York for him—consisting of one unheated room. A kitchen table brought from home was his desk, a box his chair, grocery cartons his filing cases. For the first two years, the AFL did not provide a typewriter and a secretary for its chieftain. He would get some help in handling business affairs from the AFL vice-presidents, secretary, and treasurer. But the overwhelming bulk of correspondence, negotiations, lobbying, editing a journal, and pushing new organizations would be his. To take the job meant a further commitment to poverty. It meant eighteen- and twenty-hour days with either a sandwich for lunch or no lunch at all. It meant walks of two and three miles between home and office, because there was not even a nickel to spare for carfare. It meant continued family penury, which had already forced his oldest son to forsake school for work, as Gompers himself had done so long ago in London.

And what was more, to take the job was to take on an uncertain future, as the Knights of Labor was still powerful. Nothing in its formal structure really eliminated the possibility of its organizing powerful unions that would successfully challenge the Federation. The pressure for political action by labor, on Socialist or other lines, was still felt in every hall where workingmen gathered to debate the future.

Outside the world of shop and mill, public opinion still regarded the entire labor movement with suspicion and malice. Furthermore, another major depression like that of 1873 could once again cripple the union movement. (Though nobody could have predicted it in 1886, such a depression was just seven years in the offing.) Even knowing all this, Gompers took the job. "I felt that the trade union movement stood or fell with the success of the Federation," he recalled later, "and gave everything within me to the work." In that spirit, he

## THE PRICE HIS FAMILY PAID

In many ways, Gompers' family took it even more on the chin than he himself did, during the long, lean years of his early struggles for unionism. In 1950, J. R. Rich wrote in *Liberty* magazine:

"Mrs. Gompers had a trick of her own for keeping the bareness of her cupboards a secret from her family and neighbors. She would put a couple of pots to boil on the stove and pretend that there was something cooking in them. Often there was nothing but a gruel of water and flour in one of the pots and only plain water in the other."

In 1886, Gompers accepted the AFL presidency knowing that it might be months before he received his first pay in his high-sounding new post. According to Lucy Robins: "When Gompers returned from the convention to his wife and six children, he realized that he had committed an act that was only short of criminal. How was his family to live without any income? But Mrs. Gompers was of the same stamina as her husband. She insisted that he should follow his life's work at *any* sacrifice to the family. She went to the [Hand-in-Hand] society to secure a loan. . . . Thus the great American Federation of Labor was born—through the sacrifice of Gompers *and* his family. And, actually, Gompers did not possess much more wealth when he died, in 1924, after having been president of the American Federation of Labor for thirty-seven years."

Holding office in the AFL did not require taking an oath of poverty, but Gompers never exploited for profit his position as labor's chief spokesman. There were many temptations, offers of large sums of money for the use of his name—in the formation of a land-grant enterprise in Mexico, for example, and in the organization of an industrial-accident insurance company. Such offers were rejected.

"In my presence," Miss Robins recalled, "he was offered $40,000 a year to write twelve articles on world affairs for a national magazine. He refused on the ground that whatever of him was of value, he owed it to the labor movement. It was not his to sell. Nor did he permit his children to use his name to secure advantageous positions."

threw doubts aside and simply dismissed his own and his family's poverty as an unimportant distraction from the central effort that energized his life. In that spirit, he moved forward with the AFL into a crucial struggle for survival, as the nineteenth century in America drew toward a stormy, dramatic, and supremely important closing decade.

# Chapter 4

# LEADERSHIP TAKES A MIDDLE COURSE

F OR THE FIRST six years of its life, the American Federation of Labor slowly gathered strength in its infant limbs. Critics as well as friends of the organization, and all of its historians, have always agreed that the vital spurt of growth was furnished by the leadership of Samuel Gompers. It could hardly have been otherwise. The very structure of the AFL was such that its early existence depended almost entirely upon the wisdom, energy, and dedication of its president. He was the organization's only full-time paid official. For the Federation *was* a federation—a league, and not a supergovernment. (An analogy to the United Nations would not be altogether wrong.) While it included a number of city and state labor councils, the bulk of its voting delegates were members of individual trade unions. And among these, in turn, power was further centered, not in the independent locals, but in the steadily rising number of national unions.

Nineteen of these national unions were represented at the AFL's 1888 convention, and twenty-seven by 1890. These "great powers"— such as the Miners, the Carpenters, the Machinists, the Typographers—were almost always represented by the election of their leaders to the executive council, which consisted of Gompers, two vice-presidents, a secretary, and a treasurer. Gompers and the council were pledged to respect the autonomy of the individual unions, to enlist no competing (or

"dual") unions in the same trade, and to issue no commands, fines, or punishments. If a union persistently refused to support a decision made in convention, it might be thrown out of the AFL (or "disaffiliated," as the ritual phrase went). But in the case of a powerful and numerous union, the punishment would hurt the membership-hungry Federation more than it would the culprit.

Success for the Federation, therefore, rested on the ability of the president to function as a peacemaker, troubleshooter, educator, coach, inspirational spokesman, strategist, and scapegoat. His efforts were required to settle jurisdictional disputes. For instance, should factory workers producing metal-and-wood objects be organized as metalworkers or carpenters? Should men who moved beer barrels become members of a union of teamsters, brewers, or coopers? Such jurisdictional questions were of agonizing importance to the unions involved. Gompers was also needed to coax funds out of slow contributors, to coordinate the assignment of organizers to expanding unions and the allotment of support money to unions in trouble. He was needed to placate those who were asked to postpone strikes, and to try (not always successfully) to persuade them to agree on delay. He was often badly needed to encourage those already involved in strikes. He was even more often needed to poll member unions to find out which objectives the Federation should urge most strenuously on lawmakers, and to give an impression of AFL unity and confidence at all times.

He was expected to be a tiger in dealing with the Knights, the Socialists, the employers, and the politicians. At the same time, naturally, he was expected to be diplomatic, saying nothing in his tigerish roarings and tail-lashings that would upset the fragile balances within the AFL. Diplomacy was hardly an easy job, for many of the Federation's dominant figures were union men who still had shop grime under their nails, who replied to fine points of logic with four-letter words, and who had learned in youth, as the price of survival, to answer real or imagined injuries with a punch in the mouth. Again, it might be useful to compare Gompers to the Secretary-General of the UN, struggling to keep an organization alive while enmeshed in countless great and small sensitivities. Another figure of speech would describe him as the general of a feudal army, whose division chiefs might pull out of line at will, or even raid unattached regiments and battalions for troops and supplies. In such a force, the successful commander *is* the army. His failure dissolves it into separate, warring bands of brigands.

Gompers was successful. Working incredibly long hours in his cubby of an office, writing and copying letters by hand, walking miles to meetings at night, and occasionally dashing off on a long and grueling train tour, Gompers coaxed life into new and young unions. Then he drew them by the elbow into the AFL fold. The Iron and Steel Workers, the Brewers, and the Flint Glass Workers all came in during the Federation's first year. In the same period, the receipts from the per capita tax of half a cent per member per month put more than $2,000 into the treasury. To encourage other unions to join the AFL, this tax was cut by half. Fortunately, the financial report submitted to the 1888 convention showed over $4,000 in receipts.

It was not always easy to collect funds, however. The Typographers, for example, loftily refused at first to pay anything more than their share of convention expenses, though they later changed their tune. The unkindest cut of all, for Gompers, may have been the slowness of the Cigar Makers to pay up in 1887. This led the AFL chieftain to write his old friend Strasser: "Do you think it the wisest policy to assist in starving the Federation out of existence?" Such prodding eventually achieved results. By 1891, some $17,000 was collected (of which Gompers was allotted $1,800 in salary). By the end of October 1892, the fiscal year had seen 277 charters issued to various locals, city labor councils, state federations, and also to eight new national unions. There were some

DEVOTED TO THE INTERESTS AND VOICING THE DEMANDS OF THE TRADE UNION MOVEMENT

Founded in response to Gompers' prodding (next page), the *American Federationist* was—and is—the official AFL magazine.

forty of these "nationals" represented at the 1892 convention. And they were beginning to look to the Federation for very genuine help.

## Gains and ordeals

Gompers intended that Federation membership have tangible rewards, and that these should be felt as quickly as they could be

---

**DOUBLING AS AN EDITOR**

Gompers gave impetus to labor's growing strength not only with his voice but also by his pen. He wrote for and edited a variety of publications, the first one being *The Picket,* a crudely written and ungrammatical journal of his own Cigar Makers' Local in New York. John Swinton, then regarded as the dean of labor journalists, remarked whimsically that Gompers seemed to edit with an axe.

Delegates to the first AFL convention voted to authorize funds for an official Federation periodical, and the *Union Advocate* came into being with Gompers as editor. It was basically a one-man enterprise: Gompers wrote stories in longhand; his son Henry, the AFL's first paid office boy, delivered them to the printer. At the AFL's second convention, in 1887, it was clear that few representatives shared Gompers' conviction that a labor journal was essential, and the *Advocate* ceased publication. Never one to accept defeat, Gompers continued to argue that a labor journal was needed to present the worker's side of public issues as well as to inform workers of AFL activities. But the Federation turned a deaf ear to him, and some labor leaders rebuffed him coldly. Peter J. McGuire, whom he had known for years, wrote him candidly and somewhat harshly: "The *Journal of the Knights of Labor* even now is prostituted by Powderly to create dissension in the labor movement, and I see no reason why we should have a journal of our own simply to answer back and perpetuate these dissensions at a cost of thousands of dollars for its publication annually."

Gompers' persistent lobbying finally paid off, however, and in 1894 the AFL voted to publish the *American Federationist.* Predictably, Gompers became both editor and leading contributor. He wrote all the editorials and at least one major piece in each issue; many issues contained excerpts from his speeches. In theory, the *Federationist* reflected the collective viewpoint of all facets of American labor. But disgruntled observers often referred to it as the official voice of the *president* of the American Federation of Labor.

---

financed. In 1888 the convention voted for a new tactic to use in waging the battle for an eight-hour day: to single out one union that would strike for the shortened workday—and to lend it full support. The Brotherhood of Carpenters and Joiners moved to the attack in 1890 and scored some local successes. It was helped in this endeavor by a grant of more than $12,000 from the Federation, raised from a special one-shot assessment. The 23,000 carpenters in thirty-six cities who won their fight had substantive proof that federation was a thing of value.

In 1890 the Federation paid the expenses of an organizer for the hard-pushed coal miners' union. In 1891 it lent fresh sums of several thousand dollars to the carpenters and to the United Mine Workers. In addition, the executive council settled a jurisdictional fight among separate unions of brewery workers on the Pacific Coast. It turned down an application from a local group of cornice makers who refused to join the national union of their trade. In less publicized moves, it headed off several strikes that were planned by weak locals. "Lost strikes break up your organization faster than any other cause," Gompers wrote the head of one of these locals; undoubtedly he was thinking of the grim days of the 1870's. Negative as some of these actions appeared, they built up the Federation's credit with the practical and professional men who were pushing their way to the top in various national unions. Such actions edged union leaders gradually toward affiliation with the AFL.

By 1892 the future of the Federation appeared promising, if not radiant. Then a series of events threw the organization—and Gompers—into a period of long and fiery trial. The whole nation, breathless from the pace of industrial change, was seared as well. Names and slogans—Homestead, Pullman, "free silver," Populism—were burned into the consciousness of a people who till then had been generally complacent. Americans suddenly found themselves plunged into a depression and a social war. Out of the tumult and uproar of

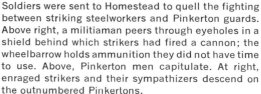

Soldiers were sent to Homestead to quell the fighting between striking steelworkers and Pinkerton guards. Above right, a militiaman peers through eyeholes in a shield behind which strikers had fired a cannon; the wheelbarrow holds ammunition they did not have time to use. Above, Pinkerton men capitulate. At right, enraged strikers and their sympathizers descend on the outnumbered Pinkertons.

the far-from-gay nineties, a twentieth-century nation would emerge. In the vortex of those years, however, the enemies of Samuel Gompers were all besieging him. These included the courts, the hard-core employers who hated all unions, the political reformers who found the AFL too narrow in its intentions, and the radicals who found it too timid. Sometimes they besieged him in succession and sometimes simultaneously. If Gompers came through the era successfully, it was at some cost both to his flexibility and to his tolerance for alternative viewpoints. Survival under fire changed him from a rising young leader to a stern old boss.

There were storm warnings in 1892. First came two brutally fought strikes. In July,

workers at the Homestead, Pennsylvania, plant of the Carnegie Steel Company struck against a series of wage cuts and other appalling work conditions (a workweek of over seventy hours in some departments, for one example). Andrew Carnegie himself was in England at the time. But his partner and lieutenant, Henry Clay Frick, a tough and mortal hater of unions, prepared to man the shops with strikebreakers. On July 6, Frick sent two barges containing three hundred armed Pinkerton detectives up the Monongahela River to occupy the works and "protect" them. The strikers had secured arms, too. During a savage gun battle, ten men were killed, and many wounded, on the two sides. The Pinkertons finally surrendered.

*49*

But the victory of the strikers was hollow. Within a week, eight thousand Pennsylvania militiamen were in Homestead to restore order. Next, an anarchist named Alexander Berkman attempted to shoot Frick as he sat in his office. This act, for which the strikers bore no responsibility whatever, provoked a violent wave of public hostility to labor. By autumn, the strike was broken. But by then the union—the Amalgamated Association of Iron and Steel Workers, one of the key building blocks in the AFL—had been weakened beyond recovery. It would be forty-three years before the steel industry was thoroughly unionized.

Almost at the same time as the Homestead strike, silver miners who had been locked out at Coeur d'Alene, Idaho, fought a pitched battle against scabs. Federal troops moved in and herded hundreds of workingmen into a barbed-wire bullpen, where they languished and starved for months. The ability of a powerful alliance between capital and government to tear savagely at labor had been demonstrated twice in one week. Moreover, in the case of the iron-workers, an apparently strong craft union had been helpless against a floodtide of unorganized and unskilled immigrant strikebreakers, mobilized by labor's enemies.

Then, on July 4, 1892, members of a brand-new political entity, the People's party (better known as the Populists), convened in Omaha. They adopted a platform whose fiery preamble proclaimed that they met "in the midst of a nation brought to the verge of moral, political, and material ruin." The Populist platform added that "urban workmen are denied the right to organize for self-protection; imported pauperized labor beats down their wages; a hireling standing army, unrecognized by our laws, is established to shoot them down; and they are rapidly degenerating into European conditions." The backbone of the Populist movement was provided by hard-driven wheat and cotton farmers. But the Populists were sounding a clarion call for unity among all the producers of America's wealth. "The interests of rural and civil labor are the same," the plat-form continued, and then it spelled out a series of demands designed to meet the grievances of millhand and plowhand alike. It was a trumpeted challenge to America to preserve the virtues of a vanishing era, that period in the nation's youth when equality among men was not a wild dream, but a near reality.

The Populist platform called for an inflated currency through the unlimited coinage of silver, government ownership of railroads and telegraphs, postal savings banks, a graduated income tax, the secret ballot, the initiative and referendum (to make politicians more directly responsible to voters and less so to corporate lobbyists), immigration restriction, the eight-hour day, and the direct election of senators. This all-embracing package of reforms carried echoes of the old National Labor Union as well as the Knights of Labor. And representatives of the Knights present at the Populist convention in 1892 were clearly gratified by a final statement of sympathy with their cause, which concluded the platform.

### A great depression

The rise of a new political faction signaled trouble to Gompers. To be sure, the stated ideals of the People's party were the same as those he had voiced to many an audience. He was openly sympathetic to the Homestead workers, and the AFL contributed $500 toward relief of the imprisoned silver miners. But he dared not follow the suggestion of some who wanted the AFL's constituent unions to call sympathy strikes. Nor would he enlist labor in the crusade against "the money power" that was gathering force and speed like a Great Plains tornado. The Federation was too fragile for a head-on collision with capital. And yet Gompers could not simply ignore the disasters experienced by unions that risked too much too soon. Such setbacks did nothing to support the argument that the AFL's approach offered salvation to the workingman. As for Populism, it provided a powerful emotional charge for the numerous opponents of Gompers who advocated a political approach to the problem.

Why strike at the employer shop by shop? the Populists asked. Although labor would win a battle now and then, it would steadily lose the war, as employers themselves tended to gather into powerful industrial combines with limitless resources for smashing unions. Why not, instead, go for the jugular? Why not go for the political power that lay in control of the government—the power that alone could check the unfair employer, just as it was now being used to brutalize and undercut the worker? True, the Knights themselves were declining in number. The AFL had already turned down one peace feeler from them, holding tight to an insistence that the Knights give up any part in the direct economic struggle with the employers. Yet the vision conceived by the Knights—of an aroused "producing" citizenry uniting to sweep away not only the occasional injustices but also much of the very structure of large-scale industrial capitalism—looked promising whenever the trade unions fell on hard times.

So did the plans of the Socialists. Like the Knights, they capitalized on a certain disgust with chaffering, bargaining, compromising, nose-counting, and nickel-collecting of "pure and simple" AFL trade unionism. In days of crisis, such tactics seemed not only ignoble but doomed. To make matters worse, hard times struck like an earthquake in 1893. A business panic signaled the start of the worst depression the country's history had yet recorded. With hundreds of thousands unemployed, the root problem for trade unions was not how to advance; it was how to keep from being destroyed as they had been in 1873–1877. Gompers was in fact proud to report to the 1893 AFL convention that the unions were weathering the storm, whereas in "every previous industrial crisis" they had been "literally mowed down and swept out of existence."

Survival of this kind was achieved through restraint. It was easy enough to arouse men to action with speeches, but of what use was it to

Jobless, snow-sprinkled victims of the depression of 1893 stand in line on New York's Bowery, seeking food and shelter.

The abolishment of sweatshops, where women worked long hours under appalling conditions, was an early union goal.

provoke them to self-destructive action? One night in 1893, at a mass meeting in New York's Madison Square Garden, Gompers himself, stung by the misery of the unemployed who thronged the city's soup kitchens and shelters, launched into a peroration that denounced the capitalists (see page 205). Suddenly he became aware that his audience, roaring its approval, was changing itself into a mob, ready for some violent move. That was not the way, and Gompers knew it. He drew back and spoke more calmly. "The responsibility of my utterance," he remembered later, "haunted me not only that night but for many a day after." Yet he could not avoid pressure from within the Federation itself to assume the political offensive. The convention was confronted, much to his discomfort, with a sweeping "Political Programme" for endorsement.

The program was a set of proposals for organized labor to support. It was introduced by a Chicago delegate who noted that the British trade union movement was preparing for independent political action. He added that because of the existing situation in the United States (with Populism setting the farm belt afire), the time was ripe for American workers to adopt the British labor technique. Of the eleven "planks" the Chicago delegate proposed, many duplicated the 1892 Populist program. Others demanded such reforms as sanitary inspection of factories, employer liability for injury on the job, municipal ownership of utilities, and an end to sweatshops. Almost all these demands would be enacted eventually by the legislatures of major industrial states, though not for several decades. But the tenth plank was overtly socialistic. It demanded "the collective ownership by the people of all means of production and distribution."

Gompers and those other AFL leaders who instinctively distrusted politics and political alliances with farmers or any other non-union group were unhappy with the program. But they were quite unable to have it voted down altogether. Gompers, writing to a friend that "in revolutionary times . . . better go out of the way than try to stem the torrent," had enough influence with labor delegations to get a breathing spell. It was agreed to submit the proposals to the unions for discussion and to review them when the next annual convention met in Denver in November of 1894. The Socialists raged. Daniel De Leon, one of their leaders, called the AFL president an "entrapped swindler" and the organization itself a "cross between a wind bag and a rope of sand." Gompers' bank account of support and goodwill was dangerously lowered. On the vote for president in 1893, he won by only 1,314 to 1,222. (The delegates cast weighted votes in accordance with the size of their unions.) In the year that followed, events in Chicago were to bring him into temporary eclipse as a leader.

While various union leaders were discussing the Political Programme in the pages of the AFL's official publication, the *Federationist*, trouble was brewing in the Chicago industrial suburb of Pullman. There, George M. Pullman, inventor and manufacturer of the magnificent "palace cars" that made long-distance rail travel a comfortable adventure, had built a model village for his employees. But during the depression, while rents remained high, the wages of the Pullman hands had been sharply cut. Grumbling, the men appointed a grievance committee, whose members Pullman proceeded to fire. In June the inhabitants of Pullman's paternal community went on strike. Some of them appealed for sympathy to a new organization in which they were enrolled, the American Railway Union.

### Eugene V. Debs

The dominant spirit in the American Railway Union was a tall, thin, saintly radical named Eugene V. Debs, who was thirty-nine years old in 1894. The child of Alsatian-German parents, Debs was from Terre Haute, Indiana. He had dabbled in business and in state politics, but found his first love in labor organization. Having worked as a railroad fireman, Debs had entered the Brotherhood of Locomotive Firemen and become one of its officials. But he found himself constricted by the temper of the BLF. Like its three fellow railroad "brotherhoods" (embracing the engineers, trainmen, and conductors), it was craft-centered and so exclusive that the brotherhoods had not—nor have they since—joined the AFL. Debs was a man who kindled to words like "brotherhood," which he interpreted in a far more comprehensive sense than the railroad unions did. He dreamed of, and organized, a union of all who worked on the railways—an army of industrial peace and liberation, open to everyone who toiled to keep the trains moving. (Or *almost* everyone. Negroes were excluded. In the 1890's idealism in America almost always seemed to stop short at the color line.)

The American Railway Union was regarded warily, not only by competing brotherhoods, but by Samuel Gompers. He wrote to a friend that the union was "a second edition of the K of L except that they propose to confine themselves to the railroad men." In fact, with a membership possibly as high as 150,000, the ARU may well have been larger than the dying Knights, and almost as large as the AFL. The ARU was in a position to become the country's most important labor organization, for potentially it controlled the nation's arterial system. The railroads were no longer simply a business. They were indispensable to the life of an industrial society. One blockage on any main line, and the chill of economic death could seize an entire region in a matter of hours.

Now, in June of 1894, that precise disaster occurred—or was provoked. Answering the call of the Pullman strikers for sympathetic action, the ARU voted to instruct its members not to handle Pullman cars. But the managers of the twenty-two major railroads converging in the Chicago area had also been watching with concern the growth of the ARU. They struck back by insisting that Pullmans be attached to

The Pullman strike's leader was depicted as "King Debs," enthroned on—and paralyzing—the "highway of trade."

trains when and as management saw fit. Workers attempting to cut out and sidetrack Pullman cars were fired. ARU train crews quit in retaliation. By July 1, it was no longer just the Pullman strike, but the Chicago rail strike and a major crisis. Moving quickly and purposefully, the railroad managers secured the intervention of the Attorney General of the United States. A federal court in Chicago hastily produced an injunction against any interference with interstate traffic. In effect, this commanded the rail workers to get back on the job. Then, claiming that clashes between ARU members and strikebreakers were uncontrollable violence, Attorney General Richard Olney persuaded President Grover Cleveland to order federal troops into Chicago.

Passions boiled throughout the country. Conservatives insisted that the strike must be broken. They said it was intolerable for a "labor boss" like Debs to have the power to squeeze the country's windpipe until it gasped and squealed for mercy. But almost every friend of labor was outraged at what certainly appeared the calculated murder of a union. The American Railway Union had never for a moment expressed unwillingness to haul any train from which Pullman cars were omitted. The railroads themselves had dictated terms—and had then persuaded federal courts and federal troops to compel workers to perform on those terms. This was no lockout; it was involuntary servitude. As John Lennon, the AFL's treasurer, wrote to Gompers: "If we must be Slaves let us fight first."

Lennon was not the only one to raise his voice. Debs, faced with the smash-up of his beloved ARU and with a jail sentence for defying the injunction, had only two cards left to play. One was to get all the railroad brotherhoods to stage sympathy walkouts all over the country. But the brotherhoods' officials sat by in grim satisfaction, unwilling to help their "rival." The other card still in Debs's hand was to see if the AFL would authorize a sympathy strike by its member unions. The clamor for

Bitter at management reprisals, railroad workers attempt to halt train traffic by derailing and upsetting freight cars.

such a strike was rising hourly among violently angry AFL unionists throughout the country. Sam Gompers resisted that clamor as long as he could. Maintaining that all the facts were not yet in, he sidestepped one invitation by Debs to meet with other labor leaders on July 8. Finally, he was pushed into calling a meeting of the executive council in Chicago on July 12.

Gompers was convinced that the strike was lost. Besides, he was sure that a general walkout would destroy the existing labor movement. Given the temper of the times, few historians could claim that his fears were not soundly rooted. But Gompers also feared the ARU, was wary of Debs both as an "idealist" and "intellectual," and was anxious to maintain the favor of the brotherhoods. To what extent he was yielding to the inevitable, and to what extent enjoying the chance to let an enemy perish, will never be known. The fact is that, after a long session with Debs and discussions lasting into the small hours of July 13, the AFL executive council led by Gompers refused to recommend sympathy strikes to the member unions. Debs asked that the AFL send an intermediary to the General Managers' Association (the railroads' board of strategy) and propose a means of peaceful surrender. What Debs had in mind was that, if all Pullman strikers could be reinstated without prejudice, the walkout would end. But the executive council refused to act.

No hope was left for Debs. The strike and the ARU alike collapsed. He himself spent six months in jail for criminal conspiracy to defy the government. He emerged from prison as a Socialist leader. Years later his recollection was: "Gompers did everything he could to break the strike." And Gompers, as an old man, said that Debs "lost all faith in the power of constructive work and became the advocate of revolt." Both statements were exaggerated, yet both showed how deep, divisive, and lasting were the passions aroused in 1894.

### Losing the presidency

So the battle ended. But when Samuel Gompers appeared at the Denver convention four months later, he was, in many eyes, the man who had sold out the railroad strikers (despite the AFL's formal gesture of a $500 contribution to Debs's legal defense). Nonetheless, his power was not entirely gone. When the Political Programme came up for a vote, the long years of Gompers' educational work in the principles of practical trade unionism bore fruit. The delegates were not interested in a political crusade. Each individual item in the program had plenty of support—except plank ten, the collective-ownership statement. That one was shot to bits by friends of Gompers, who festooned it with ridiculous amendments—such as proposing that socialization of the means of production be endorsed "as rapidly as the people of the United States shall declare in favor thereof by means of the initiative and referendum." But in the end, while the convention endorsed each plank (except number ten), it refused to adopt the program as a whole.

Sam Gompers' letter writing, speechmaking, handshaking, committee appointments, organizing assignments, and financial donations to member unions from the Federation treasury had built up a machine that could defeat the most formidable enemies of "pure and simple" unionism. But his long, hard work was unable to deliver him the vote for the presidency that year. (He denied all his life that he had ever sought support for the office, a statement quite properly believed by nobody.) Delegates seeking reprisal against Gompers—not all of them Socialists, though Gompers laid the blame at their door—elected John McBride, of the United Mine Workers, to the top office for the next year. And as if to move the Federation out from under the very suggestion of Gompers' influence, they voted to transfer its headquarters from New York to Indianapolis.

Going on forty-five, the veteran warrior with the fierce eyes, bristling moustache, and strong appetites had come a cropper. He had beaten his political enemies in the field, but now, in 1894, he had been knocked out of the AFL saddle. It was a bitter season for Gompers. Sadly, like a man watching a bit of his life being cut away, he stood in the AFL's main office with the new secretary, August McCraith, shortly after the convention, supervising the packing of the entire AFL files for shipment to Indiana. McCraith, eager to save freight charges, discarded two six-foot-high piles of material. To Gompers, every scrap of the AFL record was precious. He salvaged some papers, and returned with two suitcases for the rest, only to find that the janitor had disposed of it.

For Gompers, another turning point had been reached. His defeat did not signal the end of his life in labor, only a brief interregnum; his influence ran deeper than even *he* realized. It took only one year for the Federation to call him back. At the 1895 convention in New York, the delegates adopted a resolution that "party politics shall have no place in the conventions of the American Federation of Labor." They also reelected Gompers as president, by a tissue-thin margin of 1,041 to 1,023. He was never to lose the AFL presidency again in his life. And with the Federation's official endorsement of political noninvolvement behind him, Gompers was able to hold the line of neutrality in the hotly fought national election of 1896.

The Populists and Democrats united behind William Jennings Bryan, a youthful Nebraska spellbinder whose sonorous voice thrilled rural audiences as he attacked the sins of the plutocrats who aimed to "press down upon the brow of labor this crown of thorns." Time after time, in his grand climax, the silver-supporting Bryan declared: "You shall not crucify mankind upon a cross of gold." Since the Republican candidate, William McKinley, was very evidently a spokesman for business interests, almost all Americans who had grievances (real or fancied) against that order tended to be Bryanites. Bryan himself wasted much of his power to attract new recruits by concentrating narrowly on the issue of free silver. He made the mistake of neglecting other groups who had their own discontent with a changing social order.

Nonetheless, large elements of the laboring population were drawn to him. The remnants of the Knights (falling rapidly below the 75,000

mark and now led by an agrarian radical named James R. Sovereign) and of the American Railway Union officially supported Bryan. So did a number of unions who were AFL members. But Gompers refused categorically to commit the Federation to Bryan. He never had much confidence in courts, legislatures, or parties, though he was willing to urge that labor should support individual legislators who were friendly to its interests, or vote against those who were hostile.

Gompers, in fact, was as suspicious of government as any arch-conservative advocate of *laissez-faire* (letting people do pretty much what they choose). He looked dubiously on government-sponsored boards of arbitration as well as on laws regulating working conditions. For while he would accept whatever benefits accrued, he strongly believed that workingmen profited most by what they gained through their own power to organize and to bargain. Hence the Democratic warriors of 1896 wooed him in vain. There were rumors that Bryan was ready to offer him a place in the Cabinet if he won. And Gompers did once or twice indicate that his sentiments favored the Nebraskan *and* free silver. But he refused to endorse any candidate. Instead, he warned AFL members generally to beware of "the effervescent, bucolic, political-party, cure-all sophist and fakir," and to avoid such "Middle Class issues" as the currency problem. And to this line he held, amid the tumult and the shouting of a campaign that saw Bryan roundly defeated in November and the country committed to the acceptance, once and for all, of the industrial order.

### A respectable new phase

The decision at the polls accorded entirely with the basic outlook held by Gompers. It is essential to emphasize once again that he had come around to recognizing that large-scale capitalistic organization plus the wage system were permanent features of the social scene. His entire scheme of businesslike unions, negotiating within a relatively unregulated economy, harmonized with the mandate of the voters in 1896. The American people had voted for the factory and the city. They were willing to improve the poor conditions of life in the urban-industrial world by eventually voting to enact Populist reforms one at a time. But they would not reject the basic financial and legal structure underlying the age of steam and steel. And Gompers, with his allies in the AFL, had brought his organization through the crisis of the depression without capitulating either to the agrarian middle class or to socialist radicalism. Thus he had made the AFL an acceptable instrument to both government and business. The AFL would be able to voice labor's needs in the new century that lay ahead.

So the Federation entered a new phase. Though not one of unbroken success, it was at least one of respectability. Symbolic of the change was a fresh move of headquarters. Gompers' reelection to the presidency depressed him in only one respect: it necessitated a move to Indianapolis. He went there by himself, for he did not feel secure enough in his renewed relationship with the Federation to take his family to Indiana. It was a lonely exile and, for a person London-born and New York-bred, a painful one as well. Gompers' reaction to it may have made him vulnerable to the severe illness he contracted shortly after the move. A year later, however, the very next AFL convention voted to transfer the headquarters to the hub of national politics: Washington, D.C.

Early in 1897 Gompers rented a two-story brick home in the capital and moved the AFL files and a few pieces of furniture into a three-room suite in an office building downtown. As the Federation grew, its administrative functions multiplied, and the need for additional headquarters space became critical. Finally, the AFL had sufficient funds to put up a seven-story building in Washington, during the Woodrow Wilson Administration. Its completion received considerable fanfare and a dedicatory speech by President Wilson himself. Gompers' son Henry, who had been the Federation's first office boy and was now a granite cutter, made the building's cornerstone. On it he carved his

## THE CONSTANT WIFE

From her memory of Gompers, Lucy Robins could state that he set so strenuous a pace that he "never had the time to be present when his children were born, nor to be at funerals when members of his family died." He was devoted to his wife and the children she bore him, but most of his activity centered on the world of labor.

Sophia Gompers did not compete for her husband's attention. Her world, so much smaller than his, revolved around *him,* primarily. She was there when he needed her—to comfort him, cook for him, and care for him. When, as AFL president, he left his family in New York and went to live briefly in Indianapolis in the 1890's, he became ill with gastritis and was bedridden for several weeks. He lost so much weight that his doctor said only "bulldog strength" pulled him through—ignoring the fact that Mrs. Gompers had rushed out to nurse her husband until he recovered. She was short and round, a motherly looking woman who endured decades of hardship without complaint. Her job, as she saw it, was to make her husband's lot easier—a full-time occupation with its share of surprises. He had a habit of bringing his associates home to dinner unannounced, or inviting them for breakfast, to discuss labor matters. But Sophia's gracious spirit never wavered. She was so delighted to have her "Sammy" at home that she happily entertained anyone who came with him.

Gompers traveled extensively for the AFL; he worked late at the office; he attended night meetings. And he craved entertainment as a relief from these activities far more than he craved a warm hearth. Consequently his homecoming was a rare occurrence. Rowland H. Harvey, one of Gompers' biographers, wrote that he "drank beer in Ebbitts Café, or went to the 'Gayety' in the evening and watched the antics of comedians. . . . Behind the scenes, he, the good fellow, was always welcome. His fine, mellow voice and his eloquent shrugging of the shoulders never failed to delight the players. Sam's heart was always tender toward the girls of twinkling toes. . . . After the show came the supper, with Sam in Falstaffian mood, flanked by pretty girls, consuming almost endless drinks and more nearly endless cigars. Mamma Gompers never worried. 'Sammy' always came back, but sometimes very tired and even ill; for his oak-like body, strong as it was, often gave way before such treatment."

Miss Robins recalled that Gompers "often used to say that a woman is as old as she looks, but that a man is old when he stops looking!" Gompers wasn't a rake in the traditional sense—for none but his wife enjoyed his affections—but he never did stop looking.

Gompers sometimes tried to keep in trim by riding a bicycle. Here he stands next to British labor leader Ben Tillett.

to acquaint himself with the theaters, the restaurants, the parties—and the saloons—of the thoroughly pleasant city of Washington. His salary rose by gradual increments. His living quarters improved. He himself developed a new and more statesmanlike appearance. He shed his moustache, donned spectacles, and complacently accepted the growth of a generous paunch, the result of his lusty appreciation of good food and drink. (Vaudeville comedians began to draw laughs by patting padded bellies and referring to them as "my Sam Gompers.") By the time he reached his mid-fifties, he had the style—and look—of a patriarch.

His new appearance was appropriate, because the Federation was taking on a new image, too. It pulled far ahead of its rival unions in membership, sprinting from some 278,000 in 1898 to about 1,676,200 six years later. Heartening as these numbers were, they represented only a fraction of the total labor force. In 1904 the Federation comprised 114 international unions, 828 directly affiliated locals, 549 city centrals, and 29 state federations. Its receipts for that year exceeded $220,000. No competing organization could even come close. Socialist enemies

father's words: "This edifice is erected for service in the cause of Labor, Justice, Freedom, Humanity." Gompers, dressed to the nines and seated on the speakers' platform next to the President of the United States, remembered with wry amusement how, in his youth, "the morning of a labor gathering [used to find] travel-stained labor men sleeping on the benches in the station."

The AFL building, which Gompers called "substantial proof of the stability and influence labor has achieved," was a thing of the future in 1897. Yet the future began to take palpable shape then, as the headquarters office staff grew from two to four. Gompers himself, though he adhered to his killing work schedule, found time

To Gompers, who found pretty women delectable, these "Ziegfeld Follies" girls were a feast for the eye: well endowed, provocatively dressed, and occasionally even talented.

of the Federation had organized a Socialist Trade and Labor Alliance in 1895, but its membership was always tiny. The boisterous and fighting-mad Western Federation of Miners, after briefly joining the AFL, led in the formation of the Western (later the American) Labor Union in 1898. But it, too, had more sound and fury than voting strength. A fusion of these organizations (and several others) in 1905 was to furnish something of a challenge to the AFL, in the form of the Industrial Workers of the World (known also as the IWW and the "Wobblies"). But until that date no other alliance of unions remotely threatened the Federation.

As labor became more vocal in expressing its grievances, those in power and high places in the government began to listen. In 1898, President McKinley solemnly received a visit from the Federation's executive council and heard their request for pro-labor legislation. As a result, the President included some recommendations of this nature in his next message to Congress. Here was a kind of recognition that the unions had not previously enjoyed. More significant (and more provocative of dispute among labor leaders themselves) was the invi-

tation to Gompers and other AFL officials—John Mitchell of the United Mine Workers and James O'Connell of the International Association of Machinists, among others—to join the National Civic Federation. The purpose of this group, which had been created in Chicago in 1896, was to bring together capitalists, workers, and philanthropists in efforts at voluntary conciliation of industrial disputes.

While the Civic Federation did not formally endorse unionism, and admitted non-union (and anti-union) employers to its membership, it nevertheless gave official recognition to the existence of an organized-labor point of view. This very visible departure from conservatism promised much for the future. A few farsighted employer-members may even have foreseen a day when vast industrial combinations would negotiate binding agreements with large-scale trade unions—to their mutual benefit. Whether or not this viewpoint pervaded the organization at the time, Gompers saw distinct opportunities in membership. The Civic Federation was eminently "safe." It had a sound public image. And its members had ready access to those who really pulled the levers in the business world.

### The middle way

Yet to join meant that Gompers and his fellow labor leaders would sit at the same table with bankers and bosses. These included men like Mark Hanna, the Cleveland iron magnate who had been McKinley's campaign manager in 1896 and had been unfairly caricatured by the radical press as the embodiment of the big-bellied tycoon with a strongbox for a heart. To accept an active role in the Civic Federation meant a sharp and irrevocable break with any lingering notion that the laboring class could achieve its goals only by the route of class struggle. Gompers made the break. Thus he became finally and forever a bitter enemy of the Socialists, with whom he was to have several more duels in the Federation before his death.

Gompers' reward for his action was participation in attempts to negotiate favorable settlements of a national steel strike in 1901 and a coal strike in 1902. In neither case did the Civic Federation's efforts win a better settlement for the workers. The steel strike was lost. The coal strike was finally settled by a commission chosen after direct intervention by President Theodore Roosevelt. And yet the very fact that the AFL's leaders were consulted by the overlords of giant corporations about labor problems spelled a victory to Gompers. He still had vivid personal memories of Tompkins Square, Haymarket, Homestead, and every other crisis in which labor had been treated as a pariah, an outcast despised by "decent" society.

There were other bleak and bloody episodes to come, certainly. In the years from 1900 to Gompers' death in 1924, he and the Federation would face defeat and frustration many times in their struggles with capital. And he would be assailed savagely by radical elements in the nation as having sold out to the enemy. Yet he would grip the wheel firmly and steer the AFL down what he insisted was the only road—the middle way between radicalism and submission. It was a road full of pitfalls, and its final destination was not for Gompers to see. Its triumphant milestones—as well as its twists and depressions—made the journey of his life through its last quarter century as interesting as anything in his first fifty years. For Gompers, it would be as stimulating—and more satisfying. For history, it would be even more replete with significant questions.

# Chapter 5

# GOMPERS BECOMES
# THE VOICE OF LABOR

THE MEANING of success for Samuel Gompers was an almost total merging of his life and career with that of the Federation. It is almost impossible to disentangle the pattern of his later years from the history of the AFL, and from the labor movement in general.

He was, during his last two decades, a winner by the standards of his time. From obscurity and dark little flats, from days without lunch and miles-long hikes to save carfare, he rose to a position of enjoying comfort and esteem. Gompers was never rich, and never cared to be. But his salary climbed gradually to a very respectable $7,500 annually—respectable in those low-cost-of-living years prior to the First World War—rising to $12,000 before his death in 1924.

He could indulge his taste for late suppers and for concerts whenever his schedule allowed. But sweeter to him than either comforts or money was the widespread recognition that now came his way. There was hardly a legislative committee or a party convention after 1905 that did not solicit his views on what organized labor wanted, nor a President with whom he could not get an appointment at the White House. In fact, he could speak to Presidents not as a hat-in-hand beggar for consideration, but as a leader in his own right. He wore his self-assurance everywhere, the White House included. Once, Gompers himself reported, he was granted an interview with Theodore Roosevelt, in which he protested a public statement on

labor by the forceful, opinionated "Teddy." Voices rose. Then Roosevelt hit the desk with his fist and said: "Mr. Gompers, I want you to understand, sir, that I am the President of the United States." At once Samuel Gompers' hand also slammed explosively against wood. "Mr. President," he shot back, "I want you to understand that I am the president of the American Federation of Labor."

When the reality of World War I erupted upon America's consciousness, Gompers committed himself wholeheartedly to American intervention. When the United States finally declared itself a belligerent, he became the official representative of labor in wartime planning. He went abroad during and after the war, cushioned by the flattering rituals of high-placed official travels—motor cars to convey him here and there, official receptions, banquets, and toasts. Gompers would have been less than human if he had not relished having such blandishments bestowed on a one-time cigarmaker. Yet there was always something curiously incomplete about his triumphs. The road of accommodation and business unionism was not always easy to travel. Gompers' power was in no way equal in measure to his formal recognition. His influence on wartime and peacetime labor policies did not always have the full impact he so fervently desired.

Laws that he and the AFL favored—laws that restricted immigration, limited anti-union

The 1911 fire in New York's Triangle Waist Company emphasized the need for laws to protect factory workers. John Sloan's grim "In Memoriam—The Real Triangle" charges that the 146 fire dead were sacrificed to greed.

injunctions, controlled child labor, and set up minimum standards of safety and health in mine and factory—were eventually passed by state legislatures. Yet their passage owed much to the pressure of progressive middle-class reformers with whom Gompers had little in common. The courts often struck down such laws, with the enthusiastic approval of public opinion. Hostility to unionism continued to be an important theme in local politics everywhere, and the AFL's attempt to exert direct political pressure by endorsing candidates failed as often as it succeeded. Great strikes were smashed and workers imprisoned even while Gompers was attending White House conferences.

His life was not all laudatory speeches and public ritual. He had mellowed with the passing years, but his regard for workingmen's rights had not softened. He fought to uphold his principles, and though he did not always win, he never compromised his beliefs. Nor, when he met setbacks, could he indulge in denunciations of capitalistic injustice to ease the fullness of his heart. He had cast himself as a responsible

conservative and could play no other role. What he achieved as labor's chief spokesman had to be defended against the constant criticisms of the radical wing of the labor movement. The radicals delighted in denouncing Gompers as a man who had sold out the ideals of universal justice in economic life for a few concessions to the skilled workers, or for a few laws to lighten the worst abuses of factory labor.

Gompers could at least answer his radical critics without pulling punches. The very intensity of his debates with the Socialists reflected his need to come to grips with *some* enemy without quarter. It was somewhat difficult for him to do this with his more powerful opponents in the worlds of business and national politics. It was not that he became timorous. His dislike of radicalism and of "intellectuals" (a word that he himself used often with derisive quotation marks) was not feigned. But he operated under the restraints of "realistic" leadership, and the burden of such restraints is not light for a strong-minded man. What was more, Gompers could never advance the labor movement faster or further than America was willing to accept. National acceptance came about, to be sure, but slowly and piecemeal. Gompers, like Moses, led a people grumbling for a Promised Land that he could not bring any closer by his unaided will. It was not surprising that his impatience with those in labor's ranks who, he thought, waxed fat while still complaining, often seemed greater than his irritation with labor's enemies.

The Federation itself prospered. Membership went past the million mark at the opening of the century and climbed to about 2,000,000 by 1913. The AFL continued to have difficulties as member unions fought over jurisdiction. In some cases it could not settle these fights "in the family" without real ruptures. The United Garment Workers, for example, were led by a group of officials who fell further and further out of step with the predominantly East European rank-and-file members who manned the sweatshops of the industry. After much bitter fighting at conventions, a large number of garment makers seceded and formed the Amalgamated Clothing Workers of America, in 1914. Gompers himself was not blind to the importance of cultivating the special sensitivities of immigrant workers. The work force in the garment trade was largely Jewish, and there was even a federation of Jewish unionists, the United Hebrew Trades. It was noticed that whenever Gompers addressed this organization, he wore a black skullcap. As it happened, he wore one on many other occasions as he grew older, mainly to cover his thinning hair. But a skullcap, or *yarmulke*, is worn often by Orthodox Jews as a matter of ritual. Gompers, though in no way pious, did not mind letting his Jewish constituents assume that he was in close harmony with them—even though his *yarmulke* was sometimes worn with a very formal, American-style Prince Albert coat!

But true to the official promise of the Federation to recognize no dual unions, he refused to accept the Amalgamated Clothing Workers into the AFL fold. He even used his powers to prevent unionists in New York and Chicago from helping the Amalgamated's members when they were on strike. Nevertheless, the new organization weathered its childhood and, through a series of rancorous strikes, won major improvements in working conditions in the clothing industry. The AFL, all the while, played no more than a spectator's part. The very nature of the AFL dictated limits to its scope. Essentially a league of strong unions run on "business principles," it had no room for mass-based, industry-wide unions made up primarily of unskilled workers who could not afford high dues, and who had less of a stake in the overall success of business enterprise than the skilled workers did.

The fact that many of these unorganized workers outside the AFL fold were recent immigrants widened the gap between them and the "pure and simple" trade-unionist leaders of the Federation. The AFL's official reaction to immigration was one of distrust edging easily into hostility (see pages 177–180). It saw only armies of potential strikebreakers in the boatloads

## "AN ACTOR OF NO MEAN CALIBRE"

That Gompers served as AFL president for thirty-seven years was a tribute not only to his staying power but also to his talents for leadership. John P. Frey, his loyal AFL lieutenant, remembered that Gompers had a "remarkable" voice. "Normally it was pleasant and subject to constant modulation and emphasis. It was on the public platform that the range and appeal of his voice were most effective. . . . It was Samuel Gompers' custom to begin a public speech slowly and in a low tone, sometimes not much above a whisper; yet his words carried to everyone in the audience. As he developed his theme, his voice would become more animated, and as he presented his summation his voice could become thunderous. . . . It was this appealing, challenging voice which enabled him to express more fully his thoughts and convictions and indicate the dramatic instinct which moved him."

Florence Thorne wrote that he excelled at human relations: "S. G. always kept contact with the producing workers. He traveled widely and wherever he went, he made contacts with local people. . . . His mind seized and stored any key information or developing trend. . . . In addition S. G. presided over a convention with an eye to dramatize important events and decisions so they would be remembered. He himself was an actor of no mean calibre . . . not just for purposes of display or to carry a point but for an educational purpose of explaining situations."

William Z. Foster, an ardent Marxist in the labor movement, normally spoke contemptuously of Gompers. But on at least one occasion he had kind words for the way the AFL president handled people who worked for him: "One of many manifestations of the conservative A.F. of L. bureaucracy is the so-called chairwarmer type of organizer. Such organizers draw big wages and do nothing constructive. . . . [They] have long been targets of attack by progressives and revolutionaries in the labor movement. But I never knew a criticism more effective than one made offhand by Samuel Gompers . . . to a typical A.F. of L. conservative, do-nothing organizer. . . . Gompers happened to be in Pittsburgh, and in the course of his conferences, the organizer, an old veteran, requested that he be granted a month's vacation. Gompers, with a drink or two under his belt, listened to his request and then inquired:

" 'Now, let's see, Tom, how long have you been on our payroll?'

" 'It'll be twenty-five years next November,' replied the organizer.

" 'Well,' said Gompers with a sly grin, 'don't you think that's vacation enough?' "

landing at Ellis Island or, more dramatically, in the illegal importation of Oriental laborers to the West Coast. No matter how much Gompers and others might claim they hated only the principle of cheap labor, not the foreigner himself, immigrants could not feel much warmth toward the AFL. Federation leadership deliberately avoided the bold policy of organizing the newcomers and instead took the safer line of agitating for legal restrictions on immigration. What was more, the foreign, the transient, and the unskilled workers were, in general, much less afraid of socialism and other forms of "radicalism" than were those high in the councils of the AFL.

Movements were always brewing in the first dozen years of the new century. Powerful factions asserted their strength to challenge the Federation—and Gompers—for the leadership of labor's forces, especially those four out of five workers who remained outside AFL ranks. The most spectacular movement reached its climax in 1905 with formation of the Industrial Workers of the World. The IWW was an organization like no other one in American history. It began as a counterforce to the AFL, with the blessing of the Socialist party and the Western Federation of Miners, one of the largest unions then outside the AFL. The IWW gradually broke with the advocates of almost any kind of political or peaceful trade union activity —Socialists and WFM included—and became a tiny army of militant workers.

Membership in the IWW was drawn mainly from the mining and logging camps of the West, where company police and workers alike used clubs, bullets, and bombs to settle arguments. The IWW leaders were working-class evangelists, singing radical songs set to evangelical hymn tunes, and preaching a gospel of unity among all "working stiffs." They were certain that the ordinary laborers would one day take over the machinery of production by direct action. As one of their leaders put it, they were "Socialists with working clothes on." In 1905, at the founding convention, the IWW left no doubt as to its purposes and enemies. William

## CLASHES WITH THE WOBBLIES

"We, the IWW, stand on our own two feet—the class struggle and industrial unionism—and coolly say we want the whole earth." These words, by William "Big Bill" Haywood of the Western Federation of Miners, served as a rallying cry to the left-wing dissidents in labor, and to the feuding Socialists led by men like Debs and De Leon, to join in a new federation—the Industrial Workers of the World—whose goals were more far-reaching, if less realistic, than those of the AFL.

The IWW was the outgrowth of a secret meeting held in Brand's Hall, Chicago, in January 1905. In his book *Labor in America*, Foster Rhea Dulles described the two hundred delegates at this conclave as "militant western miners, socialists of various persuasions, advocates of industrial unionism and anarchistic exponents of direct action [who] closed their ranks for a unified and direct attack upon capitalism. Events were to prove that they agreed upon little else than their mutual scorn for the program and tactics of the AFL. Accepting the thesis of class struggle as their common starting point, however, they set up an economic organization whose aim was to work on both the political and industrial front for the final emancipation of labor. . . . While other independent radical unions were officially represented, including the American Labor Union, the United Metal Workers and the United Brotherhood of Railway Employes, individuals rather than organizations were primarily responsible for the establishment of the IWW and the convention was enlivened by the clash of their divergent personalities. . . . Among these varied and colorful figures, the most arresting was Haywood. A massive, stoop-shouldered, lumbering giant, his generally tough appearance given an almost sinister cast as a result of the loss of one eye, 'Big Bill' was a powerful and aggressive embodiment of the frontier spirit. He had been cowboy, homesteader, and miner, but at the turn of the century left the mines of Silver Creek, Idaho, to become an active organizer for labor and the Socialist party. . . . He accepted violence as a necessary phase of the labor struggle. He stood forthrightly for direct action."

To the IWW—or "Wobblies," as they came to be called—"direct action" meant battling hand to hand with soldiers or policemen to protest violation of their rights of free speech and assembly—or deliberate and destructive carelessness on the job.

64

As chairman of the IWW's founding convention, Bill Haywood opened the proceedings by stating: "The aims and objects of this organization shall be to put the working class in possession of the economic power, the means of life, in control of the machinery of production and distribution, without regard to capitalist masters." After addressing the convention as "the Continental Congress of the working class," Haywood sounded a declaration of war against the AFL, which "is not a working-class movement," he said. "It does not represent the working class.... What we want to establish at this time is a labor organization that will open wide its doors to every man that earns his livelihood either by his brain or his muscle.... When the corpora-

Wobblies marching in New York in 1913

tions and the capitalists understand that you are organized for the express purpose of placing the supervision of industry in the hands of those who do the work, you are going to be subjected to every indignity and cruelty that their minds can invent. You are also going to be confronted with the so-called labor leader, the man who will tell you and other workers that the interests of the capitalist and the workingman are identical."

Those at the convention knew that Haywood was alluding to Gompers, for it was no secret that Haywood despised the AFL president as a leader and as a man. In his autobiography, Haywood wrote of having seen "this squat specimen of humanity" for the first time in 1898 at a convention

of miners in Salt Lake City: "He had small snapping eyes, a hard cruel mouth, wide with thin drooping lips, heavy jaws and jowls. A personality vain, conceited, petulant and vindictive. Looking at him, I could realize the passion of cruelty with which this person would wield power if he had it.... One could realize that he might even refer jokingly to the defeat of a great labor struggle, if it were being conducted by an organization that was not strictly in accordance with his views."

Haywood later mused that "Sam Gompers, in an issue of the *American Federationist*, had tried to belittle the first convention of the IWW, but he paid the organization the great compliment of imitating some of its plans, that is, to the extent of establishing departments in the AFL."

The IWW was organized not by skill but by industry, with separate departments to govern workers in such general areas as mining, manufacturing, and transportation, for example. By IWW design, a walkout in one shop could be expanded on a scale vast enough to cripple an entire industry.

The IWW had Socialist origins, but not all the Socialists in the labor movement became Wobblies. Max Hayes of Cleveland, leader of the Typographical Union, was among those who held back. To him the IWW was "another running fight between Socialists on the one side and all other partisans on the other.... If there is any fighting to be done, I intend to *agitate on the inside* of the organizations now in existence." This view was shared by a great many trade union advocates in the Socialist party who were as much opposed to dual unionism as Samuel Gompers and, at the same time, were loath to antagonize the AFL. They were particularly unhappy over the fact that their chief spokesman, Eugene V. Debs, was one of the IWW founders. The AFL was anathema to Debs. Trying to win over that organization to his idea of industrial unionism, he said, was "as wasteful of time as to spray a cesspool with attar of roses."

But Debs's disenchantment with the IWW was quick in coming. After a year in the organization he allowed his membership to lapse. The Wobblies remained a powerful and vexing force in opposition to the AFL until World War I. Afterward, its members and sympathizers began splintering off into other areas of dissent that were more in keeping with the temper of the times. Some followed the lure of communism; "Big Bill" Haywood himself lived out his last years in the Soviet Union.

"Big Bill" Haywood, president of the Western Federation of Miners, and later IWW boss, announced that this was "a revolutionary movement and the capitalists are not the only foes that you are to fight, but the most ardent enemies have been the pure and simple trade unionists."

There could be no compromise between a unionism that looked for fair contracts with the bosses and a movement that called for the end of capitalism and the abolition of the wage system. Gompers understood the challenge and picked it up. In a labor pamphlet he described the meeting that organized the IWW as "the most vapid and ridiculous in the annals of those who presume to speak in the name of labor." He ridiculed the concept that workers should be organized not by crafts but in great divisions of industry, linked finally in "one big union," with every worker directly concerned with the welfare of every other worker and ready to use the ultimate weapon, a paralyzing general strike. Under that system, Gompers wrote, "the tinker, the tailor, and the candlestick maker would legislate upon every minute detail affecting the interests of the workers." But despite all his scorn, the IWW remained in existence as a militant segment of the labor movement for at least a dozen years, always threatening to force a quicker pace on the AFL than Gompers might otherwise have chosen.

### Socialist opposition

The Socialists argued their way through various positions regarding the Federation. Sometimes they attempted (without success) to elect candidates to AFL offices. Sometimes they appeared to accept a compromise whereby they would operate primarily through political channels and leave worker organization to the unionists. Whether their actions were overt or implied, Gompers never let up his fire on them. In 1903, in a convention speech, he shouted to those delegates who also happened to be Socialists: "Economically, you are unsound; socially, you are wrong; industrially, you are an impossibility." The official journal of the National Civic Federation, greatly gratified, printed a picture of him under the caption "Socialism's Ablest Foe." Eleven years later, in a debate with Socialist leader Morris Hillquit before a congressionally created commission on industrial relations, Gompers launched another attack on the theoretical orientation of social-

Facing eviction from company-owned houses, striking Colorado miners in 1913 built a tent colony at Ludlow for 1,200 workers.

ism. "The intelligent, comprehensive, common-sense workmen," he said, "prefer to deal with the problems of today . . . with which they are bound to contend if they want to advance, rather than to deal with a picture and a dream which has never had, and I am sure never will have, any reality in the affairs of humanity."

Hillquit, who was cross-questioning Gompers, then asked if the AFL, in the absence of a general social philosophy (as Gompers seemed to imply), simply worked "blindly from day to day." To Gompers, the question was an insult. "If a man should ask me whether I still beat my wife, any answer I could make would incriminate me," he said. He went on to insist that the Federation spoke for working people, not the abstraction of a "class"—for human beings who needed and wanted practical improvements in the conditions of life "from day to day." Once more Hillquit pressed in with sharp questions. Was there no limit to the meaning of "a better life from day to day?" If the union movement always pressed toward a larger share of production as the worker's reward, wouldn't it eventually demand the full product of working-class labor, with no reward to private investment, just as the Socialists did?

Gompers refused to speculate on that possibility. He said the effort for a better life each day would go on without limit and without any theoretical ultimate goal, since it is not given to men to see what the future holds. "In other words," Gompers told Hillquit, to laughter and applause from the audience, "we go further than you. You have an end; we have not." Seldom has there been a better statement of a particularly American point of view, one that subordinates ideology to practical results.

Yet despite Gompers' obvious and deep commitment to a program that demanded only a fair share for the workingman—under the existing political system—there were those who fought unionism of any kind. If some industrialists in the National Civic Federation were willing to sit down to discussion with labor union representatives, many other "tycoons" glowed at the very thought of such union-busting drives as the "open-shop campaign" launched by the National Association of Manufacturers in 1903. Under the guise of sincere interest in the freedom of workingmen, employers involved in the campaign put heavy pressure on politicians, courts, and police agencies to hamper labor organizers in their

Early in 1914, company guards at Ludlow fired on the strikers (killing twenty-one), burned the tents, then patrolled the ruins.

Fallen power lines and charred debris surround the *Times* building after a small bomb set off an unpremeditated blast.

Gompers heard the news with tears in his eyes and uttered a classic of understatement: "It won't do the labor movement any good."

There were a number of other events, early in the century, that did the labor movement no good. One resulted from the fact that an anti-union employer could turn to the courts and obtain an injunction against a strike or boycott on the grounds that it was a restraint upon trade. This legal device had a long history in the courts of individual states. Since 1890 the Sherman Anti-Trust Act had also made it possible to seek such injunctions in federal courts, though the framers of that law had not intended it *primarily* to affect unions, if at all. Just how potent a weapon the injunction could be was something Gompers discovered in the most personal way. In what was known as the Buck's Stove & Range case, he found himself a convicted and sentenced lawbreaker, in the very city of Washington where important doors were finally opening to him. Nothing could have illustrated better the ambiguous position of the labor cause in the early 1900's—or more deeply hurt Samuel Gompers, who was nothing if not respectful of orderly and legal processes.

### A boycott backfires

In 1906, a strike was called by metal polishers at the plant of the Buck's Stove & Range Company in St. Louis. After an investigation by the executive council, the name of the company appeared on what was called a "We Don't Patronize" list in the AFL's official magazine, the *American Federationist*. Such a listing was an open invitation to all AFL members to boycott the firm's products. The corporation's president, James Van Cleave, was a tough anti-unionist. When, in the early 1900's, he became president of the National Association of Manufacturers as well, he energetically spurred the open-shop campaign. To protect his company's interests, and possibly to set an example to other manufacturers, Van Cleave had his lawyers secure an injunction, in the District of Columbia, commanding the AFL to cease listing the Buck's Stove & Range Com-

work, and to turn public opinion against unions. More directly, some strikes—particularly in the mountain states where frontier turbulence and violence had not receded very far into the past—were still being broken by the forthright application of force.

In turn, force begot force. One of the AFL's most awkward moments came in 1911 when two officials of a building-trade union, the brothers J. B. and J. J. McNamara, confessed to setting off a bomb in the plant of what was then a violently anti-labor newspaper, the Los Angeles *Times*, killing twenty people (see pages 215–217). Prior to their trial and confession, the McNamaras had convinced Gompers of their innocence. Gompers, always a battler, had stirred himself mightily in raising a defense fund for them. He stormed that he was "more convinced than ever" that there was "a 'frame-up' and a plot behind their arrests." And then, incredibly, the brothers admitted their guilt.

pany as an unfair employer. Moreover, the AFL was directed to refrain from any discussion of the strike that would in any way, shape, or manner do harm to the company's sales. The injunction took effect in December of 1907.

Gompers, outraged, removed the company's name from the list. But he continued to write impassioned editorials against the injunction in the *Federationist* and to condemn the company for its part in provoking the strike. To do any less, he held, would make it impossible for him to be true to his belief in the American principle of free speech. He wrote: "Until a law is passed making it compulsory . . . to buy Van Cleave's stoves we need not buy them, we won't buy them, and we will persuade other fair-minded, sympathetic friends to cooperate with us and leave the blamed things alone. Go to —— with your injunctions." After the effective date of the court order, he published its text and warned "the people" of "the serious invasion of their liberties which has taken place. That this has been done by judge-made injunction and not by statute law makes the menace all the greater."

Gompers was playing with fire. The result was predictable, for judges are not easily defied. A charge of contempt of court was brought against him and two other officials of the AFL. The case was tried before Judge Daniel T. Wright, who, in December of 1908, delivered a verdict of "guilty" and a stinging, scalding tongue-lashing. The issue, said Judge Wright, was "between the supremacy of law over the rabble or its prostration under the feet of the disordered throng. . . . There is a . . . defiant conflict . . . between the decrees of a tribunal ordained by the Government of the Federal Union, and of the tribunals of another federation, grown up in the land; one or the other must succumb, for those who would unlaw the land are public enemies."

Samuel Gompers listened, white-faced then red, twitching and working his hands. In his own eyes, he had given so much to America, had been so much a part of its best traditions, and had sacrificed so much for its ideals as he

## "A CREATURE OF POETRY"

Shortly after the AFL set up headquarters in Washington, Samuel Gompers hired a young typist, Rosa Lee Guard, to work in the office. She had no knowledge of the issues confronting American labor and, further, she was in frail health, convinced that she had but a few years to live. However, she soon grasped the scope and detail of her work—and miraculously regained her health. Her rise to prominence in the AFL office was chronicled by Gompers' biographer Bernard Mandel: "Miss Guard was quickly promoted to chief clerk over the growing headquarters staff, and then to Gompers' private secretary. She handled his correspondence, ran the office, and even looked after his personal financial affairs. Gompers spent his money recklessly. If Miss Guard had not withheld enough to make the payments on his house before she gave him his paycheck, he probably would not have been able to meet them."

Miss Guard, who outlived the man she served, was at his side through every labor crisis that involved him. Her concern was great during the tense period when the courts were acting on the AFL boycott of the Buck's Stove & Range Company. The case against Gompers reminded her of stories she had once read of the many attempts to corner the canny Br'er Rabbit, and she even saw some resemblance between Gompers and that fictional creature with a knowing look in his eye. So she bought a small brown cotton-stuffed rabbit, with legs of cork, which delighted Gompers.

Her devotion to Gompers was total. She once wrote that he "stands apart from his fellows, a myriad-sided nature; a creature of poetry and practical action; a dreamer, yet a doer of the world's work; a soul of storm while diffusing sunshine—a combination of wholly opposing characteristics. . . . I love him next to my mother." Miss Guard lived up to this pledge of affection, for during Gompers' last years she was as much a nurse as a secretary, forcing him to take his medicine, admonishing him not to depart from his diet, and helping him conserve his strength.

saw them, that it took every ounce of restraint he possessed not to break down in the face of this unjust attack. He did deliver a long statement before receiving sentence, brilliantly defending freedom of speech in general and the specific right of laboring men to struggle for American advantages without being legally enchained (see pages 211–215). Judge Wright

Sophia, Gompers' wife for fifty-two years

then sentenced Gompers to a year in prison. He never served it. A long, grinding legal battle ensued, with appeals, new trials, more appeals, and an ultimate argument before the Supreme Court, which received the case in 1914. The justices decided that the statute of limitations had intervened—that Gompers' "crime" was no longer punishable after all the years since 1907. During that period, it should be noted, the strike had been settled and the Buck's company put under new and friendlier management.

But during the long interval, Gompers, so often condemned by radicals as a trimmer and compromiser, also stood out as a frontline leader for the cause of workingmen everywhere. At the AFL's 1909 convention, while still under the weight of a jail threat, he received a stormy, fifteen-minute ovation after his unanimous re-election to the Federation presidency. Tears rolled down his cheeks as he stood on the platform trying, without success, to speak. Finally, he covered his face with his hands and with-

drew. His wife, too, wept uncontrollably at the tribute. Although the jail sentence imposed by the courts was ultimately lifted, Sophia's anxiety for her husband's welfare never ceased. The Buck's Stove & Range case produced but a minimal gain for labor, and it no doubt shortened Sophia's life. She suffered a nervous collapse before its final resolution and was in declining health for many years.

The overwhelming vote of confidence given Gompers in 1909 was just the support he needed. He remained full of the London street-boy's defiance to the last, for he actually insisted on bringing the case to the Supreme Court even though he had had a chance to get it dismissed. Though this course would renew the risk of jail, he hoped to get a decision against labor injunctions. Later he scorned the highest court for having "evaded the fundamental issue" by basing its decision on minor grounds. A nephew recalls Gompers' saying: "They didn't have the guts to decide on the merits."

### A move into politics

The Buck's Stove & Range battle focused attention on a fact known for some time: that labor needed to have the law on its side. Economic pressure might be a more desirable technique than political campaigning, but the dead-weight of statutes interpreted against unions by unfriendly judges needed, somehow, to be lifted. This inevitably meant turning to the legislatures that had enacted those statutes and trying to change their composition. In 1906, the AFL under Gompers had moved somewhat cautiously into the arena of national politics. Gompers and other labor spokesmen announced that they would urge workers to "stand by our friends and administer a stinging rebuke to men or parties who are either indifferent, negligent, or hostile." A shortened, popular version of the policy was: "Reward your friends and punish your enemies."

The AFL presented to President Theodore Roosevelt and to Congress a so-called Bill of Grievances. This lengthy statement called for legislative protection from the competition of

At an age when most men willingly retire to rocking chairs, Gompers kept vigorously and continuously on the go—piloting the *Afel* (a ship he named for the Federation), flying in an open-cockpit biplane to keep a speaking date, posing between sets of tennis, and tossing deck quoits on a cruise.

convict labor, a more tightly restrictive immigration policy, as well as laws that would improve the working conditions of seamen, who were virtual prisoners once they signed a ship's articles. The bill also proposed to forbid child labor and deny employers the use of injunctions to crush strikes and boycotts. Congress was not disposed to act on any of these proposals. The blunt, profane, and reactionary Speaker of the House, Joseph G. Cannon, flatly declared that Gompers could expect nothing from him. "You are not the only pebble on the beach," Cannon shouted. Nor, at that time, was Theodore Roosevelt ready to risk his national popularity by waving his well-known "big stick" at Congress and demanding pro-labor legislation. So nothing happened immediately. The fuse that had been lit under Congress sputtered out. By 1908 the situation seemed even more urgent. The Supreme Court, in what came to be known as the Danbury Hatters' case, upheld a lower-court

decision to fine a union of hatmakers nearly a quarter of a million dollars for restraining the trade of an "unfair" company by a boycott. The basis of the court's action was the Sherman Anti-Trust Act of 1890, which, in order to curb monopolies, declared that every "combination . . . or conspiracy in restraint of trade or commerce" was illegal. Anti-union attorneys had been arguing that the language of the act applied equally to unions. Now the highest court seemed to have embraced this line of thinking. A few more such devastating pronouncements under the Sherman Act, and the trade unions would be fined out of existence. Congress, the President, and the Supreme Court alike seemed to be blind to workingmen's needs. Once more the AFL pushed away from its traditional anchorage in political neutrality. A program that was essentially a modified version of the Bill of Grievances was presented to both political conventions in 1908.

The Republicans virtually ignored the program, and nominated William Howard Taft, a man massive in flesh and judicial conservatism. The Democrats, on the other hand, appeared willing to incorporate planks in their platform that, Gompers recalled, "were substantially identical with our principal demands." The Democrats were making their first gestures of courtship toward labor. Eventually, the two would enter a stormy but long-lasting marriage. In fact, while Gompers sat in the convention hall listening to the report of the platform committee, the veteran Democratic leader Champ Clark (who would presently succeed "Uncle Joe" Cannon as Speaker of the House) tapped him on the shoulder from a seat just behind, and passed him a newspaper in whose margin he had penciled: "Isn't that report all right?" It was. Moreover, the Democrats nominated the old hero of 1896, William Jennings Bryan, who personally telephoned Gompers an invitation to visit him. Soon thereafter, Gompers and other members of the AFL executive council endorsed Bryan and the Democrats. That was just twelve years after Gompers had firmly insisted on official neutrality, despite a personal predilection for Bryan, in the great political battle of 1896.

## GOMPERS AND POLITICS

From his earliest years in the labor movement until, with his death, he relinquished the reins of leadership, Samuel Gompers was under continual pressure to make organized labor a third force—in government, in society, and especially in politics. That he was firm in resisting this pressure was the result of his belief that a trade union should not impose a particular philosophy or political bent on its worker-members. He believed the bond that united workers would remain strong only if workers were permitted to retain freedom of choice in all matters. Through the years of his labor leadership, he vigorously opposed those factions who would have him endorse—and openly campaign for—the Greenback party, for example, the Workingmen's party, the Populists, or the Socialists. However, in the words of his biographer Bernard Mandel: "Pure and simple unionism did not mean to Gompers, as was often charged, complete abstention from political activities. It meant that the trade unions should be the sole agency of the labor movement, that labor should not form its own political party, that it should not endorse or support any other party, and that its political activity should be confined to agitation for or against particular men and measures in particular elections" (see page 161).

In short, Gompers believed that labor reform could be achieved best by continued and concerted efforts *within* the existing political order—by dealing with whatever party happened to be in power at a given time, rather than by labor's attempting to place a party or a candidate of its own into power. As it happened, Gompers did not always stick to this precept, and had reason to be sorry when he deviated. The only two presidential candidates he publicly espoused—William Jennings Bryan in 1908 and Robert La Follette in 1924—went down to defeat, and Gompers' aggressive electioneering for the congressional candidate of his choice in 1906 was no more successful.

In this 1906 campaign he assembled some of labor's biggest guns to do battle with incumbent congressmen who had been especially unfriendly to labor. And he himself masterminded an attempt by Daniel J. McGillicuddy to unseat Representative Charles Littlefield in Maine. McGillicuddy, a Democrat, had been a state legislator and at one time the mayor of Lewiston. Littlefield, a four-time Republican incumbent, was a foe of labor, a man personally repugnant to Gompers and, worse, a friend and ally of the antilabor Speaker of the House Joe Cannon.

Gompers threw himself into the fray as though he himself were running for office, making speech after speech in McGillicuddy's behalf as he followed Littlefield around the district. In 1907, the Garment Workers' Henry White offered this assessment of the outcome of the campaign: "Mr. Gompers accordingly stood up and was counted. The result seems farcical. Into each one of the districts selected for the battle, his ablest lieutenants were sent, and the chief in person directed the fighting. Not a man was defeated whom he and his campaigners opposed. Mr. Gompers selected his own battlefield, and not even those who openly defied him suffered appreciable harm. Littlefield, Cannon . . . and all the others went back to Congress with pluralities as large as ever before, or if reduced, only by such as may be attributed to the diminished vote of an off year." But White's evaluation was unduly harsh, at least so far as Gompers' participation was concerned. For Littlefield's plurality was less than 1,000 in 1906, whereas in 1904 it had been 5,400. Gompers regarded McGillicuddy's narrow margin of defeat as a victory of sorts for labor—a "victory" he did not attempt to repeat.

Gompers' change of heart represented a major policy shift for organized labor, and he knew it. What was more, he knew that the effectiveness of the shift would be limited. For by then many urban workers had learned to regard the Republican party as the working-man's ally because it wooed industry and espoused the tariff (which restricted competition from foreign producers by imposing a duty on imported goods). The result was that Gompers could never deliver a compact labor vote to any party. In addition, he would now be criticized for exactly the kind of plunge into politics that he had long denounced as a distraction and snare. Nevertheless, he went ahead with his plans to campaign personally not only for Bryan, but also for the defeat of anti-labor congressmen, including Speaker Cannon. Cannon's usual tactic with bills for the relief of labor was to entomb them in a committee from which they would never be reported.

The 1908 campaign was a failure in a sense. The Republicans swept the election and controlled both the White House and the two chambers of Congress. Yet the GOP had reached and passed a high point, and the history of the ensuing eight years reads as if the Gompers policy change had been a brilliant success. In 1910 the Democrats did capture the House of Representatives. In 1912—aided by a split in the Republican party—the Democrats elected Woodrow Wilson to the Presidency, with a majority in each house on Capitol Hill.

It was a campaign electric with future significance for Gompers, but he was not very happy at its outset. As he frankly said later, Wilson was "not my choice for the presidential candidate for the Democratic party." The reason was that, early in his career, Wilson had appeared to show little sympathy toward unions. Nevertheless, Gompers requested an interview with the nominee, and met him in August 1912 to discuss what labor and the Democrats might expect from each other. It must have been a picturesque meeting. Gompers looked every bit the battle-scarred sixty-two-year-old he was. His face was roughened by eczema. His hair,

As these pages and this cartoon show, Gompers' chief congressional foe, Joe Cannon, could squelch bills he opposed.

according to one observer, "looked like a piece of worn-out buffalo robe which has lain in the garret and been chewed by the moths since 1890, and then been thrown out in the rain and laid in the gutter for a year or two, and then been dragged back by a puppy dog to cut his teeth on."

Wilson, on the other hand, was lean-faced, dignified, an intellectual gazing through glasses at a world to which he seemed constantly to be lecturing. And yet Gompers, while impressed with his "beautiful English, the perfect enunciation and modulation of his speaking voice," and his "personal dignity that made me feel when the door swung open to admit him that a real President of the United States was entering," sensed something else, too—"sincerity" and "obvious humanitarianism." The part-time night-school student put his trust in the former university president, and kept it there. The trust was justified. Under Wilson, Congress proceeded to turn out a legislative record that appeared to meet most of the grievances labor had rebelled against in 1906. In 1913 a Department of Labor was created, and William B. Wilson of the United Mine Workers became the first Secretary of Labor.

### Pungency on pork

In 1914 a new antitrust bill, the Clayton Act, specifically exempted labor unions from prosecution as conspiracies. It declared flatly: "The labor of a human being is not a commodity or an article of commerce." This sentence boldly dismissed a century of classical economic argument to the effect that wages, or the "price of labor," could only be set by the "law of supply and demand," which knew no mercy. Or, as Samuel Gompers himself had put it in a characteristically pungent speech: "You cannot weigh a human soul on the same scales on which you weigh a piece of pork" (see pages 217–219). Small wonder that Gompers called the Clayton Act "the industrial Magna Charta," even

Though shipowners attacked it as being monstrous, the Seamen's Act ended many age-old abuses inflicted on sailors.

though it did not in fact protect unions entirely from strikebreaking injunctions. In 1915 the La Follette Seamen's Act vastly improved the conditions of those who went down to the sea in the fo'c'sle. In 1916 Congress forbade the use of child labor in establishments involved in interstate commerce—though the Supreme Court would soon thereafter strike down this law. In 1916 the Adamson Railway Labor Act made an eight-hour day mandatory for workers on railroads engaged in interstate commerce. Gompers was less happy with this than with the Clayton Act. As much as any *laissez-faire* businessman, he distrusted government regulation of hours and wages, for he felt it could too easily become a two-edged weapon.

Finally, in 1917 (though in this case over President Wilson's veto), Congress passed the first of a series of acts restricting immigration. These bills would culminate in the severely prohibitory immigration law of 1924, an enactment thoroughly offensive to modern liberalism in its frank discrimination against southern and eastern European peoples. Nevertheless, it did give labor organizations something they had sought for nearly thirty years—a kind of "protective tariff" on job competition. It was hardly a wonder, then, that the AFL supported Woodrow Wilson's bid for a second term in 1916. Nor was it surprising, when the Democratic victory was assured after a nip-and-tuck election, that Samuel Gompers should send a telegram to Wilson brimming with superlatives. "The cause of labor, justice, freedom, American patriotism, and humanity has been vindicated," it read. Gompers was not one to stint either his anger or his praise, and though this message might seem bombastic, he had reason to be grateful for Wilson's reelection.

Yet 1916 was also a year of gathering storms. War was casting its shadow across America. Riding the crest of legislative success, Gompers now moved to what he regarded his grandest effort. He would cement his partnership with Wilson, and labor's with the nation, by joining heart and soul in the crusade against the Kaiser, thus bringing his career to a glowing apex.

# Chapter 6

# THE WAR, THE VICTORY, AND THE DECLINE

WHEN THE GREAT WAR that began in 1914 reached out to engage America three years later, it marked the end of an important period in American politics—the so-called era of progressivism. Samuel Gompers might well rejoice over the favorable labor laws that Congress passed after 1912. He must have realized, however, that this legislation did not spring from a deep feeling among Democrats that their party owed a debt to labor, but from a new current of political thought among the middle-class Americans who put parties into office. Gompers, with a streak of shrewdness that ran steadily between his idealism and pugnacity, had deftly floated the labor movement on that current. For the AFL's move into politics in 1906 coincided with the upsurge of progressivism throughout the land. Twentieth-century Americans began, temporarily at least, to accept the proposition that the government owed protection and support to those outclassed by corporate wealth.

Editors, preachers, and politicians who had little social kinship with factory workers voted for legislators who went down the line in behalf of conservation, regulation of trusts, and inspection of food and drugs for purity. During the same period the same progressive voters and legislators gave their backing to control of insurance, banking, utilities, and transportation companies. They also established new machinery to break up alliances between unscrupulous businessmen and politicians. Both Republicans and Democrats were involved in the progressive movement, in cities and states as well as in Washington. The pro-labor enactments of the Wilson Administration, therefore, were not isolated. They were part of a trend that had not only seen the Democrats embrace progressive ideas, but had also witnessed Republican insurgents dethroning Speaker Cannon and bolting away from Taft in 1912 to run Theodore Roosevelt on a Progressive ticket.

By calculation or by intuition, Gompers had abandoned nonpartisanship in the right way at the right time. The public would accept neither a labor party nor socialism, though nearly a million votes had been cast for Socialist candidate Eugene Debs in 1912. But Americans would, nevertheless, endorse acts of public policy that would once have been deemed socialistic. Therefore, some lobbying by the AFL—clearly a group of businesslike unions that accepted capitalism and the two-party system as well—was entirely safe during these lively years. Gompers, in short, had identified labor's cause with middle-class reform. Once labor unions were seen not as sinister conspiracies but as special-interest groups like organizations of farmers or businessmen, they, too, could be entitled to government help. Gompers had accomplished this identification of the goals of labor with those of America at large without sacrificing the basically economic structure of trade unionism, as the political reformers of the

To dramatize Gompers' patriotic, pro-war stand, a Brooklyn *Eagle* cartoonist drew him as "The New Uncle Sam."

international cooperation of laboring men everywhere, partly on idealistic grounds and partly from the point of view of expediency. For if labor standards were raised throughout the world, then newly arrived immigrant workmen in the United States could not so easily be exploited by employers, to the disadvantage of American laborers. In 1909 Gompers had attended the Paris meeting of a body later to become the International Federation of Trade Unions. On his return to America, he successfully urged the AFL to affiliate with it. He also established a working relationship with the Mexican trade-union movement—a tie that became even stronger after Mexico's 1911 revolution. In 1916, during a period of tense relations between the United States and Mexico, President Wilson employed Gompers as a kind of informal go-between in negotiations with the existing Mexican regime, because of his close contacts with important labor officials south of the border.

Yet at the outset of World War I in 1914, international cooperation among workers was more a dream than a reality, for the labor movements of all the major powers were immediately carried away on a surge of patriotism and, with few exceptions, endorsed their own countries' war efforts. And Sam Gompers was no more cosmopolitan in his outlook than his European counterparts. When the fighting broke out, he had a collection of antiwar utterances about to appear in book form. With typical impetuosity and frankness, Gompers rushed to the printer to halt publication of "that damn-fool stuff." In point of fact, he had always felt slightly uncomfortable because the trade-union federations of so many European nations were hospitable to, or even controlled by, Socialists and other political activists. His speeches to meetings of international labor bodies were often polite exhortations to see the light and follow the path of pure and simple trade unionism, which was so clearly the great American contribution to the cause of labor everywhere. At home and abroad, his attitude won him enemies as well as friends.

1870's would have done. Now, reaching the climax of his career, he planned a final step in sealing the bond between the nonlaboring public and the organized-labor movement. He chose to align the AFL squarely behind Wilson's crusade to make the world safe for democracy. Even before America's declaration of hostilities in 1917, Samuel Gompers blew the trumpet and marched his legions into participation in World War I (see pages 220–222).

At the outbreak of war in Europe in 1914, Gompers, like many labor leaders of his time, had been an avowed pacifist. He had supported the Spanish-American War in 1898 as an act of sympathy for Cuban workmen in their struggle against "Spanish tyranny." But he had opposed follow-up actions by the United States in 1898, which led to the annexation of an overseas empire. He was also a professed believer in

But with almost no difficulty at all, Gompers decided that the German and Austrian labor movements were somehow more reprehensible than all the others in underwriting the efforts of their "autocratic" and "militaristic" governments. By early 1916, he had become an all-out enemy of pacifism and a full-scale supporter of the Allies. As the United States moved closer to war against Germany, he became more clearly than ever the labor spokesman with whom officialdom could deal in comfort. One reason for this was that the Socialists, the IWW, and some independent union spokesmen continued to denounce the entire American drive toward military preparedness and war participation. The union dissenters thought the end result would be to fatten war profiteers to the detriment of workingmen, who would become "cannon fodder" or conscripted toilers.

Gompers fought these views with all his traditional vigor. He tongue-lashed as deluded victims of German propaganda those who opposed preparedness. In 1916 the government created a Committee on National Defense, consisting of the Secretaries of War, Navy, Interior, Agriculture, Commerce, and Labor. An advisory commission of seven was to assist these Cabinet members in mobilizing the country, and Samuel Gompers was named to it. Another adviser recalled that after a long and apparently meandering discussion at the initial meeting, Gompers leaned back in his chair, held up a cigar with two fingers, and in fifteen minutes dictated to a secretary a plan of organization. It was so thorough and so orderly that his fellow members broke into a round of applause.

Years of organizing protests, lobbies, strikes, conventions, and federations had stood the old man in good stead. Now he sat with the heads of the nation's highest executive departments, bringing to them as the spokesman of labor its promise of cooperation in preparing for war. There was no doubt in his mind that he could get the support of the unions in the Federation, though many of their leaders were less than enthusiastic. In March of 1917 Gompers presented to the AFL's executive council a statement for endorsement, entitled "American Labor's Position in Peace or in War." It pledged support for the coming struggle. But, in exchange, it urged the federal government to make certain that trade-union standards would be maintained in war work, that profiteering would be discouraged, and that labor would be represented in all bodies charged with industrial planning. Even friends of Gompers' position were somewhat resentful of the fact that the chieftain would accept almost no alterations in his wording. The viewpoint of opponents was summed up by Andrew Furuseth, veteran leader of the Seamen's Union, who told Gompers that the declaration wiped out "forty years of work for labor." Yet the council, and then a conference of most of the AFL union heads, adopted the statement Gompers had prepared. When the declaration of war came a few weeks later, labor had already put on its uniform.

These women making airplane parts wanted to keep home fires burning—and also to release male workers for war.

Once again, it is hard to say whether Gompers' vision of labor's wartime role was due more to his idealism, to his practical politicking, or to his own soaring vanity. Undoubtedly he had convinced himself that the future of mankind depended on victory over the Central Powers. When he believed something, he impatiently sought to set afire with his own glow whatever organization he was part of. In the abstract, he did want workingmen to give their all for victory. Moreover, Gompers believed that the war would be a turning point in the relationship between government, capital, and labor in the United States. If the government recognized organized labor as a partner in the war effort, if it admitted labor representatives into its inner councils, it would have made a commitment that could not later be wiped out. Or—as Gompers put it in a wartime speech—if labor did its part, "our appeal for justice will take on redoubled force when this terrific conflict shall have been brought to a close."

It would have been inconceivable in the Civil War, for example, to petition special labor representatives for their views on how best to step up the economic aspect of the war effort. In 1917, their opinions would come to be expected, Gompers felt. And, he also believed, no nation that appealed to working-class citizens as a body to support it in crises could easily revert to regarding labor as an article of commerce or a plaything of the market. Nor would it consider labor organizations as conspiracies to be checked by injunctions and military force. War would also give labor a national standing. Last, but far from least, the war of 1917 would be one in which America's highest-ranking spokesman for labor—the man whose stamp of approval would invariably be needed before any other union official was appointed to a planning committee—would be Samuel Gompers of the AFL!

The outcome was a gamble, for a strong-handed government could punish as well as reward labor. But at first it looked like a successful gamble, and events seemed to fulfill Gompers' predictions in the short run. A busy

## GOMPERS GOES TO WAR

The role Gompers assumed during the Wilson years was that of a statesman and patriot. When American involvement in the First World War seemed imminent, he strove to marshal labor's support of pro-war policies so he could make a grand gesture of compliance with the President's call for national unity. Early in 1917 he summoned an advisory group of union leaders to Washington to discuss and ultimately define labor's attitude toward the war. So sensitive was the issue and so obvious were his motives that he met resistance even before the meeting began.

Daniel J. Tobin, president of the Teamsters' Union and soon to be elected AFL treasurer, wrote Gompers that he had "no confidence in a committee that you are endeavoring to organize because of the fact that things will have to run as you want them to run or they can not run at all." And Marsden Scott, the typographers' president, wrote tersely: "Having no confidence whatever in your integrity, I decline to serve on your committee."

The meeting was held, despite the absence of some key officials, and a labor manifesto was drawn up and adopted—by a conference whose members included the AFL executive council and representatives from the railroad brotherhoods and from seventy-nine affiliated unions—on March 12, less than a month before the United States declared war. The manifesto (drafted by Gompers himself) said in part: "We, the officers of the National and International Trade Unions of America in national conference assembled in the capital of our nation, hereby pledge ourselves in peace and in war, in stress or in storm, to stand unreservedly by the standards of liberty and the safety and preservation of the institutions and ideals of our Republic. In this solemn hour of our nation's life, it is our earnest hope that our Republic may be safeguarded in its unswerving desire for peace; that our people may be spared the horrors and the burdens of war; that they may have the opportunity to cultivate and develop the arts of peace, human brotherhood, and a higher civilization. But despite all our endeavors and hopes, should our country be drawn into the maelstrom of the European conflict, we . . . offer our services to our country in every field of activity to defend, safeguard, and preserve the Republic of the United States of America against its enemies whomsoever they may be, and we call upon our fellow workers and fellow citizens in the holy name of Labor, Justice, Freedom and Humanity, to devotedly and patriotically give like service."

A month later, at their St. Louis convention, the Socialists, many of whom figured prominently in labor, proclaimed an opposite view: "The Socialist Party of the United States, in the present grave crisis, solemnly reaffirms its allegiance to the principle of internationalism and working-class solidarity the world over, and proclaims its unalterable opposition to the war just declared by the government of the United States. . . . Wars bring wealth and power to the ruling classes, and suffering, death and demoralization to the workers. . . . The Socialist Party of the United States is unalterably opposed

Gompers at the front, with gas mask and helmet

to the system of exploitation and class rule which is upheld and strengthened by military power and sham national patriotism. We, therefore, call upon the workers of all countries to refuse support to their governments in their wars. . . . The only struggle which would justify the workers in taking up arms is the great struggle of the working class of the world to free itself from economic exploitation and political oppression. . . . In support of capitalism, we will not willingly give a single life or a single dollar; in support of the struggle of the workers for freedom, we pledge our all."

With such antipodal thinking among his labor constituents, Gompers knew trouble lay ahead at the AFL's November convention in Buffalo. To

add strength to his views on labor and the war— and for prestige purposes as well—he invited the President to speak to the delegates, and Wilson agreed to come. It was Gompers' finest hour, and a significant one for Wilson, too, for he was the first Chief Executive ever to address an American labor convention. Wilson, no less a politician than Gompers had become, made the most of this occasion. The United States had been at war with the Central Powers for more than seven months by then, so the President took the opportunity to restate what he expected of labor in the continuing crisis:

"If we are true friends of freedom, our own or anybody else's, we will see that the power of this country and the productivity of this country are raised to their absolute maximum, and that absolutely *nobody* is allowed to stand in the way of it. . . . Our duty, if we are to do this great thing and show America to be what we believe her to be—the greatest hope and energy of the world—is to stand together night and day until the job is finished. . . . Now to stand together means that *nobody* must interrupt the processes of our energy if the interruption can possibly be avoided without the absolute invasion of freedom. To put it concretely, that means this: *Nobody* has a right to stop the processes of labor until all the methods of conciliation and settlement have been exhausted."

In effect, Wilson was exacting a "no-strike" pledge from labor and, predictably, not everyone in labor was willing to give it. In subsequent debate, opponents of the war denounced Wilson for having involved the United States in the conflict and complained that Gompers was attempting to chain them to the workbench for its duration. The hostile factions were never reconciled, but the convention ended on a note of resignation sounded by James A. Duncan, a delegate from the Seattle Central Labor Council: "I believe you will all agree with me that almost to a man we are for peace and opposed to this war. However, conditions are radically changing, and no matter how much we may have been opposed to war and for peace, we are forced by force of circumstances to change our attitude somewhat. . . . Today, many holding union cards have gone into the trenches, have been forced into the trenches against their will . . . and they are calling upon us for munitions and supplies in order to defend their lives. . . . We have a very bitter pill to swallow." And so, with Gompers' blessing, swallow it they did.

## "SAM IS IN TOWN"

Florence Thorne first met Gompers when, as a University of Chicago senior in 1910, she was assigned by one of her professors, Robert F. Hoxie, to do a term paper on the AFL's role in politics. Her research required interviewing "those who had lived trade unionism." "One Saturday morning I was up early and on the Illinois Central, reviewing a series of questions which I planned to put to George W. Perkins, president of the Cigar Makers' International Union. . . . But Mr. Perkins [was busy and told me]: 'Sam is in town. You need to talk to him anyhow.' . . . I called the hotel. A voice with the volume of a pipe organ answered. 'Have breakfast with me here at eleven o'clock.' . . . Over to the old Briggs Hotel I hastened. . . . Finally the door of the elevator opened on a short, squat figure in a buttoned Prince Albert coat. His short legs moved with extreme dignity, and with a courtly gesture he invited me into the dining room. The unhurried interview lasted about three hours and ended with this offer: 'Come to Washington and all the files of the Federation will be available to you.' When I reported to Dr. Hoxie, his comment was: 'How soon can you go? This is an unparalleled offer.' . . .

"As soon as possible I went to Washington to complete my thesis, and so began a new discipline in my own education. . . . Mr. Gompers made good on his promise to open everything. He formed a habit of dropping in as he passed by my door to see what I was doing and to make suggestions. As he fingered lovingly the old records, he told me stories about each, reliving episodes in Federation history. He told me not only what he did but often why he did it, so I could follow his mind through problems that recurred in the successive years. He occasionally referred with obvious pride to the instruction in trade unionism which he gave me. It was an invaluable seminar. . . . Intellectually he was honest and undeviating. As a man of action and a participant in our complex society, he had many personalities. . . . For many years I had the privilege of working with him in confidential capacity, first as an editorial and research assistant and as writing assistant when he prepared his autobiography. He used to say to me: 'Girl, if you want to work with me, you must understand what is in my mind.' . . .

"Mr. Gompers' wisdom was not from books but from personal contacts and exchange of experience and thought with others. . . . In addition he had rare power of drawing from some reservoir of human experience and wisdom—a power essentially primitive and organic—the essence of some spiritual communion. This I felt often and had the rare experience of seeing once. In his leadership in connection with World War I, he was most careful to be restrained enough not to be in advance of political leadership, yet positive and forceful enough to help workers not to be misled. He timed his national conference of union executives by President Wilson's schedule, to follow immediately the declaration of war by Congress and to be supplemented by the first meeting of his Advisory Committee on War Labor Problems. Suddenly President Wilson changed his schedule. S. G.'s letters fixing dates of his meetings had gone out. . . . It happened to be my responsibility to convey information of change to him. My eyes were on my memorandum. There was a deep silence so intense I looked up with concern. He had turned and sat looking in the opposite direction and somehow had shrunk into himself. His lips moved as he talked with himself—in a sibilant, scarcely audible tone. The inner communication with his conscious and subconscious lasted at least fifteen minutes. When his decision was reached, he turned and gradually became normal. It was a privacy to be respected—and was. No order to countermand meetings was issued—they were held and were of outstanding service."

assortment of committees, boards, and councils spun a web of regulation over the nation's industries. Best known of these bodies was the War Committee on Labor, a great superagency created to settle disputes that threatened production. There were also many others in the assortment, and union representatives sat on all those dealing with labor relations. There were no major labor upheavals during the nineteen months of active American participation in the war, and relatively few strikes. In many projects undertaken on government contract (such as the building of bases, camps, hospitals, and other military installations), hours, wages, and working conditions were on the high plane that unions had strived for years to attain. However, tentative efforts to persuade government contractors to make closed-shop agreements, which stipulated the hiring of union members only, were repulsed.

On the whole, there was a kind of mutual truce between government and organized labor that was helpful to both sides. Washington used its influence to build up work standards in war industries, while the unions refrained from vigorous campaigns of recruitment backed by strike threats. More significantly, from Gompers' point of view, the government tended to punish "uncooperative" labor elements as readily as it rewarded the faithful. Strict sedition and espionage laws for wartime were used as a basis for prosecuting Socialist and IWW leaders who continued to battle the war effort and the draft. Eugene Debs was sent to jail. IWW spokesmen were also imprisoned, their offices raided, their files destroyed, and their members harassed. In November 1918 only the AFL and the railroad brotherhoods were healthy and truly effective labor organizations. The long-time "enemies on the left" had been broken in the storms of war.

### Sweet sounds of praise

This was a victory that Gompers had long desired, but he was bitterly reproached for "selling out" to wartime hysteria. To this day, some historians list his hand-in-glove partner-ship with government as a black mark against him. But to counterbalance criticism, there were sweet choruses of official praise. The Secretary of the Navy said that Gompers' "wise and patriotic councils" [sic] had kept navy-yard workers "alive to a sense of their duty as American citizens." Senator John Williams of Mississippi, a state hardly notable for its warmth towards organized labor, gave major credit to Gompers "for harmonizing our national purposes and unifying our national effort." But most impressive of all was the appearance of President Woodrow Wilson himself at the AFL convention of 1917 in Buffalo, where he declared: "I want to express my admiration of [Gompers'] patriotic courage, his large vision, and his statesmanlike sense of what has to be done." The President undoubtedly knew that he was praising a man who, until just three years before, had still been under a federal jail sentence for defying a court injunction!

Though workers often had reason to feel exploited during World War I, management—in posters like these—continued to proclaim the triumphant partnership of capital and labor in aiding the Allied cause—a viewpoint Gompers shared.

Steadfast but incongruous in cutaway coat and wing collar, Gompers visits American troops in a trench at the front.

Then Wilson added a comment that perhaps symbolized the relationship between himself and Gompers better than whole paragraphs could have done: "I like to lay my mind alongside of a mind that knows how to pull in harness. The horses that kick over the traces will have to be put in a corral." While the enemies of the war effort in labor's ranks were herded off to federal "corrals," Samuel Gompers, willing to accept a harness, became American labor's representative to the world. In August of 1918 he was sent to Europe, along with several other AFL officials, to meet with Allied labor leaders and bolster their morale, badly frayed after four agonizing war years.

A trip in convoy through the submarine-menaced North Atlantic was followed by a month in England attending labor conferences and a steady round of public functions. Gompers, who had been one of the London poor of Victorian days, glowingly sat at a banquet and heard Prime Minister David Lloyd George hail him as a lifelong fighter for progress. Moreover,

he had an audience with King George V at Buckingham Palace. Buoyed by such attentions, he told one English audience that he would "rather have one day facing the Huns on the field of battle than twenty years of this."

From England the Gompers party went on to France and made a brief visit to the front. There he amused his companions and embarrassed himself by rescuing, from a pile of rubble, a souvenir "German" helmet that turned out to be a French fire-chief's hat. Then the group visited Rome. Everywhere Gompers' message was the same: Allied workers must support their governments to the hilt, resist any peace movements not based on total German and Austrian surrender, and beware of the sinister potentialities of socialism, which, to his satisfaction, was now a discredited and disgraced movement in the United States. As one American on the scene remembered, "He told British, French, and Italian labor leaders, quite positively, what they must do to be saved." But for the past fifty years he had been doing that to whatever groups he faced.

The official accounts of his trip held that it was a great success in stimulating Allied morale. A less flattering estimate was made in some quarters, however. Veteran European labor leaders were deeply concerned with the repair of war's ravages and the launching of long-delayed movements for social justice in their countries. They regarded socialism as intellectually quite respectable. Also, they were thoroughly tired of the "up-and-at-'em" war propaganda that Gompers, representing a nation still fresh and relatively unblooded, delivered so zestfully. In point of fact, Gompers never could convice his European counterparts that AFL-type unionism was the salvation of working classes the world over—or that suppression of radical labor movements had not harmed the democratic process in the United States by closing off certain alternatives for discussion. Many British and Continental unionists believed that a labor movement, like any other movement, thrives on free debate between various and conflicting points of view.

Gompers, in 1918, represented but one—and his country recognized only that one. In his own mirror he saw a spokesman for triumphant Americanism. But many onlookers saw only a vain old man—a captive warrior, not even aware of his government "harness."

It may be that his unilateral approach made him perform unremarkably when he returned to France in 1919 as part of a team sent to advise the United States delegation to the international peace conference. American labor experts (a new academic breed), functioning under Gompers' nominal leadership, helped to write a kind of international code of fair labor standards into the Versailles Treaty. But Congress never ratified that treaty. The United States also refrained from joining the International Labor Organization set up under the peace terms. And the AFL—with Gompers' unofficial approval—refused to rejoin the International Federation of Trade Unions when it was resurrected after the armistice, November 11, 1918. Gompers was convinced that he had much to teach the international labor movement. But by 1919 he was both too old and too impatient to realize that a good teacher must be willing to listen and learn. He placed himself above the need for give and take, for, as president of the AFL, he had supped with prime ministers and spoken with kings. An American workingman had risen that high! Few things could have convinced Gompers more dramatically of the soundness of his faith in America and in the kind of labor movement that he had helped to build. Now approaching his sixty-ninth birthday, he captured still another honor—election as head of the newly created Pan-American Federation of Labor. Seemingly the time had come for him to reap the rich harvest of all the years of struggle and growth, and of wartime cooperation. Gompers' heart was still young and hopeful, but his body was aging rapidly. He did not know, in January 1919, that he had not quite six years to live—or that, during those years, the very nature and extent of his success would be questioned as America returned to peaceful pursuits. In the

## "A POWERFUL SQUAT FIGURE"

Gompers' 1918 mission to Europe as an emissary of President Wilson had mixed results, for he was only partly successful in promulgating the AFL "message." The fact that Gompers considered the expedition a triumph, however, is evident in a report of his appearance in London and on the Continent, published in the London *Daily News* by Ray Stannard Baker, who later became Woodrow Wilson's official biographer: "I see him now striding down the street, a powerful squat figure followed a step behind by a looming bodyguard of labor leaders. He was scattering the assembled and gaping subjects of King George, however well inured to the sight of potentates, to the right and left. His hat was set well back upon his head, his chin was thrust forward, and he was throwing aside humorous remarks to his followers. So I saw him once again in Paris. So he strode full-fronted throughout Europe, so sure of himself and his entire equipment of ideas, so conscious of the immense power of American labor behind him, that he scattered to the right and left all peoples of all nations."

In Rome, Gompers was to speak at a workers' meeting—widely regarded as a test of strength between those who, like Gompers, favored war and those who did not, namely the Italian Bolsheviks. All arrangements had been made when it was discovered that cancellation notices had been pasted on posters announcing the event. Gompers and his labor delegation countered by placing an advertisement in the afternoon newspapers, but what appeared in the press, in place of the ad, was a notice to the effect that Gompers had not arrived in the city. John Frey, one of the AFL delegates, later wrote: "Gompers was like a caged lion. His enemies had tricked him and brought about a situation which, in addition to being a personal humiliation, would work against the patriotic purpose which had brought him to Italy. . . . His emotions were so strong that for a while he did not care to speak. Some one suggested that it might be well to postpone the meeting, but the fighting spirit which had made Gompers so strong a character would not consent to this. He was determined to speak, though . . . he dreaded the occasion."

Much to Gompers' surprise, the auditorium was filled to capacity; the crowd listened attentively and cheered him with gusto. What Gompers did not know, and never suspected, was that the seats were filled not by workers but by soldiers and sailors recruited especially for the occasion. Also, an Italian officer was standing in a little alcove, behind the speakers' platform, signaling audience response. After Gompers left the auditorium, the troops were marched back to their barracks.

final phase of his career, a hard light would be cast on his triumphs and failures.

Old age, that grim nonrespecter of persons, showed no special favoritism to Samuel Gompers. His sturdy physique at last began to show signs of deterioration and strain. It had taken him years to recover completely from a bicycle accident that occurred in Washington in the 1890's. In 1919, he was injured once more. A streetcar struck the taxi he was riding in, and the bruises, fractures, and lacerations he received from this misfortune kept him in pain the rest of his life. He suffered as well from Bright's disease (leading to kidney failure), and, worst of all, from gradually dwindling vision. He literally forced himself to maintain the old pose, however, and hid his illnesses from the world. "Socialists have always called me blind," he told a young friend. "What a field day they would have if they knew the truth!" Yet it was clear to all that he was no longer the old tiger, though he still tried to eat and drink as of old and to smoke twenty-five cigars a day.

His personal life, too, was touched with sadness. While in Italy in 1918, he learned that his favorite daughter, Sadie, had died in the influenza epidemic of that year. It was a blow from which he never really recovered. In 1920 his wife, Sophia, whose companionship bridged the years of struggle and success, also died after a long illness. Like many older men, Gompers tried to fill the new void in his life by remarriage. But it was a failure. His younger second wife was enamored of money and status, neither of which had ever interested Gompers even remotely. Sharp, cruel quarrels disrupted his declining years, and divorce proceedings were begun before his death. Increasingly he spent his days in travel or at his desk, where documents and books were read to him by secretaries because of his bad vision. He spent parts of four years dictating his autobiography, but it was published posthumously.

As for *his* labor movement, it faced many difficult problems. Postwar economic contraction created a depression in 1920–1921, and jobs became extremely hard to find. By 1921 the number of unemployed approached 4,500,-000—about 1,500,000 more than the total membership of the AFL. The earlier war-induced inflation had boosted the cost of living to record levels, but the end of fighting had not automatically restored prices to prewar norms. Now, as depression set in, hunger and destitution were driving men to form picket lines around factories and plants across the land.

Yet the great issue of the day to the average American was not industrial democracy but Prohibition. Sam Gompers was driven to impatient fury once by a "dry" congressman who said that drink was the workingman's curse. "It is the misery of poverty and undernourishment which has driven men to drink," he snapped in reply. It was poverty and undernourishment that caused the two biggest strikes of this period right after World War I: in the coal and steel industries. The coal strike was thwarted by an injunction, despite the existence of labor's Magna Charta—the Clayton Act. The steel strike, desperately fought by largely unorganized workers, was broken by the steel corporations after long, bitter months.

What was more, the progressive mood of the years from 1910 to 1916 had given way to a sudden nationwide yearning for what the 1920 Republican presidential candidate, Warren G. Harding, called "normalcy." This desire boiled over into a major "Red scare," in which suspected "Bolsheviks" were arrested, deported, expelled from government and private positions, and harassed in other ways. Gompers had labored for almost his entire career to dissociate himself and the AFL from "radicalism." Now, in the 1920's, he became an ardent foe of Soviet Communism at a time when many younger laboring men were attracted by its vaunted claims of creating a workers' republic. Yet the fickle American public, its romance with progressive reform cooling, now made no distinction between radical and conservative labor leadership. Gompers' position gained him no new ground among nonlaboring Americans. It simply lost him the support of the more aggressive elements within labor's ranks.

Marital troubles (opposite page) came soon after this 1921 wedding portrait of Gompers and his young second wife.

On another front, new open-shop campaigns were launched in certain industries. A movement to establish state courts of industrial arbitration, which would force unions to accept their proposed settlements of disputes or face legal penalties, attracted widespread and favorable press notice. Kansas actually had such a court for a time. Some industrial leaders spoke of an "American plan" of improving working conditions in their plants without the intervention of outside unions. Such a plan, of course, threatened Gompers' entire philosophy. He believed that workmen were most secure if their rights were gained by bargaining and pressure through their own independent organizations.

### Vanishing fruits

The fruits of labor's wartime cooperation, in short, did not materialize. In 1924, both major parties chose conservative candidates for the

Chorus girls parade along a Broadway sidewalk during the 1919 strike by Actors' Equity, a union Gompers helped organize.

Presidency. The Republicans named Calvin Coolidge, who had first achieved national fame by using the Massachusetts National Guard to break a strike of Boston policemen in 1919. The Democrats selected John W. Davis, a corporation lawyer. Those who, for one reason or another, were discontented with an America that seemed to be run primarily in the interests of business, united to form a third party, which took the old name, Progressive. They ran the veteran Republican insurgent, Senator Robert M. La Follette. The AFL, with Gompers' resigned backing, endorsed him.

The old chief knew that 1924 was not 1912, and a maverick candidate was not going to win in the new climate of opinion. Yet he had been warned that both major parties had turned their backs on labor, that labor's friends and supporters of many years were now Progressives, and could not be abandoned without the AFL's being forever branded reactionary. "All

right," Gompers agreed wearily. "I'll play the reckless game, but I know we're going to lose." La Follette carried only his home state of Wisconsin, although he did win nearly 5,000,000 popular votes. Gompers had been right—only now, unlike 1896, the year of Bryan's first campaign, he had not been stubborn enough to avoid playing "the reckless game."

Another problem arose from well-founded claims within the AFL itself that certain unions (especially in the building trades) were falling victim to racketeers. Gompers could only deny such charges. In cases where they were proven, he was helpless except to point out that redemption would have to come from the affected locals themselves. The Federation was founded on the principle of respecting the full autonomy of each group among its members. Gompers had built the AFL by fighting for that principle and safeguarding it for more than a third of a century. Moreover, while Gompers could not smash crime within local unions, he was charged with at least partial responsibility for its existence. For men argued that Gompers' "bread-and-butter" unionism had destroyed both the idealism and the community of purpose that would have helped rank-and-file members to reject dishonest leadership, whether or not it "buttered the bread."

And so in 1924 an aged and infirm Samuel Gompers attended his final convention of an American Federation of Labor that had fallen heir to certain infirmities of its own. The AFL appeared old and sick and rigid, too. Yet it was a success in terms of its numbers, solidity of financial resources, and general acceptance on the American scene. Gompers' critics often forgot what a spectacular achievement these facts alone represented. They were too young to have known the grim days of the 1870's.

However one looked at it, the record defied easy judgment. The AFL had helped to lift the dark shadows of the Haymarket, Homestead, and Pullman era; that achievement could not be forgotten. And yet it had only reached a small fraction of the labor force—namely the skilled workers, that fraction best able to take care of itself. It had not mobilized fully the political power of labor. It had ignored—even compounded—such general evils as racial discrimination. It had done little, in short, to transform the quality of the society of which it was part. By making itself conform to the basic standards of American life—and by underscoring material progress as the workers' main goal—the AFL had renounced the opportunity to criticize freely and democratically the beliefs of that society. But American history was strewn with the wreckage of labor organizations that had challenged or defied the system—from the National Labor Union to the IWW. Wrecked organizations have never helped a worker achieve human betterment. For Samuel Gompers, progress began with step-by-step gains for the individual, and not with grandiose blueprints for perfection.

That was his faith, and it was characteristic of his time and his adopted country. Facing the

AFL delegates for the last time, on the seventh day of that 1924 convention, he declared: "I want to live for one thing alone—to leave a better labor movement in America and in the world than I found in it when I entered, as a boy, the field of industrial and humane struggle for the right."

It was a farewell. Everyone in the hall knew it as they looked at the weak, white-faced, trembling old man. Immediately after the convention adjourned, Gompers proceeded from El Paso, Texas, where it had been held, to Mexico City for a meeting of the Pan-American Federation of Labor, and to be a representative at the inauguration of a new Mexican president. Within a few days, the exertion had taken its toll. With failing heart—he was gasping for breath, almost unable to move—Gompers was rushed by special train from the high, thin atmosphere of Mexico City to San Antonio, Texas. On the morning of December 13, 1924, he spoke to a bedside attendant. "Nurse, this is the end. God bless our American institutions. May they grow better day by day." It was his last and shortest speech—and it perhaps summated all the others he had made. Then he was gone. His body was taken to Washington where thousands of his old enemies, friends, and those who knew him only as a name, saluted him before he was buried in Tarrytown, New York.

Few words can describe Gompers' character better than his own dying blessing on America, and his hope that it would "grow better day by day." His life had been full of action, directed by the ideals of service and fraternity that he conceived as a boy in the ghettos of London and New York. He had been a worker of unsparing energy, and a tough combatant. His personal triumphs had been enjoyed immensely and without false modesty. Indeed, his self-importance in later years had made him the butt of jokes by those who could make fun of him but could not challenge his control of the AFL. One detractor was a union official who said: "Sam . . . likes to be played up. . . . In fact, if he were going to walk around the block, he would want to be preceded by a brass band."

## The human touch

Although that judgment was partly true, Gompers had another side. He could never be totally stuffy, or totally hostile. Certain stories are representative of his later years. In 1908, during a strenuous AFL campaign against Speaker of the House Cannon, Gompers found himself seated in a railroad smoking car not far from the congressional autocrat. Cannon leaned over. "Mr. Gompers," he said, "why the hell don't you come over here and sit beside me?" Gompers did, and shared "an interesting conversation for the balance of the evening." One could hardly conceive of a more self-conscious man—say, Woodrow Wilson—doing that.

In 1916 a young lady named Lucy Robins with an interest in liberal causes was attempting to see Gompers to secure his help for a pacifist labor leader convicted of bombing a prepared-

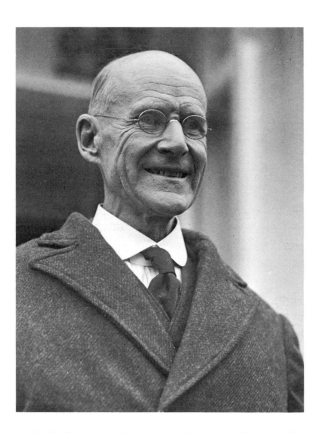

Debs, the Socialists' five-time presidential candidate, polled 920,000 votes in 1920 while he was still in prison. On hearing that Gompers was lobbying for his release, Debs said: "Tell him that I am grateful and will never forget."

ness parade in San Francisco. After being turned away by secretaries, she sent him a sizzling note in a Western Union envelope: "I now understand why the great masses of workers despise you, curse you, and eagerly await your death." Promptly Gompers summoned her to his office. He rose from his seat and peered at her over his spectacles. "Suppose I should die," he asked her, laughing. "What would you do? If you have any good ideas, I might be willing to cooperate." Miss Robins stammered, blushed, then joined with Gompers, and two office workers who were present, in roars of laughter. Miss Robins became Gompers' devoted friend, and remained so for the rest of his life. And, despite his personal enmity to pacifism, Gompers urged the AFL to intercede for Tom Mooney, the accused "bomber." Mooney's sentence was commuted to life, and he was pardoned twenty years later.

Toward the end of his life, flouting the Red scare of 1920 and his own strenuous conservatism, Gompers helped in the fight to secure Presidential amnesty for Socialists and other "radicals" jailed under wartime sedition acts. And when told that his old friend Woodrow Wilson had closed his mind to such pleas, Gompers dryly remarked, "The professor of history has lost his historical perspective." In September of 1921 he went to an Atlanta penitentiary to visit his old adversary Eugene Debs (about to be pardoned), and threw his arms around him. "It used to be Gene," said Gompers—who had not seen Debs since the Pullman strike twenty-seven years earlier. "Yes," replied the Socialist leader, "and always Sam."

These were acts not of a saint but of a human being who lived, struggled, and sweated for the working classes from which he came, in the America to which he was wholly dedicated. Gompers gave the American labor movement a sense of direction and sufficient impetus to weather the depression and war that followed his own death. His achievements stand as his monument, representing a mixture of good and bad—the mixture that is in all who share the pain and glory of being human.

# PICTURE PORTFOLIO

A bust by Frederick Louis Roslyn stands among mementos of Gompers' lifelong efforts on behalf of the AFL.

# THE INDUSTRIAL REVOLUTION

THE TEEMING CITY of London, where Samuel Gompers was born in 1850, epitomized the Industrial Revolution. Squalor and splendor have always dwelt together in cities, but in London the revolution that held sway monstrously magnified the contrasts. When the Great Exhibition opened in the Crystal Palace (right) on May 1, 1851, Queen Victoria was moved to write in her diary: "The glimpse through the iron gates of the Transept, the waving palms and flowers, the myriads of people...gave a sensation I shall never forget.... God bless...my dear country which has shown itself so great today." But Britain's industrial greatness fed on human misery: Manufacturers considered poverty and a vast pool of unemployed essential to the system. Artisans displaced by machinery worked—if they were

lucky—in smoke-belching factories to produce the goods of which the Queen was so proud. They toiled from dawn to dark, or longer, for wages so low that their children had to take full-time jobs, as Gompers did. They had to crowd their families into dark flats in grimy row houses such as the nineteenth-century French artist Gustave Doré pictured (below) when he visited London. Though denied human dignity, some of these people nevertheless refused to accept the status quo. Their unrest spurred the trade union movement.

A great glass cathedral, the Crystal Palace (above), which displayed British technology and culture to the world when Gompers was an infant, stood in Hyde Park. In East London's Bishopsgate Street, pictured below in a Doré engraving, Gompers, aged ten, began work for a shilling a week.

91

A steamer with sails, the *City of London* (above) was new the year Gompers crossed in her. "We boys found the boat a bit restrictive," he later wrote. How restrictive such a voyage could be is depicted in A. B. Houghton's wood engraving (below): "Between Decks in an Emigrant Ship—Feeding Time."

From 1855 to 1890, European arrivals in New York made their first contact with America at Castle Garden (right), an immigration station on the Battery that had been a fort in the War of 1812 and then a concert hall. Thieves and swindlers swarmed nearby, waiting to prey on the many bewildered newcomers.

# AN ANTI-IMMIGRATION IMMIGRANT

**B**RITAIN'S ENTRAPPED WORKERS shared one hope with their brethren in other lands: escape to America. A popular song Gompers often bellowed fervently as a boy—before his family abandoned London for New York in 1863—expressed this dream. It began:

"To the west, to the west, to the
  land of the free
Where mighty Missouri rolls down to
  the sea;
Where a man is a man if he's willing
  to toil,
And the humblest may gather the fruits
  of the soil."

Millions, from all over Europe and even the Orient, pursued the promise. It seemed so easy of fulfillment; steerage passage to New York from Liverpool, for example, cost but $25. For those too poor to pay, prospective employers were eager to advance the fare. The reality of the journey proved grim, however. Aboard ship, travelers were jammed by the hundred in fetid belowdecks compartments with the barest minimum of light, ventilation, and sanitary facilities. There, sometimes for two months or more, they ate, drank, stored and cooked their food, answered calls of nature, and slept. "A perfect pesthole, calculated to kill the healthiest man," the New York State Commissioners of Emigration described one wicked example. Nobody died on the voyage Gompers made, but of 544 Germans who set out from Hamburg in the *Leibnitz* in the fall of 1867, only 436 arrived alive in New York seventy days later. Ironically, Gompers—an immigrant who knew the immigrant's problems and motivations—would eventually fight to cut immigration to a trickle.

Once past Castle Garden, the immigrant often encountered a reception less benign than that pictured at right by the cartoonist Joseph Keppler. Vienna-born, Keppler had done well in America with the comic weekly *Puck,* which he founded, and accordingly portrayed Uncle Sam as a genial Noah welcoming couples from everywhere aboard his great Ark. Economically, however, many immigrants were hardly better off in America than they had been in their native lands. Competing for jobs, they found themselves sweating for low wages in steel mills, coal mines, and slaughterhouses. As immigration swelled in the 1880's, Gompers feared the newcomers would overwhelm the nation's resources and create a labor surplus like that in Britain when he was a boy. Gompers fought, reasonably, to forbid "contract labor" immigration—importing workers who agreed to accept lower-than-standard wages—and, unreasonably, to exclude all Chinese, whom he definitely considered an inferior race. As he grew older, his views grew more extreme. In 1915, he helped to push through Congress a law imposing literacy tests on immigrants. By 1924, he was arguing for a total halt in immigration for five years, and, failing in that, he supported the notorious quota system, which was finally repealed in 1965, to be effective in 1968. Both the literacy tests and the quotas were designed to admit only a trickle of eastern and southern. Europeans, whom Gompers scorned as unlikely union members and undesirable citizens. Time has, of course, shown how wrong he was.

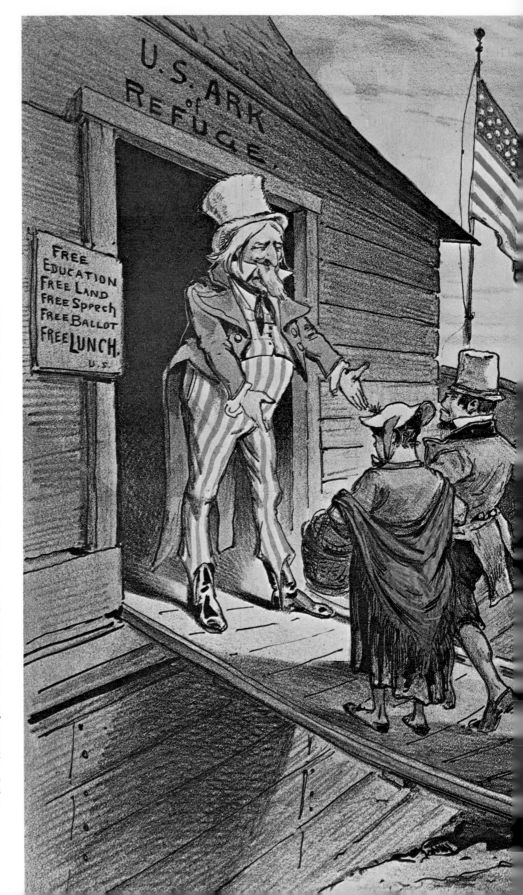

# THE BURGEONING OF INDUSTRY

**T**HE CIVIL WAR'S OUTCOME freed America at last from the economic grip of the cotton-minded South, and, bestirred by technology and high tariffs, industrialization soared at an unprecedented rate. Foundries, shoe factories, textile mills, and packing plants sprang up and thrived. Railways, aided by government subsidies, crossed the continent. Job-seekers poured into cities from farms and far-off countries to make the new productivity possible. But the demand for jobs far exceeded the supply, and skilled workers found themselves competing with vast numbers of the unskilled who flooded the labor pool. Hours were long; mill workers, like the girls portrayed by Winslow Homer (lower right), toiled from 5 A.M. to 7 P.M. Wages were cut when business sagged, and no job was ever secure against a boss's whim. Inevitably, more and more workers joined the labor movement in an attempt to better their lives.

The exuberant vigor of industrialization, suggested in John Ferguson Weir's 1866 oil, "The Gun Foundry" (lower left), presented American cities with all the problems of too-rapid growth. In the decade following the end of the Civil War, 3,500,000 immigrants poured in, pushing the population of New York, the gateway city, above 1,000,000 and creating a building boom in every major city. "Construction Work in New York" (at left), painted by Alexander Mario in 1868, shows the city in transition: excavation along 46th Street east of Lexington Avenue. One reality of nineteenth-century life was that neither the speed nor the volume of construction could keep pace with the demand.

97

# THE NEW YORK GOMPERS KNEW

THOUSANDS OF IMMIGRANTS arriving in New York stayed within a few miles of Castle Garden—prominent near Manhattan's southern tip in the 1867 lithograph above. Like the Gompers family, these newcomers settled between Broadway (center foreground) and the East River (right); some never went as far as the Hudson River (left) or the East River's far shore, Brooklyn. The area favored by immigrants—the Lower East Side—was a slum. One part of it, the notorious Five Points (upper right, in an oil by Frank Melville), teemed with thieves and derelicts who infested five-cents-a-night lodgings. The sight of squalid Chatham Street (far right, in a watercolor) moved an 1852 visitor to suggest that the showman P. T. Barnum "would do well

to buy the whole concern, men, women, and goods." This was the world from which Gompers (at right, in his earliest known portrait, 1881) emerged to give strength and direction to the fledgling labor movement. His first home on the Lower East Side was near Five Points, but residence there was not always demeaning. Many of his neighbors were honest, hardworking folk whose sons (like Gompers himself) studied art or engineering by night at Cooper Union's free classes. There was as much intellectual ferment as corruption. Some notorious criminals came out of the tenements. But so did a greater number of musicians, writers, artists, judges, and industrialists, whose influence on American culture has persisted right up to the present day.

# WOES OF THE WORKINGMAN

WAGES AND WORKING CONDITIONS in the 1870's and 1880's, deplorable all over industrial America, hit bottom in the tenement workshops of New York. Gompers and other cigarmakers employed in small factories had to compete, for example, with such hapless folk as the family at right, whose boss was also its landlord. Jacob A. Riis, a noted journalist and reformer, described the plight of these slum workers in his book *How the Other Half Lives.* Riis wrote: "The manufacturer who owns, say, from three or four, to a dozen or more tenements...fills them up with these [Bohemian immigrants] charging them outrageous rents, and demanding often even a prelimi-

nary deposit of five dollars 'key money'; deals them out tobacco by the week, and devotes the rest of his energies to the paring down of wages to within a peg or two of the point where the tenant rebels in desperation. When he does rebel, he is given the alternative of submission, or eviction with entire loss of employment. His needs determine the issue. Usually he is not in a position to hesitate long [for] he has seldom much laid up against a rainy day."

Gompers, posing as a book salesman, surveyed the tenement workshops on behalf of a union campaign to eliminate them. He reported that more than seven thousand persons

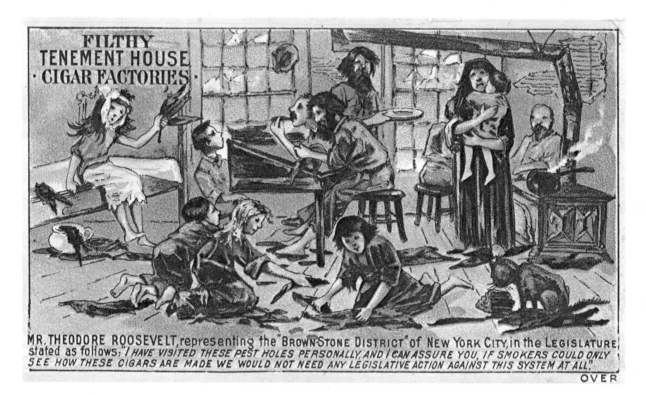

MR. THEODORE ROOSEVELT, representing the "BROWN STONE DISTRICT" of NEW YORK CITY, in the LEGISLATURE, stated as follows: *'I HAVE VISITED THESE PEST HOLES PERSONALLY, AND I CAN ASSURE YOU, IF SMOKERS COULD ONLY SEE HOW THESE CIGARS ARE MADE WE WOULD NOT NEED ANY LEGISLATIVE ACTION AGAINST THIS SYSTEM AT ALL.''*

OVER

Cigar Makers' International Union of America

This certifies that

M... *Samuel Gompers.*

No. *1* was initiated by Union *No. 144*

*New York Nov 1.st, 879.*

Jacob Riis's book on slum life contains pictures he took as well as his verbal impressions. In describing tenement shops where the cigar mold was used (right), he wrote: "Men, women, and children work together seven days in the week...from the break of day till far into the night." After Theodore Roosevelt had visited tenements —Gompers was one of his escorts—he was quoted in material the Cigar Makers distributed urging smokers not to buy tenement-made cigars (above). A portion of Gompers' dues book, which notes that he held union card No. 1 issued in 1879, is reproduced at left.

toiled in dark, odorous, filthy rooms, and that nearly three fourths of the young girls became ill within six months, and that many of the workers suffered from contagious diseases. Moreover, he noted that "there was nothing in those tenements to stimulate cleanliness and discrimination of mind and body."

But practical more than humanitarian considerations motivated the union's opposition to the tenement shops; starvation pay in the tenements endangered pay scales in the factories. The problem remained basically the same throughout American industry, though it took varied shapes, as is evident in these Lewis Hine photographs: In the Georgia tex-

tile mills (far right), pay rates were kept down by child workers so small that they had to clamber up on their machines; in hatmaking, prison factories provided the competition; in garment manufacturing, it was the East Side sweatshop (above), to which boys like the lad in the center lugged cloth for stitching.

The Cigar Makers' campaign against tenement shops constitutes a classic case history of labor's struggles. The tactics and the strategy employed by Gompers set a pattern that the AFL followed long after it had become powerful. And the tribulations the campaign encountered were typical, too. The Cigar Makers decided in 1878 that tenement shops

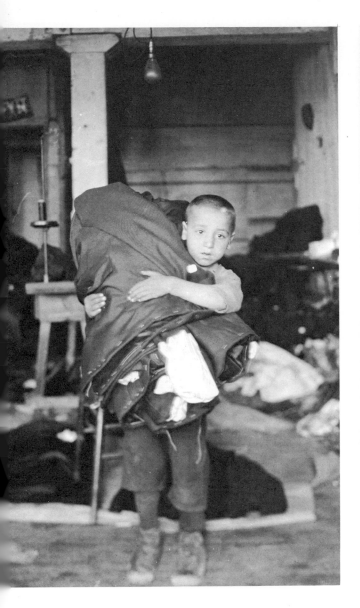

should be abolished by federal law, and next year a New York Congressman, Abram S. Hewitt, pushed a measure to that end through the House of Representatives. The Senate killed it. When Gompers resumed the presidency of his Cigar Makers' Local in 1880, he renewed the campaign with redoubled vigor, but made state, rather than federal, legislation the objective. To achieve it, he lobbied persistently in Albany, where he found an unlikely ally in Assemblyman Theodore Roosevelt. When the legislature failed to act in 1881, he mobilized unions all over the state to work to elect the bill's supporters and defeat its opponents. As a result, the State Senate in

1882 voted to ban tenement workshops. But in the legislature's last hours, the bill's official copy vanished and never reached the Assembly. (The manufacturers had legislative friends, too.) Next session, the bill did become law, but the courts ruled it unconstitutional. Amended, it passed again. Again, under pressure from manufacturers, the courts nullified it, contending that the law interfered with a laborer's right to work where he chose. Ultimately, the tenement cigar and clothing workshops, and child labor and prison labor all disappeared because organized labor had become strong enough to achieve its objectives—either by economic pressures or by law.

# THE STRIFE
# AND STRIVING

**O**RGANIZED LABOR'S eventual strength was fathered by oppression and nurtured by blood. The great railway strike of 1877 (left) erupted spontaneously when the Baltimore & Ohio cut wages 10 percent for the third time in three years, and the Pennsylvania followed suit. Many lives were lost in pitched battle as the strike spread, halting most of the nation's rail traffic. President Hayes finally put down the protest with federal troops, but the strikers' courage, even in defeat, inspired workers all over the country to demand better conditions. Gompers' cigar union scored a wage

An 1877 rail-strike leader, Robert M. Ammon, telegraphs his orders.

Massed New York police open the way for a horsecar. Strikers often dumped coal on the tracks to make them impassable.

breakthrough soon after 1877, but for other workers, improvement was slow to come. The New York horsecar drivers' strike of 1886 (below) began with a few employees defying an army of police, and eventually involved fifteen thousand men. This time, the strikers won: $2 for a twelve-hour day, with half an hour off for dinner. A court injunction—and labor's own divisiveness—crushed the Pullman strike of 1894 (below). But in 1897 an injunction had no effect on striking West Virginia miners. Gompers himself first unified support for the walkout, then defied the injunction as unconstitutional, and the United Mine Workers won a strike for the first time. The mine guard who took the picture at right gave it to Gompers after discovering they were both affiliated with the Masons.

Gompers, snapped during the mine strike of 1897

Federal troops, with guns cocked, are ready to defend a train against assault by railway men in Chicago during the Pullman strike.

The discord that beset the labor movement in its formative years is sardonically preserved in Frederick Burr Opper's cartoon for the December 22, 1886, issue of *Puck*. Titled "Wanted, a Leader!—The Labor Agitation Orchestra on the Go-As-You-Please Plan," it appeared the very month the AFL was organized, with Gompers (clanging cymbals in the center background) as president.

Opper's imagination ranged the ideological spectrum. At left (physically but not politically) sits Terence Powderly of the Knights of Labor, plucking a harp. Powderly believed all conflicts between capital and labor could be settled through arbitration, without strikes. Next to Powderly's harp, the Reverend Heber Newton, a "liberal, humanitarian" Episcopalian, tootles a flute in support of Henry George's bass viol (far right). George, founder of the Single Tax movement, believed the root of all evil lay in private ownership of land; he proposed that, for the common good, land be taxed at its full value, and all other taxes be abolished. As a candidate for Mayor of New York in 1886, George ran behind Abram Hewitt but well ahead of Theodore Roosevelt. Sourly viewing the whole scene stands Father Edward McGlynn (left), a Roman Catholic priest who fiddles more or less in tune with George and Newton. Excommunicated the following year, McGlynn was later reinstated. Drowning out the oompahs from the walking delegate's tuba (right, rear) is the blaring trombone of one anarchist, behind Newton, and the angry drumming of another next to the unconcerned Henry George. Shortly before this cartoon appeared, the anarchist martyrs of the Haymarket affair had been convicted. Anarchism was still a serious movement whose adherents believed that if governments were abolished, the innate goodness of man would triumph. But they were divided on whether to hasten utopia by violence, or to agitate from the sidelines. At center, Robert G. Ingersoll has ceased trumpeting and is covering an ear to bar the din. A renowned agnostic orator, Ingersoll was essentially conservative. Though he opposed anarchism, he thought the Haymarket anarchists had been tried unfairly.

Opper's cartoon sums up the dilemma of labor in 1886. It knew it had to take a stand but did not know how; it knew it had to take positive steps but lacked a precise direction. Only Gompers, among the players in this "Benefit Concert," would learn the score well enough to assert needed leadership. From percussionist he would, in due course, rise to leader of the orchestra.

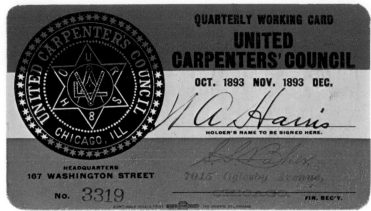

The AFL's characteristic handclasp and a union label adorn a badge (left) owned by a member of a union local. A typical union membership card appears above. Below is a 1902 advertisement for the merits of union-made clothing.

GOMPERS

BY PERMISSION: *Saml Gompers.*

COPYRIGHT 1914 BY SAMUEL GOMPERS, REG. IN U. S. PATENT OFFICE.

CIGARS

HIGH GRADE GOMPERS HAND MADE

## SYMBOLS OF GROWING STRENGTH

For centuries men who follow the same calling have banded together for their mutual good. The modern trade union descends spiritually, if not lineally, from the *collegia* of Roman times and the artisans' guilds of medieval Europe. Commonly the guild stamped a symbol or hallmark on its product to bespeak the maker's pride in his craftsmanship and to assure purchasers of the quality of the artifact. The union label is intended to serve similar purposes today, but its most important function is to attract the patronage of all believers in trade unionism. When the Cigar Makers' International introduced the label to America at San Francisco in 1874, the union intended it as a weapon. Unorganized, woefully exploited Chinese were threatening to monopolize employment in the cigar trade. Since then, as labor's strength has grown, union-made products have borne the label as proudly as union men have carried their membership cards and donned, on special occasions, their silk badges (far left). No one enjoyed wearing the trappings, attending the conventions, and being part of the bustle of union business more than Gompers. He remained a member of the Cigar Makers' union all his life and even allowed a good cigar to be named for him. Each box lid (above) bore an excellent likeness of him—and a rare one, too, for it showed him in his prime—and the words "high grade" and "hand made" flanked his name. No tribute could have pleased the craftsman in him more.

# THE VARIED
# RELAXATIONS
# OF A BUSY MAN

Gompers, sketched by Caruso during a backstage chat

Ellen Terry, painted as Lady Macbeth by Sargent

GOMPERS WROTE in his memoirs, "Life has never been tame for me"—and he enjoyed leisure as lustily as he enjoyed work. From childhood, he delighted in music and in the theater. He thrilled at the acting of Edwin Booth, Richard Mansfield, Eleonora Duse and Ellen Terry (left below). He went often to the opera; sometimes, having been detained by work, he missed the curtain's rise and stood in the wings while his friend Enrico Caruso sang. But Gompers' tastes were broad. He made a second home of saloons, for example, and one of the most famous in his day was McSorley's Old Ale House (shown in John Sloan's painting below). It was a decorous but strictly masculine Lower East Side retreat for New York businessmen, laborers, politicians, artists, journalists, and even stray an-

Like other famous men Samuel Gompers enjoys a morning shower. To pull the wrong cord occasionally never is a shock because Sam is continually getting into hot water.

One thing that worries Sam are his short legs. Every morning to increase his height he indulges in a little dumb-bell exercise while on tip-toe. Having juggled all kinds including human he depreciates his skill. "It's born in me," says Mr. Gompers.

"Scare 'em to death with a look," is the labor leader's motto for his enemies. Here he is cultivating that angelic expression he reserves exclusively for his Bolshevik friends.

Mr. Gompers is very proud of his scanty locks generally at rest on the back of his collar. He insists that they be curly because radicals wear them long and straight. He looks better that way too.

Here is Mr. Gompers with that shy expression he wears when called upon to make a speech. Unaccustomed to such requests still he always manages to get out a word or two.

His short legs may handicap Sam when he takes his morning gallop but when it comes to riding a hostile labor convention the old boy always sticks in his saddle. He has'nt been thrown yet.

Scattering crumbs from the rich man's table among his feathered friends is Sam's delight after dining with the high and mighty.

That much talked about battle Mr. Gompers waged with Judge Gary is historic. Eye-witnesses differ greatly regarding it but Sam says, "Why every one knows I had the Judge licked to a frazzle in the first round."

Hatred of publicity is strong in Mr. Gompers' breast. The sight of a 'movie' man or photographer sends him off at top speed. Still there are a few photographs of Samuel in existence and they're not back views either.

archists. Gompers enjoyed prizefights—then mainly a diversion of the lower classes—and once left the opera after the first act to accompany a friend to a promising boxing match. He admired well-shaped women, among whom Lillian Russell (right), with her much-envied hourglass figure, was considered one of the shapeliest. Like his favorite President, Woodrow Wilson, he also had a passion for vaudeville. Gompers never attempted to conceal his hedonistic side, but the public knew little if anything about it. When Gompers was seventy, Tony Sarg, a cartoonist and creator of marionettes, included him (left) in a newspaper series, "A Day in the Life of Famous Men." Sarg portrayed a tireless worker, galloping and glowering through endless duties. But when Gompers' associates at AFL headquarters needed to find him in an emergency, they would begin their search by peering into Washington's ribald Gayety burlesque theater, a place where even a hard-driving man found it easy to laugh and relax.

Like Gompers, the distinguished American painter Thomas Eakins found prizefights fascinating, but he did not attend fights to relax. As an artist, he studied the dynamics of boxers in action and went through the motions himself when the fighting grew hot. In the 1899 oil below, "Between Rounds," he painted the faces of several Philadelphia friends.

Lillian Russell reigned as belle of the musical theater at the time Eakins was painting prizefights. Widely known for her tiffs with producers and for her tempestuous marriages, she had a more amiable side. She worked with the Red Cross in World War I, and Gompers recalled that she once sang "song after song" at a benefit for women workers on strike.

# SOME REWARDS OF HARD WORK

GOMPERS DIVIDED HIS TIME among many causes, but his heart was always with organized labor. His name appears in the minutes (opposite) of the first meeting of the Federation of Organized Trades and Labor Unions on November 19, 1881, at which he was promptly given a responsible post. Except for 1895, he presided over the AFL, which grew out of the FTLU, every year from 1886 until his death in 1924. The gavel he used at his last AFL convention is in the foreground, opposite. Behind the handwritten minutes he proudly retained through the years is a bust by Kathleen Wheeler, which the AFL presented him in 1916. The variety of Gompers' interests was staggering in scope; he personified the perfect "joiner." He was a Mason, an Elk, a Forester, an Odd Fellow, and a member of countless humanitarian and patriotic committees. When he joined, he worked. He earned his medals, and in his early days put them to work, too. To feed his hungry family, he often pawned the gold token (first vertical row below, second from bottom) given him by the Foresters in 1873. Among the awards pictured below is one for war relief work in Belgium, one for vigorously promoting the sale of Liberty Loans, one for bringing the prison labor problem to light, and a number from unions and fraternal orders.

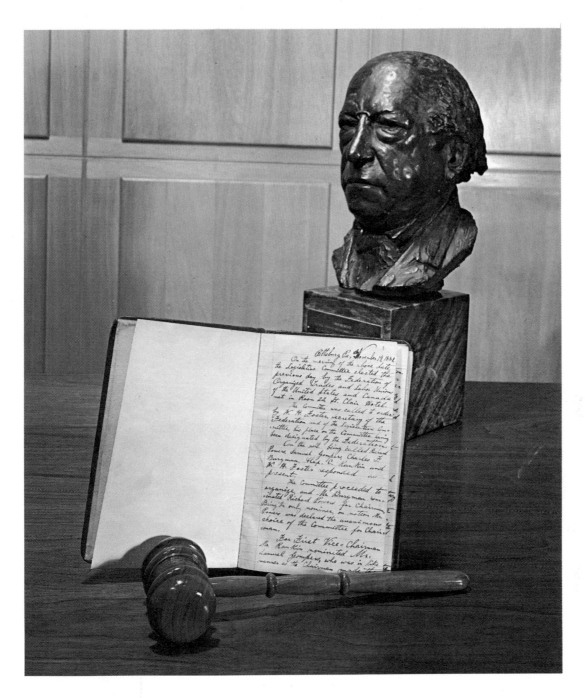

Gompers' awards (left), listed by vertical rows from the top, were: a gold medal from the National Committee on Prisons and Prison Labor, 1919; two World War I medallions he wore in honor of American men in military service; a gold medal presented by Court Empire City of the Ancient Order of Foresters, 5345, in 1873; a Liberty Loan award of 1920. Second row: a bronze medal given by August Keufer of France in appreciation of Gompers' aid "to the sufferers of Belgium," 1919; his Cigar Makers' International Union of America button; an Elks lapel pin; a gold medal from the National Institute of Social Sci-

ences, 1919. Third row: Queen Victoria Badge from the British Trades Union Congress, 1895; bronze medals signifying membership on the reception committee for Theodore Roosevelt's inauguration, 1905; an Odd Fellows badge (left) and two Masonic emblems—a Scottish Rite lapel pin over a Shriners watch fob (right). Last row: an American Legion medal, 1920; a gold badge presented for fifty years' membership in the Odd Fellows, 1923; and the badge Gompers wore while presiding over the AFL's 1924 convention in El Paso, Texas, which took place only a few weeks before he died.

# STRIKE AND RIFT

**G**OMPERS LEFT BEHIND a Federation muscular enough to survive the great depression of the 1930's, but too muscle-bound to make the most of what advantage the crisis presented. Like the imploring figures in Max Weber's "Seeking Work" (above), up to sixteen million Americans lacked jobs, and more than half the population suffered real privation. In the shadow of adversity, white-collar employees, intellectuals, actors, writers, and artists aligned themselves more closely with labor than ever before—or since. New laws guaranteed labor's right to organize, and millions of the unskilled and semiskilled in such industries as steel and auto-making clamored for unionization. There was also a clamor to reform the AFL structure, which specified membership by craft, not by industry. In 1935, AFL dissidents set up a Committee for Industrial Organization that attracted millions of new members. However, CIO victories over management did not come so easily: In a painting characteristic of the 1930's, Philip Evergood recorded (left) a bloody battle in the 1937 Republic Steel strike.

117

The AFL-CIO merger, marked by the handshake of George Meany (left) and Walter Reuther, brought together fifteen million craft and industrial union members.

# UNIONISM NOW

**W**ITH THE DEPRESSION, which increased its membership, and World War II, which relieved unemployment, organized labor became a political force, proving it could win elections for those it backed. With its strength and recognition came maturity. In most instances, strikes were called after orderly secret balloting (right), instead of rowdy outbursts. Arguments were settled by collective bargaining, or arbitration with the help of outside mediators (right, above), rather than bloodshed. A new era began in 1955 when the AFL merged with the CIO. For the two groups, divorced since 1938 when the CIO (renamed the Congress of Industrial Organizations) was expelled from the AFL, it was a remarriage of convenience—not a "happily ever after" affair. Long-standing differences between AFL President Meany and former CIO President Reuther led to Reuther's resignation from the AFL-CIO executive council in 1967. It became clear, then, that survival of the superfederation would be decided by time, moderation, vision, and flexibility. La-

bor can, for example, win still higher wages, shorter workdays and workweeks, and ever more generous fringe benefits, but in an age of automation it cannot long guarantee its members job security. Strikes can be more potent than ever, paralyzing whole sections of the economy, but their social impact hurts labor—as does labor's wide failure to accept racial integration. Though there have been efforts to organize agricultural workers and such professionals as teachers and social workers, union membership totals are declin-ing, not increasing, and so is labor's popular-ity. The New York unionists below are march-ing by a cigar store in a Labor Day scene of the 1960's. Their signs, calling for an end to immigration quotas Gompers fought for and endorsing a health program he would have opposed, suggest something of labor's tri-umph over inequities of the past. Missing, however, is an indication that labor is looking ahead to a goal Gompers defined as early as 1904: "to clear the pathway for a...success-ful advance tomorrow and tomorrow."

HIS OWN WORDS

# HIS YOUTH REMEMBERED

*Samuel Gompers was nearing seventy when he began a project on which he would work intensively during his last five years of life—the writing of his autobiography. Its two weighty volumes were not published until 1925, shortly after his death. By the time he embarked on his reminiscences, Gompers' memory was no longer razor sharp, and, since his eyesight was dimming, much of the manuscript was dictated to assistants. But his own words, as expressed in* Seventy Years of Life and Labor, *are a memorable reconstruction of his life and times. Such a strong-minded man was bound to be one-sided about many aspects of his controversial career. He was too partisan to be wholly objective, too egotistic to be entirely accurate. But no other human being could have written what he did, and his memoirs are more telling than anything else ever written about him. They begin with his London boyhood in a household that, though shabby and poor in creature comforts, was rich in family warmth:*

■ The first home that I remember was in a three-story brick house at No. 2 Fort Street, in East Side, London. I believed I was born in that house until my trip to London in 1919 when a painstaking reporter consulted the London birth registry and announced that I was born in No. 11 Tentor Street and that my parents soon afterwards moved to Fort Street. I accepted the revision philosophically, for many years of contact with reporters had accustomed me to receiving from them much novel and sometimes interesting information about myself. . . . My father and mother lived on the ground floor. My paternal grandparents lived in the second story with their four girls and one boy just ten months older than I. On the top floor lived Mr. Lellyveld, who had two sons. . . .

Our apartment consisted of one large front room and a little back room which we used in the winter for storage and for things which had to be kept cool. In the summertime father constructed bunks in the little room and we children slept there. In the wintertime we all slept in the big room— father and mother in the big bed that had a curtain around it, and we children on the floor in a trundle bed that was rolled under the big bed in the daytime. I was the oldest. Besides me there were Henry, Alexander, Lewis, and Jack. That front room was sitting-room, bedroom, dining-room, and kitchen—the center of our busy little lives as we learned the ways of childhood in East Side, London. Like all children of the poor, we early found our way to the city streets—the place where we began contacts and struggles with our fellows. It is the education of the street that produces that early shrewdness in the children of those who "have not" that often leaves an ineradicable difference between them and the children of those who "have." Life in the streets had manifold fascinations, but we were required to be home for meals and at other definite times. . . .

Our home preserved many of the customs of the Dutch community from which mother and father came. In our big room was a large fireplace in which mother had a Dutch oven that produced what seemed to us children marvelously delicious things to eat. All mother's cooking utensils were of the squat, substantial Dutch make, necessary for the old-fashioned Dutch cooking that nourished us youngsters three times a day. We had plenty of dishes—an unusual possession in our neighborhood. These mother brought to this country and I have one of her old teapots in my present home. . . . I can remember yet her roast meat and a very savory dish of baked potatoes and rice. The meat was suspended on a string and we children were often permitted to turn it. At regular intervals mother basted it—a job she never entrusted to us. Our bread came from a neighboring bakery. I was always glad to be sent to purchase the loaf. We bought a "quarten"—a four-pound loaf. In those days the bakers were required to weigh each loaf as they sold it and if the big round loaf was a bit under weight, an extra slice was cut from another loaf. That extra slice never reached home—the fresh, warm bread was irresistible to my sturdy appetite. . . .

In the evening we burned eight-penny rush lights or large candles which stood in old-fashioned brass candlesticks. These made a fairly good light for that time. On special occasions we used a paraffin lamp, which was considered a great discovery. Kerosene was too high for daily use. Every hour of the night the beadle made his round. It seems but last night when I heard "It is ten o'clock and all is well," and again snuggled under the cover for peaceful sleep. Special occurrences were heralded by the town crier.

At regular intervals our "sitting-room, bedroom, dining-room, and kitchen" was converted into a bathroom. Mother brought in the wash-tub

English children here burn a "guy" (an effigy of Guy Fawkes) as fireworks explode overhead on the night of November 5—an annual highlight of Gompers' London boyhood. Such festivities still commemorate exposure of the aborted Gunpowder Plot to blow up Parliament in 1605, for which Guy Fawkes and other conspirators were executed. Gompers recalled: "On the holiday that all England celebrates, Guy Fawkes Day, we boys were on the streets as was all London. . . . Each group of boys constructed a little dome-like grotto of oyster shells. . . . In the grotto we built a red fire and then we stood by it with oyster shell in hand, accosting each person who passed with, 'Please remember the Grotto once a year.' When we got enough money, we went to the theater. Truly, life in the London streets, though precarious, was adventurous, wonderfully interesting, and happy."

While still a boy in London, Gompers went to work making cigars from tobacco that merchant ships regularly brought to England. With this engraving of a dockside warehouse in 1856, the *Illustrated London News* published a description of the "busy group assembled round a huge pair of scales which require the assistance of a large pulley-wheel fixed to the beams above to hoist them free of the ground. Around these scales a number of workmen are busily employed [as] the Custom-house officer . . . directs one of his men to insert a sharp-pointed instrument into the mass and, by using it as a lever, to detach thick layers at various intervals, and thus to ascertain that the whole block consists of tobacco leaves and nothing else. Its weight is then taken and duly noted . . . with a view to the charging of duty for revenue."

and, with thorough-going Dutch cleanliness, scrubbed us youngsters or superintended the process. In those days they called me the sleepy-head. Mother couldn't get me up in the morning and couldn't keep me out of bed in the evening—a distinct inconvenience in that room that served all the needs of the whole family. Perhaps I was stowing up sleep for later years when I slept when there was nothing else to do. . . .

When six years of age I was sent to the Jewish Free School in Bell Lane and learned rapidly all that was taught there—reading, writing, arithmetic, geography, and history. The school was an old institution when I attended it. It provided instructions for both boys and girls, as well as for select students known as the Talmud boys—twenty-one in number. . . . When I was ten years and three months I had to go to work. When I left school I stood third to the highest in my classes. As I made rapid progress in my studies, the teacher told father that it was wrong to rob me of an education, particularly as I showed ability. But father could not do otherwise. Though I left school at an early age to help earn a living . . . I was eager to learn more and found opportunity in the Night Free School where I added to my meager equipment. French and music were among my studies there. Though I could never speak French, the rudiments and rules of grammar and fair pronunciation I never forgot. Years later they helped me during my trips to France and in those important international gatherings that began with the Paris Peace Conference. Of almost equal value

has been my knowledge of Dutch, which, without formal study, I somehow assimilated from Dutch friends and neighbors. My knowledge of this language enabled me to write grandfather's letters for him as well as to keep his accounts. . . .

At night school I learned something of the Talmud. I was taught Hebrew—not the mongrel language spoken and written by many Jews of the present age, but that honorable language that unlocked a literature of wonderful beauty and wisdom. The discipline gained from studying the Talmud is essentially the same as resulting from any legal study. It develops the more subtle qualities of mind; the student learns to deal with abstract problems, to make careful discriminations, to follow a line of reasoning from premise to conclusion. This legal training given to Jewish boys is fundamental in explaining the intellectual quality of many of the Jewish people. Again and again in after years I was told that I missed my career in not studying law.

My paternal grandfather, for whom I was named, had come to London from Amsterdam in 1845. . . . With his philosophy and his kindly generosity, grandfather was the most [potent] influence in my early life. He would illustrate his philosophy by story or incident. One quaint illustration of human proneness to talk many times has helped me to keep my own counsel. I can vividly see the old man standing by the wall with a piece of chalk in his hands. "Son," he said, "if you would keep a matter secret do not speak of it, then only one person knows it"; and he gravely chalked up on the wall the figure "1," representing secrecy. "For if you tell another person that makes"—and here he gravely chalked on the wall the additional "1" following secrecy, making "11." "That person will tell his confidant and the secret will be known by"—he chalked up the additional "1," making the total "111," etc.

Our grandfather was scrupulously clean as was shown in one peculiarity which used to afford us fun. He disliked paper money as being dirty and whenever in later years he got a dollar bill he would at once exchange it for coin. He was generous and kind and yet at times, though not often, he would be seized by manifestations of savage outbursts of uncontrollable rage which lasted but a moment. Afterwards he would not only express regret but would make more than ample amends. These outbursts of temper, I afterwards learned, are a family characteristic which I too possessed. But they grew in frequency as grandfather became older. Afterwards when we came to the United States, and grandfather followed us in 1868, I witnessed a terrible paroxysm of temper on his part—absolutely without justification. Then I seemed to see myself in the same rage. I said to myself, "Sam, that's you and that ain't good." I accused myself and for days was very unhappy. It had its influence upon me and my whole conduct. From that time I determined to become master of myself.

*The Gompers apartment was situated about a mile from the teeming ghetto where most of the slum Jews of London lived. As was customary in Jewish households, young Sam received religious training. As a boy, he went through the motions and adhered to the doctrines that made one a practicing Jew, but when he grew older his outlook toward Judaism became ambivalent.*

■ Where we lived there were endless rows of shabby houses bordered by pavements. . . . I never knew the pleasure and sense of individuality of living in a separate house, with four walls of its own, until I bought my present home in 1917. . . . Our family, though not scrupulously orthodox, observed fast days and the important ceremonials in those London days. Although educated—if the term might be applied to the slight schooling I was permitted—in a sectarian school, my nature has been in conflict with the restrictions of sects, against conformity to ritual or the idea of authority vested in superiors. Fast days invariably came at a time when I wanted to eat—and I early felt that natural instinct was of greater importance than blind obedience. By nature I am a non-conformist. I believe that restrictions dwarf personality and that largest usefulness comes through greatest personal freedom. Somehow I have never been able to separate an act of worship or service, as I prefer to call it, from some concrete human need. My mind has ever hungrily grasped ideals, and I have followed them with unflagging devotion under the inspiration of service to my fellows. Service has been to me the great spiritual purpose that illumines life.

*In his long service to the labor movement, Gompers pursued a course quite consistent with his own personal—and liberal—attitude toward religion. The first paragraph excerpted below is from an 1894 letter to a friend. The second paragraph shows that his stand on an issue, even one as sensitive as religion, usually became official policy, and he was firm in maintaining it. When the United Hebrew Trades, acting as a religious labor body, rejected an AFL trade-union ruling in 1915, Gompers overruled the group.*

■ You say that your chief glory is that you are a Jew. Mine is that I have a heart, a mind and a conscience, that I have struggled with my fellow men, and yearn to struggle on for a better day when the ridiculous divisions, questions which make man an enemy to man instead of his brother, shall be eliminated. . . . Jefferson placed this as a test of Americans: 'Is he honest, is he true, is he faithful to the Constitution?' I am willing that the test be applied to me so far as the labor movement of our country and the struggles of the people are concerned. . . .

In the United States of America there must not be the judgment of a Jewish labor movement, no more than there must be the judgment of the Catholic labor movement, no more than there must be the judgment of a Protestant labor movement, no more than there must be a judgment of a Buddhist or an atheist labor movement. The labor movement of America must prevail. . . . To me it matters not whether a man be a Protestant or a Catholic, or a free thinker, or an atheist. That is a matter of his own conscience and of his own judgment, his own hopes or his own fears, but I do say that in the labor movement we are not Jews nor Christians nor atheists but we are working men and bound by the common ties.

*Sam was "thirteen years, six months, and two days old" when his family reached America in July 1863. Guided by friends and relatives who met them at the boat, the family found a flat in the squalor of New York's Lower East Side. Within a year Sam was in a union, and before he was seventeen he was upholding his fellow workers' rights against their employer:*

■ In 1864 I joined the Cigar Makers' Local Union No. 15 which was the English-speaking union of New York City. This organization was not strong. There was also Union No. 90 of German-speaking cigarmakers which was affiliated to the German Labor Union that met in the Tenth Ward Hotel. All my life I had been accustomed to the labor movement and accepted as a matter of course that every wage earner should belong to the union of his trade. I did not yet have a conscious appreciation of the labor movement. My awakening was to come later. However, I attended union meetings and observed union regulations.

For the first year and a half after we came to New York I worked with my father at home. Father paid a deposit for materials and worked at his bench at home instead of in a shop. At that time home work was not exploited as it was later under the tenement-house system. When I determined to find work outside, I had the self-confidence that goes with mastery of a trade. In hunting for a job, I chanced to fall in with another cigarmaker much older than I. Together we went from shop to shop until we found work. With a bit of nervousness but with sure, quick skill I made my first two cigars which the boss accepted and I became a permanent workman in the shop.

My first job as a journeyman was at M. Stachelberg's on Pearl Street. I was then between sixteen and seventeen. There was much unrest in the shop. The men were discontented. They asked me to present to the employer their grievances and the new conditions they wanted. When I did so, Mr. Stachelberg told me that I, a mere boy, ought to be ashamed to be representing men old enough to be my father and that I ought to be at home where my mother could "dry me one behind the ear." I told him that the men were entitled to have whoever they chose. When Stachelberg found that I couldn't be intimidated, he tried to bribe me. He sought me out in conversation, offered to treat me to beer, and to do everything to alienate me from the men. However, I stuck by the men and finally succeeded in winning the case.

*Gompers had a forceful, outgoing personality, which—even when he was a teen-ager—attracted people and commanded their respect. His self-confidence was matched by great sociability and a profound eagerness to learn. Moreover, his lack of formal education was a stimulus rather than a handicap; it spurred him on a quest for knowledge that lasted a lifetime:*

■ When I was fourteen, judge and jury clubs were popular among young men in New York. A number of my boy companions formed an organization for pleasure and mental advancement, and named it the Arion Base

Gompers sometimes enhanced his dignity—and heightened his diminutive stature—by wearing a black skullcap. It was unmistakably a *yarmulke*, Yiddish for the skullcap traditionally worn by Orthodox and Conservative Jews engaged in worship or religious study. As his comments on the opposite page indicate, Gompers abandoned formal religious observances in his youth, and no one has ever learned exactly why he continued to don a *yarmulke*. At least occasionally he wore it to impress important Jewish figures (see page 10). At other times he may simply have wished to hide his bald spot—or keep the top of his head warm!

Peter Cooper was one of the truly remarkable Americans of his time—a time that spanned almost a century from 1791. In youth he developed a better glue than was being produced at home or abroad, and almost monopolized the American glue market. He went on to make an even bigger fortune in iron, building huge blast furnaces and being the first man anywhere to manufacture iron structural beams. In 1830 his noted "Tom Thumb" was the first practical steam locomotive built in America. A washing machine was among his numerous inventions, while his still more numerous benefactions included the founding of Cooper Union in 1857 "for the advancement of science and art." Cooper himself had only one year of schooling before going to work—even less than Gompers was able to get—and thus resolved to provide better educational opportunities for others. In 1876, Cooper was the Greenback party's candidate for President, and Gompers eagerly voted for him, admiring not only his political and philanthropic viewpoints but also the philosophy this self-made man had expressed: "I have always recognized that the object of business is to make money in an honorable manner. I have endeavored to remember that the object of life is to do good."

Ball and Social Club. We tried various kinds of athletics without a tutor. We seriously and ardently debated all the mooted public questions of the day. We held court, trying our members for all manner of fictitious crimes. As president of the club, I was intensely interested in all its activities—as a debater, attorney, and judge. This was a practical training in public speaking, argumentation, and parliamentary procedure. The study these activities required made it necessary for me to acquire information from the best sources available.

By reason of my activity in the debating club which I helped to organize, I cannot say whether I was attracted by or drifted to the debating club in Room 24, Cooper Union, the institute founded by Peter Cooper. In any event, I came in contact with young men, many of whom were striving to learn. One of these was Peter J. McGuire, then an alert attractive young Irish-American hungry for information and opportunities to discuss current problems. . . .

Cooper Union provided opportunities for formal study courses as well as lectures every Saturday evening which were usually attended by from twenty-five hundred to three thousand. . . . I was fairly quivering in my intense desire to know. Mental hunger is just as painful as physical hunger. Every Saturday night some great scholar talked to an open meeting and gave most wonderfully illuminating results of experimentation and study. . . . Truths gleaned in those lectures became a most vital part of me and gave the world marvelously inspiring meaning. . . . I attended these lectures and study classes over a period of twenty years. Classes were organized in the fall, spring, and winter. Among the courses for which I registered were history, biography, music, mechanics, measurement of speed, elocution, economics, electric power, geography, astronomy, and travels.

No one can fully evaluate the work which the Cooper Institute has been doing as year after year it has brought to the youth of East Side New York the culture and wisdom of the best minds of the nation. It has been a constructive agency for better living and better citizenship. At these lectures Peter Cooper, then in his advanced years, venerable, beaming with pleasure and satisfaction, and accompanied by the lecturer would walk upon the platform with his air cushion under his arm. His appearance was always greeted with a demonstration of affection and gratitude. The audience rose at his entrance and remained standing until he was seated. Then the lecture began.

*At sixteen, despite all his other activities, Sam fell in love—and soon began a marriage that lasted happily for fifty-three years:*

■ One day Jack Polak, a very dear friend of mine, said to me: "Sam, I've got to go away for the summer. Will you look after my girl for me?" I carelessly promised and in a few days hunted up Sophia Julian. Sophia was a stripper [of tobacco] who worked in the same shop that I did. She was very pretty, with a clear olive complexion and a glowing color like peachblow, soft musical voice, and black curls that she arranged most attractively. Sophia had been born in London and when only a young child came to America. . . . We drifted along all summer. There were Sophia Julian and Mary Ancona who were chums, and Jack Davis and I who were chums. Sophia and Mary Ancona lived in Brooklyn as did Jack Davis. Two or three times every week I went in the evening to Brooklyn and it was a journey in those days, before the subways were constructed. I took a stagecoach to the ferry, the ferry from the Battery to Hamilton Avenue. By the time I returned the stagecoach was not running and there was then no streetcar north from the Battery. I established relations of reciprocity with the driver of a milk wagon whereby I exchanged cigars for a seat on the tail end of his wagon. . . . But sometimes I was too late for my milk-wagon driver . . . and that five-mile walk after midnight through an unilluminated, badly paved section of New York noted for its holdups and rough work was a tax on loyalty.

Sometimes the girls came over to New York and went with Jack and me to our debating club. The girls were always a spur to our oratorical ability. Sometimes we planned picnics and little parties. The four of us went out together, had a pretty good time, dancing and walking and occasionally going to the theater. On my birthday, January 27, 1867, we discussed how best to celebrate the day and someone suggested that we get married. Sophia did not show any disposition to oppose. . . . On January 28, without consultation or announcement of plans, we simply went to the Justice of the Peace at the City Hall of Brooklyn and we were married. Jack and Mary stood up for us as witnesses and we stood up for them, and so both couples were married. We went to a cheap restaurant and got a bite to eat as our wedding supper and then we went to the theater to see the play "La Poveretta" or "Under the Snow." Then I took my new wife to her home and I went over to my home. I was seventeen years and one day old when I married Sophia Julian and she was sixteen years and six months. When the marriage license was published, there was a sort of a hullabaloo about it and then it was simply all right and my wife came over to our house and lived with us. She was working and so was I. We paid board and saved whatever we could until finally we concluded to put up our own little nest and bought some furniture for which we paid cash—not on time—and made our home in which we then gathered our children, one after the other. . . .

The first weeks of married life were a dream of happiness. Well do I remember the walks home at night, the day's work forgotten, talking, laughing as we sauntered along. We were both very fond of smoked sturgeon. Sometimes we bought a pound from a stand along our way, intending to take it home, but often it had disappeared when we reached home and the family worried because we didn't eat. Fifty-three long years afterward all this came back to us with startling vividness. . . . Sophia and I called a taxi and went down to Center Market in Washington. We had the joy of marketing. We bought a great thick steak—a luxury the doctor had forbidden us both. Then we saw smoked sturgeon and Sophia said to the dealer, "How much is it?" "One dollar and twenty cents a pound," he replied. I looked at Sophia—Sophia looked at me. We thought of our smoked sturgeon—fifteen cents a pound, bought and eaten in the streets of East Side New York. No, we could not pay one dollar and twenty cents a pound for smoked sturgeon, though neither had hesitated about the steak. That was the last time we went to market together.

After we had been married for a short time I was out of a job and had to find a position outside of New York. I found work over in Hackensack . . . and moved my family over there. . . .

One Saturday afternoon I went to New York and my wife gave me $25 which she had saved, and asked me to go to my mother and give it to her and ask her to buy material for two dresses. I went to New York and because it was necessary for me to meet my father-in-law, David H. Julian of Brooklyn, I saw that he had a few harps, banjos, guitars, and about forty fiddles. A longing for a fiddle, stronger than I could control, possessed me and I persuaded him to sell me one of his best violins. At first he refused to accept money, but I insisted and I paid him $25, the money which my wife had given me for the dress goods. I later visited my mother in New York and studiously avoided mentioning the fact that I had failed in my mission and had bought a fiddle instead of dress goods. But when I got home to Hackensack after midnight, of course I could not evade the questions. That I had bought a fiddle from her father was not a very satisfactory explanation to my wife, but there was no undoing the transaction. I was so impassioned with desire to learn music that I immediately took the fiddle out of the box and without knowing how to tune the instrument, I proceeded to scratch on it. . . .

But neighbors rarely appreciate the artistic temperament. I got a great deal of pleasure out of scratching upon that fiddle even before I was able to play a tune. Sometimes my scratching seemed to remind Mrs. Gompers of her lost dress—new dresses were not commonplace in those days. . . .

It was while living in Hackensack that our first-born came to us. Just before that birth I took Mrs. Gompers over to my mother's home so that she would have the proper attention. It was in New York City on September 4, 1868 my first son, Samuel J., was born. . . . In the fall I returned to New York where I again found work. . . . After I returned to New York, for a year and a half, I took lessons. . . . I was complimented by my teacher and others who heard me and told that I had made wonderful progress in music and playing of the violin. . . . About that same time one of my children died after having lived little more than a year, and I had no inclination to seek another music teacher. Thus ended my musical career.

## UNDERSTANDING UNIONISM

*To Gompers, family life "was firmly interwoven in my fiber." He and Sophia took deep satisfaction in having "our own nest. . . . We hadn't much, but we were bound together." Then and always, his wife and children meant much to him. But at that time his interest in labor matters was still only peripheral. He had his union card, yet gave it little thought. At the end of a long, hard day at the cigarmaking bench, he liked to devote his energy and attention to other pursuits:*

■ In those early years the fraternal or lodge movement absorbed practically all my leisure. It was its human side that drew me. I saw in it a chance for men to develop and to lend a helping hand when most needed. The lodge was to me a form of education extension. In time its limitations became evident, for I had been making ready to reach out for something bigger and more fundamental. I was a member of the union in my trade for practical reasons, while my idealism and sentiment found expression in fraternalism. As yet I did not understand that the philosophy and scope of the trade union movement could be made broad and deep enough to include all the aspirations and needs of the wage earner. . . .

There was a vast difference between those early unions and the unions of today. Then there was no law or order. A union was a more or less definite group of people employed in the same trade who might help each other out in special difficulties with the employer. There was no sustained effort to secure fair wages through collective bargaining. The employer fixed wages until he shoved them down to a point where human endurance revolted. Often the revolt started by an individual whose personal griev-

The Labor Day parade pictured below was one of three such events staged by the Knights of Labor in New York City in the early 1880's. With such pioneering demonstrations the Knights hoped to convince state governments, and ultimately the federal government as well, to set aside one day a year to honor the workingman. The Knights' persuasion was effective: Colorado passed a law in 1887 recognizing Labor Day; New York, New Jersey, and Massachusetts soon followed suit; and Congress later made Labor Day a national holiday, which has since been celebrated every year on the first Monday of September. Though the Knights themselves quickly vanished, this annual holiday survives as perhaps their most permanent contribution to the American scene. But Gompers, who heartily disliked the Knights, never gave them due credit for originating Labor Day.

ance was sore, who rose and declared: "I am going on strike. All who remain at work are scabs." Usually the workers went out with him. . . .

The union was generally in a precarious condition financially. Strike funds were never assured, and there were no other benefits. The union represented a feeling of community of burdens of those working in the same industry. It had to acquire a new meaning before it became an industrial agency. It had to strengthen its defensive resources and develop cohesive forces. But that was not only the embryonic state of unionism; it was the fledgling period of industry. Industrial production was uncouth, unscientific, just about as planless as unionism. Management, accountancy, salesmanship, elimination of waste were in the rule-of-thumb stage. Factory architecture and industrial sanitation were undeveloped sciences.

*It was through personal relationships within his own Cigar Makers' Local that Gompers began to grasp the multifaceted ideas behind trade unionism. In his autobiography he pays tribute to the intellectuals who, in effect, were his godfathers in the labor movement, the men whose influence helped him shape a labor philosophy that was valid and durable enough to guide the AFL for decades.*

■ Gradually I became a regular attendant of the inner group which was heart and mind devoted to the cause of trade unionism. Long and earnestly we discussed plans, policies, and theories. Out of the chaos of radicalism and revolutionary phraseology, we were seeking principles that would bring opportunities for better living to fellow workers. . . . We dreamed together and then thrashed out our dreams to see what might be of practical value. From this little group came the purpose and the initiative that finally resulted in the present American labor movement—the most effective economic organization in the world. We did not create the American trade union—that is a product of forces and conditions. But we did create the technique and formulate the fundamentals that guided trade unions to constructive policies and achievements.

At these meetings in the Tenth Ward Hotel I often saw J. P. McDonnell —an ardent worker for Irish freedom who had spent several years in London in the office of Karl Marx. McDonnell was a very striking figure— only a little taller than I, with a rather small face and clean-cut small features, wonderful eyes and an abundance of red curly hair. . . . P. J. McGuire, my old schoolmate at Cooper Union, was also a member. . . .

From these men who were genuine revolutionaries in thought and in deed, men to whom principles meant something, I learned the fundamentals of the labor movement. They were men who did not hesitate to risk something to accomplish a purpose. They were alive in minds and bodies and they did not find life dull or uninteresting. They were eagerly seeking new thought and new opportunity to bring about the betterment of their fellows. It is difficult for me to describe adequately what the New York labor movement during the seventies meant to me. There was a strikingly unusual group of brainy men of strong individuality—men not afraid to think and do, even at a risk. . . . No idea, no suggestion, was denied consideration. We were groping for principles with which to lay a foundation. . . .

In 1872 there appeared among the ranks of the labor movement in New York a man destined to have a tremendous influence—Adolph Strasser, a cigarmaker by trade, a Hungarian by birth, an organizer for the Social Democratic Party, a member of the Cigar Makers' Union. Strasser was a man of extraordinary mentality. . . . [He] had a keen practical mind and did not allow precedent to restrict his ability to utilize constructive agencies. He became a member of our little union No. 15. No one knew Strasser's early life and no one asked him questions lightly, for Strasser had a terse bluntness of expression in English and in German that made even the most venturesome hesitate to take liberties. . . .

Late in 1872, under the leadership of Strasser and others from the International group at the Tenth Ward Hotel, a new cigarmakers' organization was started. . . . We talked over the problem of organization and decided we had to work out a program to meet New York difficulties. Our plan was to reach those who were otherwise ineligible. . . . We called shop meetings and mass meetings of cigarmakers and finally launched the United Cigarmakers. The doors of this organization were open to all, regardless of sex, method, or place of work, or nationality. . . . Though we did not realize it at the time, we were starting the revival of the trade union movement. The immediate effects were not conspicuous, for we had yet to go through the panic of 1873, but our foundations had begun. . . . We held agitation meetings, first in locals, and finally, a mass meeting. . . . Our educational propaganda gave so much publicity to the health hazards of workers and consumers arising from badly regulated conditions in tenements, that the Board of Health could not refuse to take notice. The Chief of the Board directed that an investigation be made. The report of this investigation was made public in the fall of 1874. To the amazement of everybody it was a whitewashing report which endeavored to create the impression that tenements were superior dwelling places. . . . All the unions of New York met in protest in public meeting against the outrageous attempt to conceal conditions and facts that were dangerous to the health of the workers and the users of cigars. That rousing meeting inaugurated a campaign against tenement cigar-manufacturing. . . .

The story of the hardships, the laborious toil, the sacrifices of those early days can never be told. We fought for each gain and with bare hands unaided carried off victories against the protest of a hostile world. In those days the movement was very poor, not respectable, unpopular. It cost something even to be associated with a labor organization. Not only was the labor leader a marked man, but his family suffered from a kind of ostracism that placed many difficulties in their paths. . . .

The cigar factories were generally insanitary. The smaller shops, employing from one-half dozen to twenty men, were particularly so, but the idea and concept of sanitation in 1880, particularly in factories and even homes, was different from that of now. Women had come into the industry

The first appearance of a workman's square cap and of the dinner pail as symbols of the labor movement came in these two sketches by Thomas Nast, which were printed in *Harper's Weekly* on February 7, 1874. The German-born Nast, who humorously called himself a "little fat Dutch boy," was the outstanding American cartoonist of his era—and many connoisseurs deem him the best political cartoonist in American history. Born in 1840, he became a staff artist for *Harper's Weekly* at twenty-two, and his satirical caricatures of those opposing the Civil War caused Abraham Lincoln to praise him as "our best recruiting sergeant." Nast's cartoons were so true to life that they enabled the police in Spain to identify and arrest the corrupt Boss William M. Tweed when he fled to Europe disguised as a sailor. Nast was equally ingenious and imaginative in creating emblematic objects that are still the valued stock-in-trade of his successors. The Democratic donkey, Republican elephant, and Tammany tiger are among his creations.

and were working side by side with the men. I remember a factory where two hundred women and men were employed, with but one water closet, and that was dark, dingy, and filthy. There was a sink generally beside the water closet where the workmen and workwomen would wash their hands, and the bagging used on the bales of Havana tobacco and a few other grades of tobacco were the towels used. . . . The sanitary conditions in McCoy's shop in Avenue A were bad and probably worse than those that usually prevailed. There were about sixty men employed at the time when they left the shop and went on strike. The cause for their outbreak was that the water closet was in such a filthy, insanitary condition that the odor nearly overcame some of the workers and the condition was intolerable. . . . The strike was approved by Union 144 and won in less than twenty-four hours. The members of the organization generally thereafter complied with the law. Our efforts to build up No. 144 were ceaseless struggles. . . .

The union grew slowly and steadily. It was a genuinely American trade union. . . . We had faith in the democratic theory that wage earners understood their problems and could deal with them better than outsiders. We preferred to rely upon ourselves, make mistakes perhaps, but we could profit by them and thus advance along the road to knowledge and progress free to follow our best judgment.

*A significant turning point came to Gompers at twenty-three. He was still young in years though hardly callow—more than half of his life until then had already been spent at work. But new friends, notably a man named Laurrell, now forced him to think more realistically and trenchantly than ever before:*

■ In 1873 came one of the most important changes in my life. I . . . found employment with David Hirsch & Company . . . then the only union shop in the city. It was also a high-class shop where only the most skilled workmen were employed. . . . There a new world opened to me. The cigarmakers employed at Hirsch's were practically all Germans—men of keener mentality and wider thought than any I had met before. They talked and read in German, but there was enough English spoken to enable me to understand that the trade union movement meant to those men something vastly bigger than anything I had ever conceived. Many of them were men who had learned the labor movement in Europe and who were refugees because they were active for the struggle for political as well as economic freedom.

With all the energy and confidence born of my young strength, I talked from my limited experiences—fraternal idealism, the Odd Fellows Order, etc. On labor matters my thought was wild. I had been feeling profoundly the injustice that society meted out to wage earners. I was familiar with the vocabulary of revolutionists, but I had not yet attained a practical understanding of the scope and the power of economic organization. . . . Some had a better understanding—fortunately they were to become my teachers. . . .

One major influence on the thinking and discussion Gompers describes in the next three pages was the social philosopher Henry George (above). While he was a journalist in California, the railroad land grants made by the federal government led to George's criticizing the whole system of land ownership. His great book *Progress and Poverty* argues that, since social growth raises land values, allowing landlords an "unearned increment," the cure for economic injustice would be to tax the increment out of existence. This single tax, George believed, would obviate all others and eradicate "millionaires and tramps." Gompers first encountered parts of *Progress and Poverty* as magazine articles before they appeared in book form; they provoked lively argument when read aloud in his cigar shop. Though Gompers never became a Single Taxer, he backed George for political office and later recalled: "Henry George and I became warm personal friends. . . . It was due to George that I came to ride a bicycle, and frequently on our long rides on Sunday we would discuss single tax, the land question, trade unionism, Socialism, or any other topic of the day."

The man whom I loved most, and for whose brain, heart, and character I have always had boundless admiration, was Karl Malcolm Ferdinand Laurrell. He was so gentle and yet so able. I heard much of him about the shop before I met him—his was the dominating mind. Laurrell spoke with a distinct Teutonic accent and very tersely—especially when not pleased. He didn't seem to think much of me at first. But that was probably due to my enthusiasm for the fraternal orders. Karl . . . had passed through that stage of thought and had been convinced that the trade union was the fundamental agency to which working people must trust. At first he regarded me as "fresh," but soon he began talking to me, explaining a bit now and then as though he would teach me. He afterwards explained he thought he saw ability in me and he wanted to save me from mistakes. His kindly talks and warnings did more to shape my mind upon the labor movement than any other single influence. The principles of trade unionism that I learned then remained the basis upon which my policies and methods were determined in the years to come. I have always felt that he watched over me with chastening criticism, for he wanted to save me from allowing my sentiment and emotion to be perverted into the channel of "radicalism." . . .

After I had known Laurrell but a short time, I remember going to him one day and enthusiastically telling him some wild plans I had for human betterment. When I had finished, convinced that I had talked well, I sat back with manifest satisfaction to let Laurrell reply. He had been working silently, but had not missed a point, and point by point he replied. Soon my self-confidence began to ebb, and I began to feel physically smaller as Laurrell systematically and ruthlessly demolished my every statement. By the time he had finished I vowed to myself, "Never again will I talk that stuff—but I will find principles that will stand the test." . . .

I remember asking Laurrell whether in his opinion I ought to keep in touch with the Socialist movement. He replied, "Go to their meetings by all means, listen to what they have to say and understand them, but do not join the Party." I never did, though it was my habit to attend their Saturday evening meetings. There were often good speakers present and the discussions were stimulating.

As the days went by, my mind was groping for something fundamental, something upon which one could base a constructive program. I spoke to Laurrell of my need. He replied, "If you wish to know, I will give you something tangible, something that will give you a background philosophy." He placed in my hands a copy of the Communist Manifesto. As it was in German and my knowledge of the language was still inadequate, he translated and interpreted it for me paragraph by paragraph. That document brought me an interpretation of much that before had been only inarticulate feeling.

This insight into a hidden world of thought aroused me to master the German language in order that I might read for myself. I buckled down to hard work and for months read not one word of English in papers or books. By forcing myself to acquire all information through the medium of

Charles A. Dana, praised here by Gompers, was an energetic New Hampshire farm boy who was self-educated before entering Harvard. Five years among the transcendentalists of Brook Farm gave him a taste for social theorizing. In the Civil War, Dana served in the Lincoln Administration, one of his chores being to assess General Grant's drinking habits. His favorable report assisted Grant's rise to top command. Dana gained control of the New York *Sun* in 1868. The clear writing that impressed Gompers was a fetish with Dana, who told his colleagues to watch their grammar and "be interesting." He feuded with newspaper rivals who accused him of promoting sensationalism with the famous *Sun* formula: "When a man bites a dog, that's news." A cultured man who assembled one of America's finest ceramics collections, Dana was implacable on public issues, even turning against Grant because of the scandals during his Presidency. In 1895, he joined Gompers and other notable Americans in demanding recognition of Cuba's rebels. But he died shortly before Spain lost Cuba in 1898.

the German language and by daily conversations in it, I acquired a fair ability to read and speak German. I read all the German economic literature that I could lay hands on—Marx, Engels, Lassalle, and the others. . . .

Gradually, but inevitably, my interest began to center on the problems I found in the shop—the problems of daily life and the work-place where we spent the greater number of our waking hours. I began to see that the fundamental things had to do with the relations between those associated together in making things, and proper compensation for such service. Life was becoming more real and more serious. . . .

Shop life stimulated my mental development. Another impetus came through newspapers. Someone has said that newspapers are the characteristic literature of Americans. Whether that statement is an epigram or a truth, when as a lad I came to New York, I soon learned what a mine of information awaited one in New York papers. I carried newspapers with me from early morning, reading every chance I got. I read in the morning as I got ready to go to work and often I walked to the shop—for New York streets in those days were not the maelstrom of humanity found today. During this period I was reading greedily whatever came to hand on general subjects, for I was young and strong and eager to know all things about life. The New York *Sun* under Charles A. Dana was the publication I read most thoroughly and persistently. It was the great daily of the time, publishing a wider range of informational matter than the other papers. . . . Both editorial and news columns were edited carefully. From them I absorbed ideas of style, sentence structure, and the use of words. Charles A. Dana's editorials were in themselves a daily stimulus to my mind. Though I more often than not disagreed with the editorial policy of the *Sun* in dealing with local and national affairs, I found a large fund of information with which I was in complete accord.

In the shop there was also reading. It was the custom of the cigarmakers to chip in to create a fund for purchasing papers, magazines, and books. Then while the rest worked, one of our members would read to us perhaps for an hour at a time, sometimes longer. In order that the reader might not be the loser financially, each one of the other men in the shop gave him a definite number of cigars. I had a habit of saving any interesting magazine or newspaper articles to read to my shopmates. Others did the same. As my voice was strong and the men could hear me easily whenever I read, they always asked me to read more than my period. In fact, these discussions in the shops were more like public debating societies or what we call these days "labor forums." This practice had a great deal to do with developing the interest of cigarmakers in leading economic questions.

*A new Cigar Makers' unit, Local 144, was chartered in 1875 and Gompers became its president. He worked tirelessly—writing circulars, organizing meetings, making speeches—and within a few months the local's membership of 245 was the largest Cigar Makers' unit in the country. But labor conditions worsened steadily during the depression of 1873–1879. One of the most poignant sections of Gompers' autobiography is his vivid description of the events leading up to the cigarmakers' strike of 1877, the bitterness of the strike itself, and the suffering of his family when the manufacturers blacklisted him from employment after the strike was broken.*

■ During the summer of 1876 the unemployment situation grew steadily worse. A feeling of desperation was growing as week after week slipped by and still the unemployed had no dependable means of earning a livelihood. The city authorities selected that time to suspend improvements on public works. The workingmen protested against this course as a harmful, cruel policy. . . . The public was not interested in labor problems in those days and obviously felt no burning responsibility for doing a part to help solve the great labor problem.

In the fall of 1876, the seemingly impossible happened. Wages were again reduced and working forces decreased. In December about two thirds of the shops closed entirely, to remain closed until sometime in January. The others dismissed more than half their men and reduced wages. There were between five and six thousand cigarmakers idle in New York City. . . . I was fortunate in not being among those Hirsch dismissed, but that did not free me from the feeling of impending tragedy and despair. We knew that when the shops were reopened and employment offered it would be at reduced wages—a starvation level.

The year 1877 dawned on a world of unrest and gloom. We struggled on in our efforts at organization, but we saw little encouragement in the future. . . . Mass meetings for organization, and as unemployment demonstrations, continued. We tried to organize discontent for constructive purposes. Mayor Ely paid no more attention to our needs than other mayors had done, but wage earners did heed our gospel of organization and solidarity. I am recounting in some detail a picture of cumulative misery in order to bring out why revolt brought a whisper of hope. The crash that broke the months of strain came in the revolt of the railroad workers in July 1877. . . . Their rebellion was a declaration of protest in the name of American manhood against conditions that nullified the rights of American citizens. The railroad strike of 1877 was the tocsin that sounded a ringing message of hope to us all.

The railroad rebellion was spontaneous. In those days before the establishment of collective bargaining as an orderly system for presenting grievances to employers as the preliminary to securing an adjustment based on mutuality, the only way the workers could secure the attention of employers was through some demonstration of protest in the form of a strike. The strike grew steadily until it surpassed in numbers and importance all previous industrial movements. . . .

In New York we were stirred deeply. While we had put our faith in constructive methods, yet the sky of Pittsburgh, reddened by fires started by company agents and desperate men denied all other recourse, brought us the message that human aspiration had not been killed or cowed. [We] arranged for a mass meeting in Cooper Union to express our sympathy for the railroad strikers. . . . Several thousand men gathered. . . . In his speech,

Strasser referred to a statement of Henry Ward Beecher which had aroused much criticism. Beecher had declared in a public speech or sermon in New York: "Is not a dollar a day enough to buy bread? Water costs nothing and a man who cannot live on bread is not fit to live. A family may live, laugh, love, and be happy that eats bread in the morning with good water, and water and good bread at noon, and water and bread at night." Such things as this made the working people think the Church had no consideration or understanding of our welfare or problems. We resented the heartlessness and questioned whether it was personal or institutional. The statement did not make for wise deliberation in a difficult period. . . .

Heartened by the courage of the railway workers' protest against injustice, our union inaugurated a strike in the De Barry factory with a demand for higher wages—$6 a thousand, minimum. . . .

In a short time an agreement was made. This initial contest lasted five weeks and was the first successful strike in many years. It brought the first real improvement in our trade. The next step was the strike which followed in the factory of M. Stachelberg & Company and was also successful. The cigarmakers of the entire city and vicinity were elated over our unprecedented victories. The same tactics in other organized shops were equally encouraging. Members began flocking into our union. . . .

Under the elation of victories gained by organized workers the tenement-house workers, made desperate by wage reductions, determined to take a chance. They all went out on strike without organization or discipline. . . . No. 144 had only $4,000 in the treasury when the general strike broke upon us. Our Executive Committee urged that those still employed in the

"better condition" factories and tenement houses remain at work and contribute ten per cent of their earnings to the support of those on strike and that if victory came there would be little or no difficulty in securing improvements for those who remained at work in the meantime. But despite all suggestions, men and women just scampered pell-mell out of the tenements and out of the workshops so that we had nearly all the workers on strike. . . .

As the strike continued, we issued circulars to cigarmakers all over America. . . . In many cities those to whom we addressed circulars called upon other members of the trade to meet with them so as to raise funds for transmittal to our strikers. The result of these men gathering together began a movement for the establishment of local unions of cigarmakers in many of these centers. This revival of organization activity spread to other trades.

We held almost continuous meetings of strikers in order to get them to join the union, to maintain morale, and to have centers from which to issue directions as to the conduct of the strike. . . .

In order to take care of the physical needs of the strikers we established provision kitchens or relief stores from which we distributed food and money—chiefly food, which we purchased wholesale. Meat and bread were distributed daily upon presentation of tickets given by the Relief Committee. Once a week we distributed to each family a supply of groceries. To single men we gave tickets for one meal a day. . . . On October 24, the employers brought into action a terrible weapon [evicting] workers from ten tenements. We had been trying to guard against this catastrophe by helping with rent payments, but our resources could not keep pace with the demands made on them.

The union rented more than a hundred rooms for evicted strikers, but could not provide for all. Every few days the tenement-house employers brought dispossession proceedings against new groups of employes. The distress that followed was appalling. One case I remember for its shocking brutality. A cigarmaker's wife sick unto death was moved in her bed to the sidewalk where she lay for hours on a cold winter day. . . . When the strike reached its climax there were eleven thousand men on strike with more than forty thousand women and children dependent upon them. . . . Our expenditures from October 15 to February 17 were sometimes $1,200 a day—an unprecedented sum in those days. . . .

Just before Christmas [1877] came a new offensive—a staggering one. A number of firms locked out their workmen who had been the financial backbone of the strike. . . . The cigarmakers were forced to make terms as best they could by groups. The strike slowly crumbled away. It was a wonderful fight. I shall never forget the heroic sacrifices made and the burdens borne by the men and women engaged in that struggle. Although we did not win, we learned the fundamentals and technique which assured success later. The strikers had to go back wherever they could find employment and were welcomed by employers who had learned the value of [drawing upon the talents of] skilled workmen. . . .

Like thousands of other cigar-makers and their families, Gompers, with his wife and children, suffered great privations during this unsuccessful strike of 1877–1878. One fundamental problem of the period was that the entire country was undergoing a severe depression that did not really begin to ease until 1879. As in 1929, the economic collapse of the 1870's started with a tremendous crash in the stock market and then went on for many years. The cartoon above appeared on the front page of the New York *Daily Graphic* for September 29, 1873, and was titled: "Panic, as a health officer, sweeping the garbage out of Wall Street."

The Cigar Manufacturers' Association had declared that under no circumstances would any leaders of the strike be employed for at least six months. As a consequence, for nearly four months I was out of employment. I had parted with everything of any value in the house, and my wife and I were every day expecting a newcomer in addition to the five children we already had. . . . One night when there was no food in the house and our little girl was very ill I returned home to find a fellow worker . . . had called and offered my wife $30 a week for three months if she would persuade me to give up the union and return to work. I turned to my wife and said, "Well, what did you tell him?" My wife, indignant at the question, answered: "What do you suppose I said to him with one child dying and another coming? Of course I took the money." Stunned by the blow I fell in a chair. My wife, all tenderness and sympathy, seeing I didn't understand, exclaimed: "Good God, Sam, how could you ask such a question? Don't you know I resented the insult?"

Occasionally, my wife suggested the commissary—but I refused that help, for I wanted to fight my own way. My mother worried over our need. . . . Many times [she] sent us food from her none too bountiful supply.

Once I was ready to commit murder. All the children were ill, probably because of winter cold and undernourishment; they were subject to illness and fever. I walked around looking for work and could not find it, and as I left my wife in the morning again to look for work there were indications that the newcomer was about due, but by previous experience I thought that that condition would last a couple of days. But when I came home, my sister-in-law, who was living with us and sharing whatever little we had, told me that the child was born. There had been nobody to help the mother or the child. I stood by, dazed, and then rushed to the man who had acted as our physician. He was the physician paid by the Hand-in-Hand Society. But he was not in and like a madman I rushed back, but the situation was the same as it was before.

It dawned on me that there was a physician on the next block and I went to him and told him of the condition and that I wanted him to come down and attend to my wife. He asked me if I had money. When I told him I did not, he replied that he was not our regular physician. I said I knew that but my wife was in such a serious condition and the child there and I wanted him to come to attend her right away. He said, "Well, I do not feel like it and I won't do it."

I walked up to him, looked him square in the eye and said, "Yes you will, you will come and see my wife now." He said, "Well, I will not." I put my hand on his coat collar and said, "You will come now with me or you will never make another move." He said he wanted me to pay him and I said: "I have got no money. I have been out of work, but I will promise to pay you everything I can gather tonight, but you will come with me without another minute's hesitation or I will not be responsible for what I will do to you. Come along." He put on his hat and coat and he went with me. . . . He prescribed some medicine and I did not have the money to get the prescription filled and finally prevailed upon the druggist with whom I was acquainted through living in the neighborhood to trust me for it and we pulled her through. The baby was my Al. He was our strike baby, born in the forenoon of February 28, 1878.

In the course of time the foreman at M. Stachelberg & Company gave me a job. I had sat at my bench and had made about twenty cigars when Mr. Stachelberg came up to the floor where I was working and came over to me. . . . I conversed about the strike with him and he said that he regretted very much what he was about to say to me, but he could not help it; that he liked me personally and liked my work but that the Manufacturers' Association had decided that the leaders of the strike should not be employed by any member of the Association. He did not want to discharge me, but I would confer a great favor upon him if I would leave of my own accord. I recall the incident very vividly, and the remark which I made to him in reply: "Why, of course, Mr. Stachelberg, I will quit. There is no alternative left for me if I desire to retain my own self-respect. We have lost the strike. If we had won, the Manufacturers' Association would not have dared to take the position they did. Now that we have lost they want to wreak their vengeance even upon those who tried to serve their fellows." . . .

I was heavily in debt and most of the valuable trinkets that I owned, including the gold and diamond-studded medal presented to me by the Court Empire City of the Ancient Order of Foresters, had been pawned. My heavy overcoat stayed in the pawnbroker's shop all summer while I tried to get the necessary five dollars with which to redeem it. Everything of value that belonged to my family except my wife's wedding ring had followed the same course. . . .

*With the help of his friend Laurrell, Gompers eventually found employment again and decided to devote more time to his family and less to union affairs. He found this impossible (see page 30), and years later rationalized his decision by writing: "I am not unmindful of the duties which one owes to his family and to himself, but there is also a duty which one owes to his fellow workmen and his fellow men." His ever deepening commitment to labor would ultimately involve him in national and even world affairs. But for some time the challenges that faced him were largely local; one such episode landed him in the Tombs, that most noisome and notorious of all New York City jails:*

■ In the spring of 1879 for the first and only time in my life I was arrested. The cigarmakers at Kimball & Gaullieur's struck . . . and put their pickets in front of the shop. The company had a big burly policeman detailed "to protect the property." At that time I was president of No. 144, and on my way to work in the morning I stopped to ask Sam Elkins, one of the pickets, how things were progressing. As I was quietly talking on the sidewalk, the policeman arrested me and [a union associate] with me. Though I was seething with indignation at the unwarranted action of the policeman, I went quietly to the police court where the policeman charged us with disorderly conduct.

I told Judge Flammer that I was doing nothing disorderly and had used no threats to keep men from entering the shop and that I had a right to walk up and down in front of the building and talk to men so long as I used no threats. However, Justice Flammer accepted the policeman's charge as true and fined [the two of us] $10 each or ten days' imprisonment, refusing to delay examination until we could secure counsel. I would not have paid that fine if my life had depended on it, and so the alternate penalty of ten days' imprisonment began at once; I was put in the Tombs. There I immediately became the center of interest for all those held there who wanted to know who I was and what I had done. They quickly lost interest when they ascertained the nature of my "crime"—only big crime appealed to them. That was one of the most uncomfortable days I ever spent, sitting there in the dirt and filth and vermin surrounded by men of unclean bodies and minds, who used vile language. Fortunately for the effect upon me, there was only one day of it. . . . A fellow workman had seen the arrest and carried word to my shopmates. . . . They went to the police court, found out my sentence and paid the fine. That evening I was released from that place of physical misery and mental degradation.

*From the 1870's onward, Gompers and Local 144 waged a vigorous battle to rid their industry of the unhealthy and demoralizing practice of tenement-house cigarmaking. In New York City alone at that time, manufacturers employed seven thousand tenement workers, many of them diseased because of appalling work conditions. The union led the way in pressing for reform.*

*Gompers later recalled: "As we were pioneers in the field of social legislation, we had none of the precedents and data which serve as guides for present-day problems." A slow, painful process of trial and error led to eventual triumph:*

■ After years of educational work, in 1881, our union inaugurated an intensive effort to get a state law. We persuaded a member of each house of the Legislature to act as sponsor for our bill, and at the same time kept labor men in Albany, not only to watch the legislative situation, but to advise the labor movement of developments so that the legislators might constantly be made aware that their constituents were interested. . . .

Securing the enactment of a law does not mean the solution of the problem, as I learned in my legislative experience. The power of the courts to pass upon constitutionality of law so complicates reform by legislation as to seriously restrict the effectiveness of that method. [And] the [state] court declared our law unconstitutional. We found our work was nullified. The court had evaded the heart of the issue. . . . We met the check imposed by the court quickly and in a constructive way. Our machinery was still intact. A new bill passed the Legislature and was signed by the Governor in May 1884. The tenement-house manufacturers again carried the law into court. . . . In October the Supreme Court declared this second enactment null and void. . . . Through our trade unions we harassed the manufacturers by strikes and agitation until they were convinced that we did not intend to stop until we gained our point.

*During his tenement-house investigations, Gompers had been horrified at seeing hundreds of small children whose "old-young faces and work-weary figures mutely condemned the crime industry was committing against them." In 1881 he spoke fervently against child labor.*

■ While making the house-to-house canvass, I saw scenes that sickened me. Little children—six, seven, and eight years of age—were seated in the middle of a room on the floor, in all the dirt and dust, stripping tobacco. Little, pale-faced children, with a look of care upon their faces, toiled with their tiny hands from dawn till dark and even late into the night, to keep the wolf from the door. I asked the children how late they worked, but they did not or could not understand. In the simplest way I talked to them, and learned that they began before daylight and worked till long after dark. Often they would be overcome with weariness and want of sleep, and fall over upon the tobacco heap. Shame upon such crimes; shame upon us if we do not raise our voices against them.

## EFFORT ON A NATIONAL SCALE

*The manifold stresses and strains described in the foregoing excerpts made Gompers and his fellow workers painfully aware that—not only to survive future depressions but also to stand up again and again to recalcitrant em-*

William Maxwell Evarts, the lawyer who persuaded a court in New York State to declare unconstitutional the Gompers-backed tenement legislation described on this page, had already proved himself a powerful opponent of labor. As President Grant's Attorney-General in 1869, he had rendered an opinion that nullified the effect of the federal government's first eight-hour-day law. But the growing strength of the union movement by the 1880's was reflected in the fact that the manufacturers fighting this bill hired Evarts, a very high-priced leader of the nation's bar. A New Englander who had found legal loopholes against slavery before the Civil War, Evarts went to London during that conflict to state the Union case against British aid to the Confederacy. He helped prosecute Jefferson Davis in 1867 and defend President Andrew Johnson in 1868 when the latter was impeached. His shrewd legal advice during the disputed Hayes-Tilden election of 1876 led to his appointment as Secretary of State under Hayes. When he successfully defended the noted clergyman Henry Ward Beecher in 1875, he told the jury that anyone who believed Beecher had committed adultery was "wicked as it can be, wicked in heart, wicked in soul, wicked in hate to God, to society, to human nature, wicked in everything."

*ployers—they must stiffen their collective backbone even more. Yet how could any single union resist the social and economic pressures that might be applied in a labor crisis? One possible answer was federation, and Gompers helped lead the way to it.*

■ Men's thoughts were turning toward federation—all felt the need of common protection. Various plans were advocated for achieving that end. . . . Our minds were busy with the idea of national unity, but we had nothing to guide us. The British Trades Union Congress, which was the only international labor body, was organized to deal with legislative issues. The conception of a national federation of trade unions was then clear to no one. Its development, together with policies and methods, was the natural evolution of the principles we cigarmakers [had] worked out . . . and applied to widely varying problems and situations. Economic need and betterment could best be served by mobilizing and controlling economic power. This was the simple basis upon which all policies were squared. . . .

The congress met November 15, 1881, in Pittsburgh. It was the first national meeting of labor men from all the trades that I attended. I was thirty-one at that time and was looked upon as one of the youngsters. . . .

The influence of the political nature of the British Trades Union Congress is shown in paragraph 8 of our Standing Orders: "No paper shall be read except those which are required for legislative purposes." We foolishly fancied that papers in defense of trade unionism were unnecessary because the principles were so well known and so generally approved that they needed no discussion. Little did that congress realize that the fundamental

The ills of tenement cigarmaking —so poignantly described by Gompers on page 143—are depicted in this contemporary sketch of a bedridden mother watching her exhausted children strip tobacco. In 1890, Jacob Riis told of a visit he made to a similar tobacco tenement: "The mother of the three barefooted children we met on the stairs was taken to the hospital the other day when she could no longer work. She will never come out alive. There is no waste in these tenements. Lives, like clothes, are worn through and out before put aside. Her place on the bench is taken already by another who divides with the head of the household his earnings of $15.50 a week. . . . Asked how long he works, the man says, 'From they can see till bedtime.' Bedtime proves to be eleven o'clock. Seventeen hours a day, seven days in the week."

work of the labor movement was to be the development and inculcation of the principles of trade unionism—the understanding and the use of economic power. . . .

The committee on platform proposed legislation needed to protect wage earners. That report shows so concretely what was in the minds of labor men of that day, that I wish to enumerate the subjects: compulsory education laws, prohibition of labor of children under fourteen years, licensing of stationary engineers, sanitation and safety provisions for factories, uniform apprentice laws, national eight-hour law, prohibition of contract convict labor, law prohibiting the order or truck system of wage payment, law making wages a first lien upon the product of labor, repeal of all conspiracy law, National Bureau of Labor Statistics, protection of American industry against cheap foreign labor, laws prohibiting importation of foreign workers under contract, Chinese exclusion. . . .

On the last day of the congress, Charles Burgman presented the situation on the Pacific Coast, showing the need of prohibiting importation of Chinese coolies. The Pacific Coast Trades and Labor Union of San Francisco sent him to the Pittsburgh congress to present their most urgent difficulty. A declaration demanding Chinese exclusion was adopted by the congress. The Federation in 1881 was the first national organization which demanded the exclusion of coolies from the United States. . . .

The following business details show how small was the beginning from which the present organization grew: The treasurer was required to give a bond of $1,000 and the secretary one of $500. The secretary was authorized to keep on hand a sum not to exceed $50. . . . With no provision for a central office, there was grave danger that the organization would have no real existence, influence, or even records. I suggested that each member of the Legislative Committee purchase a blank book in which to record all official acts and also that each write to the secretary at least once a month. . . .

My own mind was firmly convinced that progress for labor must come through economic agencies. I did not then have a clear idea of how it was to be done, but I sensed the fundamental principles and appreciated the dangers that lay in partisan methods. . . . The American trade union movement had to work out its own philosophy, technique, and language. What has been developed is different from that of any other country. It was my purpose to bring into it the sentiment that was so completely lacking in the British trade unions. I strove to make the American movement practical, deep-rooted in sympathy and sentiment. I refused to concede one single inch of labor activity to any other movement. I held that the trade union was capable of all manner of diverse services and that there was no need of creating separate organizations for different fields of interests—for such separation would only diffuse the power of labor.

*The Federation launched at Pittsburgh in 1881 had no full-time staff, no headquarters, and almost no money. "Its future was dependent upon individual effort," Gompers wrote. At the second Federation congress, held in*

"On to Chinatown!" was a racist cry that often turned an orderly nineteenth-century assembly of workers into a howling mob. As shown in this drawing of a Denver riot in 1880, the Chinese were periodically pulled from their workbenches, driven from their homes, and savagely beaten by men who believed the "Chinese menace" was the cause of unemployment in those depression-ridden years. The Chinese first came to California in the 1850's to work in the mines and soon entered other occupations in many parts of America. The intensity and frequency of anti-Chinese rioting increased with the spreading fear that because the Chinese would work longer hours for lower wages, American laborers might be put out of business. Pressure by unions, beginning long before the FTLU was established (contrary to what Gompers implies in the passage at left), finally produced the Chinese Exclusion Act of 1882, prohibiting Chinese immigration for the next ten years. Renewed several times, the law was repealed in 1943.

145

"Labor first, last, and all the time, wherever and whenever I can strike a blow for labor, I shall do it." With this pledge, Terence V. Powderly (above) became Grand Master Workman of the Knights of Labor in 1879. His first contact with organized labor was in 1871 when, as a twenty-two-year-old, he had joined a machinists' local. Three years later, embittered by a jobless period endured during the depression that began in 1873, he joined the Knights of Labor, convinced this body would fulfill his hope "that one day in the future all departments of labor would be firmly welded together in one solid, compact organization, so strong as to repel attack from any quarter." As a speaker, he had almost magical powers. But he was a better talker than doer, and his leadership, though firm, remained utopian. The Knights favored neither craft nor industrial unionism, and could not even be called a wage earners' organization since it did not exclude employers. The *Puck* cartoon (opposite), proclaiming that skilled craftsmen were the "Knights of the Nineteenth Century," appeared in 1886, at the peak of the Knights' strength, and cheerily satirized various member units by outfitting them in farcical "armor" symbolic of their occupations.

*Cleveland in 1882, he was elected president of the legislative committee. "Thus," he declared "began my first service as leader of the American labor movement." It was hard, but not entirely thankless, work—it did, for instance, enable him to feast on delicious oysters. Then as later, Gompers enjoyed gratifying all five of his senses.*

■ The next congress of the Federation met in New York in August 1883. As I was chairman and New York was my home town, the responsibility of preparing for that meeting fell upon me. . . . There were about twenty-five delegates present when I called the congress to order. I was elected by acclamation president of the gathering and I outlined the situation with which we had to deal thus: "The object of the assembly of the delegates is to discuss grievances and hardships workingmen are called on to endure from time to time in their respective trades. Employes are attacked by employers who would subjugate the workingmen and prevent them from organizing for mutual protection. In this city there is a recent instance in point wherein a vast corporation has tried to crush out their employes' hopes. The corporation's motto, with reference to their workingmen, is 'One man is no man.' The time fast approaches when workingmen will be required to determine what rights and liberties they really have. Employers not only try to crush the manhood of the employes, but they also use their vast wealth to take away their independence. The strong arm of the government is on their side and against us. The police and the military are used against labor, and even the goodwill of order-loving citizens is employed to crush us. We do not receive a legal right to exercise our whole efforts to unite. Federal and state laws deny us the right to unite. They protect employers and their ill-gotten gains. When labor asks for protection, there is no response from the legislators in Washington or at the state capitals, where their interests are presumably attended to. . . .

"Children of employes should be kept from factories, workhouses, and mines. Our children should be superior to the present generation. A Bureau of Labor Statistics should also be organized in order that legislators who now plead ignorance and fail to represent workingmen may have a headquarters for obtaining information and be unable longer to plead ignorance."

The report of the Legislative Committee showed how inadequate our organization was to meet our needs. With no directing executive the work was sporadic, depending upon the interest and opportunities of individuals. The results were chiefly by-products of activity by other organizations and not the initiation of an organization caring for the interests of labor as a whole. Our efforts to secure the affiliation of other national trade organizations had not been successful. . . .

Next year I was elected a delegate from the cigarmakers' union to the fourth congress of the Federation of Trades and Labor Unions which met in Chicago in November 1884, but owing to the very serious illness of my wife and two of our children, at the last minute I was prevented from going. . . . I was not elected to an executive office that year. The following year, however, I attended the fifth annual meeting of the Federation in Washington, D.C. I [helped propose that America] join in a conference of nations to consider an international agreement proposed by Switzerland for the limitation of the hours of labor of the working people, the regulation of female and child labor, and factory inspection and other measures tending to the amelioration of the conditions of the workers of the world. That resolution contained the germ of an idea that years afterward I helped to formulate and have incorporated in the Treaty of Versailles. . . .

One very pleasurable incident in connection with this trip to Washington was my visit to the Bureau of Labor. . . . But not the smallest contribution to the pleasure of that Washington congress was the fact that it was oyster season and near by the hotel was a well-known restaurant (Harvey's) that served the finest oysters that could be had. I ate oysters every day.

*The 1885 congress was the last one held by the Federation of Trades and Labor Unions. The organization represented an important first step toward coalescing America's diverse and disparate labor unions, but as Gompers himself expressed it: "We all felt that the Federation had not become the orga-*

*nization that was urgently needed." Unhappily, the FTLU had grown weaker instead of stronger during its five-year life, and no one doubted that immediate action was needed to create a new and stronger federation while the old one still existed. Accordingly, the American Federation of Labor came into being. Sam Gompers, rather reluctantly, became its president—and on him fell the chief task of making the AFL "something more than a paper organization" such as the FTLU had been. One of the most moving passages in Gompers' reminiscences is his account of those years of struggle for the infant AFL.*

■ Our committee issued a call to national and international trade unions to send delegates to a conference to be held in Columbus, Ohio, December 8, 1886. . . . All were convinced that the old Federation could not do the effective work required. We needed a consolidated organization for the promotion of trade unionism under which work could go forward daily for the organization of all workers of America, skilled as well as unskilled. We needed a central office and officers who could give all their time to the Federation work. The old Federation was committed to relief by legislation. As year by year we learned the inadequacy of our program, we tried to revise our constitution to authorize action in the economic field. Now the time had come to stop patchwork, and rebuild. We had learned the need of an alliance for defense and mutual help. . . .

The Columbus meetings unanimously decided that a Federation should be formed and that all trade union organizations should be eligible, whether affiliated or unaffiliated to the Federation of Trades and Labor Unions, and the conference appointed a committee of five to confer with a committee from the Federation. . . . I met this committee and stated the Federation had resolved to turn over all moneys, papers, and effects to the new American Federation of Labor requesting only the publication of our Legislative Committee's report. Then the officers and delegates of the old Federation disbanded or merged in with the new Federation which was organized under the title of the American Federation of Labor. The revenue for the Federation work was to be derived from a per capita tax of one-half cent per member per month.

The convention provided for a president with a salary of $1,000 per year and added as part of its constitution "that the president shall devote his entire time to the interests of the Federation." I was nominated for president but I was greatly disinclined to accept any salaried labor office and therefore declined. John McBride of the Miners was nominated and he frankly stated that he could not afford to accept a position to which he would have to devote his entire time upon such a meager salary. The office fairly went begging and finally I was again nominated and persuaded in the interest of the movement to accept the nomination and election. That was the first salaried office I held in the labor movement. I knew the poverty of the wage earner and I did not like to think of accepting money for the service I gave them. . . .

This was in November and the constitution was to go into effect on March 1 of the following year, and so there was no salary paid me for the

The Executive Council elected by
the American Federation of Labor
held its first session at the U.S.
Hotel Columbus. O on Dec 11th 1886.
Present. Saml Gompers. Geo Harris,
J W Smith. G Edmonston & P J McGuire.

Resolved that the suscription
price be 50¢ per annum for the
Journal.
Resolved that an address be
prepared by the President.
No further business the
meeting adjourned. Saml Gompers
Pres.

These are the opening and closing lines of the handwritten minutes kept by Sam Gompers himself at the first meeting of the newly formed AFL's executive council. The men he lists were the infant organization's other officers. Harris and Smith served as first and second vice-president respectively, Edmonston was treasurer, and Gompers' old friend McGuire was secretary. In addition to the actions recorded at left (including an example of Gompers' rare misspellings), the five new officers agreed to spend $7.00 for handbills and newspaper advertisements to publicize a mass meeting, authorized Gompers to have an AFL seal engraved "and an electrotype of the same to be made," and "resolved that a salary of one dollar per annum be paid to the Treasurer."

intervening months. It was a difficult economic struggle for me to devote my entire time for those months without receiving salary or compensation for I had a wife and six children in addition to myself to support. Somehow I managed through it all. My family and I just put ourselves in the psychological position of a strike or lockout and somehow the period was tided over. . . .

I was president of a Federation that had been created but yet had to be given vitality. I felt that the trade union movement stood or fell with the success of the Federation and gave everything within me to the work. The new movement had to establish itself as a working agency. This could be done only by rendering service and establishing a reputation for ability to do things. To accomplish these ends I had to be active in labor matters, not only in New York, but in as wide a field as I could reach. What I could do was so terribly restricted by finances that I was constantly chafing. The story of the struggle can never be told. Early officers of trade union organizations had no such office rooms, equipment, and staff assistants as are now the rule with every national or international organization. In the pioneer days many carried their offices in their coat pockets during the day while they earned a living at their trades and gave such time as they could in the evenings to official business.

The new idea of united action by all the trades, which the Federation represented, had to make its way slowly by earning a place for itself in the minds and experiences of all workers. It got such scanty support as could be drawn from meager funds after they had served the urgent and manifold needs of the trade. The central trade office had only such equipment as was indispensable, and the Federation had less.

The first little office, which was about ten by eight, had a door, a small window, and a brick floor. It was cold in winter and hot in summer. The furniture was makeshift, consisting of a kitchen table brought down from our scanty house furnishings and a box for my chair. My second boy, Henry, who helped me when not in school, and who now takes great pride in the fact that he was the first office boy of the Federation, helped to contrive office furnishings. My daughter Rose had a child's writing desk that someone had given her. Henry took this down to the "office," put legs under it, and nailed it to the wall under the window. Thus equipped, with a box for a seat, Henry was busy during the summer all day long writing wrappers for the paper and doing many errands. He devised files for the office. Just across the street was a grocery store, the friendly proprietor of which contributed empty tomato boxes which Henry transformed into files. Our filing system was very simple. I personally marked each letter, circular, or pamphlet and Henry filed according to the designated subjects. As I was eager for information and had a reverence for the printed word, we soon collected a quantity of valuable information. One essential I had to buy during the first fall was a stove and a pipe which cost $8.50. So I managed for a few months. . . .

Money was scarce. There was not always enough for paper and ink. Henry remembers as one of his duties as office boy, going to the school around the corner to borrow a little ink until we could get money to buy a new bottle. Sometimes there was money to pay Henry his three dollars for his week's work, sometimes there was money to pay my week's salary. But whether there was money or not, in the morning we started to work from our home on Sixty-ninth Street and Second Avenue and usually walked to work with our lunch under our arms. If we had ten cents we might ride back—if not we walked. But we did the day's work, ate our sandwich apiece at noon, and got back home when we could. More often than not, it was midnight before I got home—there were meetings, speeches to make, conferences to attend, for the cause of labor is no easy mistress to serve. . . .

I often spent my own money for Federation work rather than stop work because none other was available. There was little enough for all purposes, with a family of eight to be cared for. We had no luxuries—not always the necessaries. Many a time the children had to stay home while shoes or clothes were repaired—there were no changes. When my shoes needed repairing, I wore old slippers in the office while Henry took the shoes over to the shoe shop to be mended before evening. My brother Alexander takes delight in recounting the time when I was going away to a convention, but had no clothes to wear. Finally, after arduous excitement, I succeeded in getting enough to buy a suit.

But those days of privation were not unhappy. My wife never interposed an objection to any decision I thought best. Many a night the children went to bed hungry, but I always tried to make it up to them the next morning at breakfast. That beautiful token [pictured on page 114] given me by the Foresters, if it could speak, could tell many a story of emergency relief service, service that renders it doubly precious as a life memento. I could always borrow from twenty dollars to fifty dollars on the token, but I rarely asked for more than five or ten because of the difficulty of getting money to redeem it. . . .

My earliest official efforts were concentrated in promoting stability of labor organizations. This had to be done by making the idea an inseparable part of the thought and habits of trade unionists by establishing a business basis for unionism and then driving home the fallacy of low dues. Cheap unionism cannot maintain effective economic activity. Sustained office work and paid union officials for administrative work have become the general practice since the Federation was organized. A big service of the Federation has been in crystallizing and unifying labor thought and practice.

To build the Federation we had to secure members. Numbers give confidence not only to members but to outsiders. The membership problem fell into three divisions—affiliation of existing nationals and internationals; chartering of local unions, central bodies, and state federations of labor; when a trade was sufficiently organized we launched a national organization.

When a large number of workers were organized in local unions of the same trade or industry, then I called a conference or convention to create a national or international union of these locals. I endeavored to carry out the historic development of the United States. The territory in which no state government existed belonged to the United States and out of this territory states were created and became part of the Federal government. Following this principle of development, I regarded the [local] unions as "territories" later to be formed into national and international unions and as such to form an integral part of the A. F. of L. The local unions not so

On this page Gompers recalls his tireless attempts to add as many union organizations as possible to the membership rolls of the struggling young AFL. One technique he used for all it was worth was to write letters to every labor group he heard about, urging them to join. If his first letter to an outfit went unanswered, he hammered away with more letters—and never willingly took "No" for an answer. Here are the opening lines of a missive he sent on July 7, 1887, to "the Officers of the Pattern Makers Union of New York & Vicinity." Just below the lines reproduced here, he complained: "You failed to take any notice of my letter. . . . I now again ask you . . . to send a committee to this office on Tuesday Evening July 12th at 7 o'clock. Fraternally yours." Time and again, such persistence did pay off.

organized in national or international unions hold the same relation to the [AFL] as the territories had to the government of the United States. . . .

A speech I made in Brooklyn in 1887 is typical of the educational work of that time: "The best way to defeat strikes and boycotts is to provide for them. There is no way of decreasing strikes so good as that of making men experienced. From a strong organization generous treatment follows, and with fairness on the part of the employer there is no desire to strike or boycott on the part of the men. The best method to decrease strikes is to organize to defend men in the case of strikes. The stronger the union the fewer the strikes. We do not want strikes, but if men are not organized they will have to strike. First, one employer will cut wages, then another, until the rate has fallen so low that the men must strike. We are opposed to sympathetic and foolish strikes. Ignorance is not discipline. It requires more discipline to pay an assessment of $1 a week to help those on strike than to strike in sympathy with them. The first thing a new union does is to want to strike. They overestimate the power of organization without resources. The old unions do not strike, their strength is known. They do not have to strike to resist encroachment." . . .

Economic betterment—today, tomorrow, in home and shop, was the foundation upon which trade unions have been builded. Economic power is the basis upon which may be developed power in other fields. It is the foundation of organized society. Whoever or whatever controls economic power directs and shapes development for the group or the nation.

*Although his family bore up as well as they could under the weight of privation, Gompers did not accept it without protest. In the spring of 1887, he wrote an anguished letter, excerpted in the first paragraph below, to the AFL treasurer. The second paragraph is what he wrote another AFL friend in 1890:*

■ I ought certainly [to] receive something for putting my whole time to the work. If I only had the means, I wouldn't care a straw, but as it is I will have shortly to decide upon giving up the position, take a job at my trade, or starve. If the Unions of the Country don't want a Federation, they don't and that settles it. If they do, they ought to pay a little for the protection its very existence affords and should not insist upon doing what we protest against employers doing, i.e., exacting work without pay. There can be no question that I did a good deal of that in my long connection with the labor movement and am willing to do so again if I get a chance to get back at my trade, but with a large family depending on me for support I cannot give my *entire time* without recompense. . . .

In the matter of salary I can assure you that I feel it is an injustice to me, since it leaves me at the end of the year just proportionately poorer as I hold office, but I could not and would not say one word upon the subject and followed the course that I usually pursue at the conventions of leaving the hall while the subject was under discussion in order to give the delegates free opportunity to express themselves without regard to my feelings in the matter.

*Whatever those early years with the AFL meant to Gompers in the way of poverty, they did not keep him from developing an eloquent labor philosophy. He worked long and spoke forcefully for social justice, as is manifest in the following passages from speeches he made before labor conventions in the first decade of the AFL:*

■ Of all the struggles of the human family for freedom, order, and progress, the trade unions are the direct and legitimate heirs. It is their mission to continue the battle for the right until the term "right" shall lose its relative significance by the abolition of injustice and wrongs. . . . To protect the innocent and the young, to raise man and woman from the sloughs of poverty and despair to a proper appreciation of their rights and duties, is worthy of our best efforts, our highest aspirations, our noblest impulses. I am willing to subordinate my opinions to the well-being, harmony, and success of the labor movement; I am willing to sacrifice myself also in advancement; and I am willing to step aside if that will promote our cause. But I can not and will not prove false to my convictions that the trade unions pure and simple are the natural organizations of the wage workers to secure their present material and practical improvement and to achieve their final emancipation. . . .

That we are still far from the goal for which the human family have been for ages struggling is due to our own shortcomings. There is no reason why we should not realize the highest hopes of an ideal life, where man's worth shall be measured by his real utility to his fellows, where his generosity and sympathy, rather than his cupidity and rapacity, will receive the encomiums and rewards of a nobler manhood, a more beautiful womanhood and a happier childhood; where justice and fair dealing will redound to the advantage and the ennobling of all. To the attainment of that end we should bend our every energy. . . .

Trade unionism is the soundest base yet laid for every project that gives promise to the working class for a firm and solid advance. Moving step by step, trade unionism contains within itself, as a movement and as a mechanism, the possibilities for establishing whatever social institutions the future shall develop for the workers as the predestined universal element in control of society.

*One of the most harrowing events in the history of American unionism was the bomb blast that turned the Haymarket rally into a riot (see pages 41–42). Owing to public hysteria, four anarchist leaders—no one of whom was ever proved to have been directly connected with the affair—were hanged. Though his own viewpoint could scarcely have been more opposed to either the philosophy or the practice of anarchism, Gompers did his best to prevent what he considered a grave miscarriage of justice:*

■ Since I have been associated with the labor movement, it has been my duty to direct policies during crises when violence brought discredit upon the movement. Personally, I have an abhorrence of violence. Physical

Allan Pinkerton, a Scottish immigrant, opened the world's first private investigation bureau in Chicago in 1850. The phrase "private eye" comes from the symbol of his detective agency—an open eye above the slogan: "We Never Sleep." Employers often hired Pinkerton and his agents to spy on labor groups and even to sabotage union activities, which caused Gompers and his colleagues to oppose the Pinkertons at every opportunity. In 1861 he claimed to have discovered a plot to assassinate Lincoln on the way to his first inauguration, changed the President's route to avoid this, and sent a famous telegram: "Plums [Pinkerton] arrived with Nuts [Lincoln] this morning." This feat led to the detective's being given important intelligence assignments during the Civil War, as well as to postwar operations against Jesse James and his gang, the Reno brothers, and other desperadoes. Allan Pinkerton died before the most notorious of his firm's antilabor actions: its attempt to smash the Homestead strike of 1892 (see page 49). The Pinkertons have since lived this down.

suffering is something that I cannot contemplate without personal pain, yet I never feel that I have a right to constitute myself the judge of those responsible for acts of violence. Long years of work in industry and the labor movement have brought to me understanding of the motives and the incentives that lead men to commit acts of violence. Situations that have been followed by acts of violence indicate that the major responsibility rests not upon wage earners but upon those who have control over the determination of industrial and social policies. Be that as it may, it is invariably the labor movement that suffers most from connection with violence and yet, as against all other organized groups in society, the labor movement owes it to its members to stand by them in time of need and to insist and see to it that opportunity for justice and a fair trial is accorded.

The labor movement, like all institutions whose purpose is to promote a revolutionizing ideal, has had to resist tendencies to violence. The difficulty in this country has not been lessened by that indefinable something in the spirit of America that finds expression in direct action. Sometimes we praise direct action as personal initiative and sometimes we condemn it as violence. The underlying philosophy—anarchism—has its roots in a concept of human freedom in which there is absence of repression.

Some of the gentlest, most spiritual men I have known were men who called themselves philosophical anarchists. Such a man was Jo Labadie, a poet-printer of Detroit. . . . At a gathering in Cooper Union, New York, where Jo Labadie delivered a lecture on anarchism, someone in the audience asked him whether he proposed the physical overthrow by force of the present system of government. He answered at once in the negative, saying that any such violent overthrow would bring its reaction and that unless the spirit of freedom and the concept of individualism were held by the people generally, anarchy was impossible. His questioner said, "You are a hell of an anarchist." He replied, "Yes, that's the kind of an anarchist I am." . . .

The anarchist propaganda moved along without serious results until the Chicago catastrophe which demolished the eight-hour movement and struck at the foundations of the organized labor movement. The trade-union movement was in no way responsible for the teachings or the deeds of the anarchists, and yet for years we suffered through their unwisdom. Nor could we leave them to the mercy of persecution in the name of justice. We stood for a fair trial for the underdog whether called anarchist or any other name.

The Chicago anarchists were charged with murder on the ground that advocacy of force makes the advocate responsible for actual violence that may develop, and were denied even the semblance of fair trial. Some of those charged with murder declared they did not even attend the meeting in Haymarket Square where the explosion took place. Reports of proceedings in the anarchists' trials before Judge Gary came through the daily press and other avenues, and it was a shocking story of official prejudice and clumsily disguised effort to punish men for identification with anarchy [by means of mere hearsay].

Because there was no direct evidence showing that these men were guilty of throwing the bomb, there were numbers of men who believed that clemency should be exercised by commutation of sentence from death to imprisonment. . . . About the seventh or eighth of November 1887, I was sitting in my small office back of Union No. 144 when [two labor leaders] asked me whether I would not go to Springfield to make a plea before Governor Oglesby for commutation of the sentence. . . . They presented to me the idea that because of my being well and favorably known and that I was regarded as a conservative man, my plea would help. Without further ado I closed my office door, and without any belongings other than those which I wore, I went directly to the train and with them to Springfield.

The hearing was in the Governor's chamber and . . . very earnest pleas were made. . . . I said in part: "I have differed all my life with the principles and methods of the condemned, but know no reason why I should not ask the Governor to interpose and save condemned men from the gallows. The execution would not be one of justice; not to the interest of the great state of Illinois; not to the interests of the country; nor the workingmen. I come as a representative of . . . organizations opposed to anarchy. . . .

"If these men are executed it would simply be an impetus to this so-called revolutionary movement which no other thing on earth can give. These men would, apart from any consideration of mercy or humanity, be looked upon as martyrs. Thousands and thousands of labor men all over the world would consider that these men had been executed because they were standing up for free speech and free press.

"We ask you, sir, to interpose your great power to prevent so dire a calamity. If this great country could be great and magnanimous enough to grant amnesty to Jeff Davis, it ought to be great and magnanimous enough to grant clemency to these men." . . .

At the close of my statement Governor Oglesby arose to greet me, and thanked me and added that my appeal made the strongest impression upon his mind. However, all the appeals were of no avail, for the Governor declined to stay the execution. The men were executed on November 11, 1887.

*At various times, Gompers' role as president of the American Federation of Labor required him to act as treasurer, office manager, file clerk, diplomat, and traveling pitchman. In the latter capacity, he embarked on his first long-distance tour in 1889. He lacked the passionate delivery and earthy theatricality of Eugene Debs, his Socialist adversary, but his less dramatic style of oratory matched his statesmanlike mien.*

*Speaking tours could be costly, even in the late 1880's, and at first Gompers found himself bearing many of the costs personally. As the AFL had begun life with an almost empty treasury, local unions were expected to pay proportionate shares of his travel expenses wherever he went. But often the locals, too, lacked funds, in which case Gompers' expense money often came out of his own pocket. He did not cease traveling, despite the hardships, for he was convinced*

August Spies, a German immigrant, was the ablest of the anarchists executed for the Haymarket riot. Infuriated by the oppression of the working class and placing the blame on the employers, Spies's philosophy moved from socialism to anarchism, which he defended in his radical paper *Arbeiter Zeitung.* In 1881 he presided over the Chicago meeting of leftists who founded a revolutionary party committed to direct action. His wild demands for an end to the existing social order, as well as his bitter editorials castigating capitalism and religion, antagonized businessmen, churchgoers, nativists, and even labor leaders (who felt he was harming their cause). The clash of police and workers that preceded the Haymarket affair prompted Spies to print a flamboyant circular headed, "Revenge! Workingmen, To Arms! ! !" After the Haymarket bombing, Spies was among the first to be arrested. He met the trial and the fatal verdict with fortitude. His prophetic last words from the gallows were: "There will come a time when our silence will be more powerful than the voices you strangle today!"

155

*that personal contacts were important to establish—and to maintain. "Everywhere I went," he said, "I tried to get acquainted with the active labor men of the community. I wanted to establish sources of information and to get acquainted with those upon whom I could rely to stand stanchly for trade unionism."*

*So for the rest of his career—as long as he was able—he spent a third of his time on the road, averaging 30,000 miles a year, never curbing his desire to win friends for labor, for the AFL, for his constituents, and to soothe the ruffled spirits of dissenters. The following excerpts from Gompers' speeches indicate the range of subjects that concerned him, and the flavor of his rhetoric:*

■ Doing for people what they can and ought to do for themselves is a dangerous experiment. In the last analysis the welfare of the workers depends on their own initiative. . . .

While some may assert that the strike is a relic of barbarism, I answer that the strike is the most highly civilized method which the workers, the wealth producers, have yet devised to protest against the wrong and injustice, and to demand the enforcement of the right. The strike compels more attention and study into economic and social wrongs than all the essays that have been written. . . . It established better relations between the contending parties than have heretofore existed . . . speeds the machinery for production to a greater extent; gives impetus to progress and increases power. . . . I trust the day will never come when the workers . . . will surrender their right to strike. . . . What workingmen of America have

obtained in improved conditions, higher wages, shorter hours of labor, was not handed to them on a silver platter. They have had to organize, they have had to show their teeth, they have had to strike, they have had to go hungry and to make sacrifices in order to impress upon the employers their determination to be larger sharers in the products of labor. . . .

Trade unions are organizations that instill into men a higher motive power and give them a higher goal to look to. The hope that is too frequently deadened in their breasts when unorganized is awakened by the trade unions as it can be by nothing else. . . . [The trade unions] are more concerned in deeds than words, achievements than promises, practical results than theories. . . . Wherever trade unions are most firmly organized, there are the rights of people most respected. . . .

"Freedom! Freedom is bread. Bread is Freedom." I am in entire accord with [the German poet] Heine. He did not mean simply the piece of bread such as this in my hand, that one may eat, but all that the term implies. Liberty can be neither exercised nor enjoyed by those who are in poverty. Material improvement is necessary to the exercise and enjoyment of liberty. . . . The wealth possessors are free wherever they go, and I will not begrudge them their freedom. All we insist upon is being free ourselves. There is no power or factor so potent to maintain the freedom that we now possess, and to obtain absolute equality before the law and equality of opportunity, as the labor organizations of our time. . . .

So long as man shall live and have his being, so long as there shall dwell in the human heart a desire for something better and nobler, so long as

there is in the human mind the germ of the belief in human justice and human liberty, so long as there is in the whole makeup of man a desire to be a brother to his fellow man, so long will there be the labor movement. It expresses all of the struggles of the past, all the sacrifices and bitterness that the human family has tasted in its experience. The movement embraces all the tenderness of the human family, all of its hopes and all of its aspirations for the real liberty of mankind. The labor movement is founded on the bedrock of opposition to wrong. It is based on the aspirations for right. I want you, and all of us, to cooperate with the best that is within us to make the labor movement strong and powerful and influential, and that it may grow day by day. . . .

The labor movement did not begin with my advent into it. The labor movement is as old as the ills of humanity. The labor movement is the result of the ills of humanity and a constant protest against those ills. It is a demonstration of protest against every wrong which exists and which has been long endured; it is a demand for every right to which the toilers are entitled and which they have not yet achieved. . . . The question propounded centuries ago, "Am I my brother's keeper?" is being answered by the labor movement and the social conscience it arouses. Yes, you are your brother's keeper, and unless you help to enlighten his burden yours will be made so much heavier. . . .

The trade unions are the legitimate outgrowth of modern society and industrial conditions. They are not the creation of any man's brain. They are organizations . . . born of the necessity of the workers to protect and defend themselves from encroachment, injustice and wrong. They are organizations of the working class, for the working class, by the working class; grappling with economic and social problems as they arise, dealing with them in a practical manner to the end that a solution commensurate with the interests of all may be attained. . . . To protect the workers in their inalienable rights to a higher and better life; to protect them not only as equals before the law but also in their right to the product of their labor; to protect their lives, their limbs, their health, their homes, their firesides, their liberties as men, workers, and citizens; to overcome and conquer prejudice and antagonisms; to secure them the right to life; a right to a full share in the abundance which is the result of their brain and brawn and the civilization of which they are the founders and the main stay; to this the workers are entitled beyond the cavil of a doubt. . . . The attainment of these is the glorious mission of the trade unions. . . .

Any one may say that the organizations of labor invade or deny liberty to the workmen. But go to the men who worked in the bituminous coal mines twelve, fourteen, sixteen hours a day for a dollar or dollar and twenty-five cents, and who now work eight hours a day and whose wages have increased 70 per cent in the past seven years [since 1898]—go tell those men that they have lost their liberty and they will laugh at you. Go to the wives who have received the benefit resulting from this higher wage and the companionship of their husbands; go to their children and compare them with the children who were deprived from going to school and have grown up to become miners and miners' wives, and see the difference in the standard of education and of morals. Say to these miners' wives and children today that their husbands and fathers have lost their liberty by joining the union! Go to the bricklayers, who worked formerly ten hours a day, but who for the past several years have enjoyed the eight-hour workday, with higher wages, with greater comforts, with larger enlightenment and social activity—tell these bricklayers that their liberties have been invaded! Go to the workers in the clothing trades who worked in the factories where they toiled, and who organized and fought and won, and lost and won, and lost again and again, until that healthier public judgment was formed that abolished sweatshops—go to them and tell them that their liberties have been invaded by the unions. . . .

The most real things in life are not the tangible things which we can see and touch, but they are the influences that make the spirit reverent and sweet and true, the glimpses we catch of the meaning of life, the conceptions that have left the trivial and have lost themselves in the immortal and the impersonal—the great motive powers that are felt throughout the ages. The passions, the ambitions, the yearnings of men for something better and higher are the most real things in the life of the people—nay, they are the throbbing, pulsating heart of life itself. Though so vital, so powerful, they are so fine and subtle that we are often unconscious of their presence; yet in the silent and lone places of life, in the times when we test our dreams and visions whether they be in tune with the ultimate and the infinite, these real things ring out like some rare strain of sweet music that thrills, and soothes, and comforts. Were it not for the courage and the inspiration born of deeper insight and fuller understanding of the meaning and the process of life and progress, the pain and disappointment would be too overpowering. But these glimpses when eternity affirms the conception of the present are the greatest reward granted honest, true work. If those whose faithful, often unnoted, services have given form and reality to that most real thing in the lives of those who bear the dead weight and burden of America's progress could but sense and realize the full nobility and grandeur of the structure they have reared, infinite peace and satisfaction would be their compensation. . . . The labor movement among the American workers is the result of self-sacrifice and consecration of minds and hearts to the work of bettering humanity. Though the individual work may seem inconsequential and scarcely worth while, yet the whole looms big with hope and power—the whole is impossible without each individual endeavor, however unimportant it may seem when isolated.

*A major issue that concerned Gompers for years was labor's campaign for the eight-hour workday. Some legislation in this field had been enacted as early as President Andrew Johnson's Administration in the 1860's, but industry had interpreted the law loosely and government had enforced it only spasmodically. The first paragraph below is from a Gompers statement to a Senate committee in 1883; the second paragraph is from an indignant speech he made to a group of employers twenty years later.*

Strong impetus toward the shortened workday described here was provided by John Mitchell, an Illinois-born miner who became president of the United Mine Workers in 1898. During his ten years in office he succeeded in getting the workday cut from ten to nine hours in the anthracite mines and, more drastically, to eight hours in the bituminous mines. Failing health necessitated his resignation in 1908, and there was speculation that he might become Secretary of Labor, a Democratic vice-presidential candidate, or Gompers' successor as AFL president. But he was none of these. He served with Gompers in the National Civic Federation. From 1915 until his early death (at forty-nine) in 1919, he was chairman of the New York State Industrial Commission. In many ways he was like Gompers—under whom he served as an AFL vice-president—for he was a moderate and, above all, a realist. "I did not revolutionize the industrial world," he said in retrospect. "I did not solve the labor problem. It will never be solved. We only hope to gain, little by little, more of our proper share of what we produce."

■ The general reduction of the hours of labor to eight per day would reach further than any other reformatory measure; it would be of more lasting benefit; it would create a greater spirit in the workingman; it would make him a better citizen, a better father, a better husband, a better man in general. . . .

I say to you . . . that we won't wait; we won't wait. We know what a shorter workday means; there is not any man upon this floor or anywhere who dares dispute the proposition that a shorter workday means better men, better workmen; more productive workmen; more intelligent workmen; better citizens; more humane men.

*One climax in the struggle for the eight-hour day came in the years following 1888. The AFL executive council had requested contributions equal to two cents per member from its affiliates—and also won a promise of more funds if a war chest were needed to finance the eight-hour campaign in specific industries. In his autobiography, Gompers tells how he toured America evangelizing for this issue in 1891; the last paragraph records his deep satisfaction at the public's eventual acceptance of this principle:*

■ The eight-hour educational work had been sufficiently thorough to enable each national union to carry forward the shorter hours movement in its own industry. Our work pressed home upon all the concept that the shorter workday is the initial step in better conditions for wage earners. Progress in establishing the eight-hour day has been an advantage not only for wage earners but in promoting industrial progress. There is general agreement among the medical men that poisons of fatigue caused by overwork and lack of sufficient time for recuperation are causes of physical and mental inefficiency. Shorter hours stimulate inventive genius by making necessary the introduction of improved machinery and tools in order that human labor power may be used more effectively. The shorter workday, with the attendant readjustments, invariably results in greater production. Long hours of labor go hand in hand with low wages. I have frequently pointed out this fact that if long hours and low wages were the barometer of commercial and industrial prosperity, China would stand first in the list. After the movement of 1891, it was no longer necessary for the national labor movement to sponsor specific eight-hour movements. The pioneer work had been done. . . .

When the agitation for eight hours began, society thought us fanatics, and businessmen declared that it was impossible to maintain production on that basis; but labor persisted and our campaign of education went forward, constantly gaining adherents. A high peak of success was marked when the President of the United States [Wilson] declared the eight-hour day had the endorsement of society. Now the eight-hour day seems rational and necessary, but few realize the long years in which the pioneer agitators spoke on street corners and through such articles as we could smuggle into the press, before innumerable Legislative Committees, until finally our position was accepted in social thinking.

Andrew Carnegie, seen here in a friendly caricature holding some of the many libraries he gave to cities across the nation, was one capitalist Gompers sincerely admired. On occasion, the two men worked in close, warm collaboration—and Gompers believed the Homestead steel strike "would have been averted" had "Carnegie been in the United States during the annual negotiations, or immediately after the rupture." Carnegie's poverty-stricken parents took him from Scotland to Pennsylvania when he was thirteen and put him to work in a cotton mill. A self-made man, Carnegie amassed hundreds of millions (mostly in steel) and then, fearing "the disgrace of dying rich," made vast donations to worthy causes. Even so, he "died rich" in 1919. Of his adopted land he said: "The old nations of the earth creep at a snail's pace; the Republic thunders past with the rush of an express."

# POLITICS AND POLITICIANS

*Gompers never wanted to see a labor party established in the United States. He thought it would only separate workers from the existing political community and reduce to political expediency labor's concern for the economic interests of the individual. However, he was quite politically minded, both in his personal and in his union philosophy:*

■ To the frequent queries as to my personal politics I made this answer: In religion I am a workingman. In politics I am a workingman, and in every nerve, in every fiber, in every aspiration I am on the side which will advance the interests of my fellow workingmen. I do not say this in the spirit of bravado or demagogism, but in all sincerity. Men of means have their political predilections but seldom allow their politics to interfere with their business interests. I take exactly the same position, except that I represent my side, the side of the toiling wage-earning masses, in my every act and in my every utterance. . . .

We must be partisan for a principle and not for a party, but we must make manifest the fact that we have political power and that we intend to use it; otherwise, the ballot will become an impotent weapon. Our members and friends can not expect that the officers of the Federation can impress either upon political parties or upon Congress the demands of the workers for justice and right unless those workers themselves have shown sufficient interest in the use of the political power as to make it clear that they are the potent force behind their chosen officers and representatives. . . .

There are some men who can never understand political action unless there is a party. As a matter of fact, there is no worse party-ridden people in the whole world than are the people of the United States. It is nothing but party, party, your party and my party. It is the abomination of American politics. Men vote for their party regardless of what that party stands for. . . . Labor must learn to use parties to advance our principles, and not allow political parties to manipulate us for their own advancement. The distinction is easily understood and readily carried into effect. If each worker as an individual uses the ballot for the advancement of the principles for which labor stands and has declared, there will be no question in future as to the power of labor to achieve its just demands; political apathy and partisan adherence will weaken; political activity and partisanship for labor's principles will bring strength and success. The activity, the loyalty of the workers in every part of the country is what we need in order that our political power may be used harmoniously with our economic efficiency.

*Gompers himself voted as he saw fit. Among the most graphic passages in his memoirs are those in which he narrates his successive choices for President and—with telling detail—how he himself dealt with the men who actually became President:*

Each of the three times William Jennings Bryan ran for President, Gompers voted for him. But this hostile cartoon from the 1908 campaign, titled "Where he keeps the labor vote"—depicting Bryan as a confidence man stealing ballots from the pockets of a scarecrow Gompers—exaggerates their symbiosis. The two men were never really intimate and Gompers, though praising Bryan's "remarkable, mellow, resilient voice," had sundry reservations about him. In 1908, Bryan announced that if he were elected President he would name Gompers to his Cabinet—and the latter promptly stated that, while he hoped Bryan would reach the White House, he would accept no political office whatever from him.

■ I cast my first presidential vote in 1872 . . . for General U. S. Grant. I was a great admirer of Horace Greeley, and just about a year before the nominations of either of the parties Horace Greeley said that General Grant would be better fitted and qualified for the Presidency in 1872 than he was in 1868. I could not see the consistency of Mr. Greeley's then accepting the nomination for President on the Democratic ticket. I believed at that time that the Republican party had not yet fulfilled its mission. It still had the halo of the antislavery movement, and there were a number of men who were still living and active in furtherance of the reconstruction policy caused by the Civil War. . . .

Only once have I ever been a member of a political party. When I became of age I joined the Republican organization in the district in which I lived. To me it was an organization which still had a great purpose to fulfill. Lincoln typified that purpose in my mind. I received citizenship papers October 4, 1872, and have always tried to live up to the serious obligations of citizenship. . . . When I left the Republican party I joined no other. In view of the fact that I have been charged with belonging first to one party and then to another, it may be of some interest to have the names of those for whom I have cast my ballot for President. As I have stated, my first vote after naturalization was cast for Grant; in 1876 I voted for Peter Cooper; in 1880, for James B. Weaver whom I knew personally and with whom I was on terms of good friendship. . . . In 1884 I voted for Ben Butler; in 1888, for some cause which I do not now remember, I did not vote; in 1892, for General Weaver; in 1896, for William J. Bryan; 1900, for Bryan; 1904, Judge Alton B. Parker; 1908, Bryan; 1912, Woodrow Wilson; 1916, Woodrow Wilson; 1920, James B. Cox.

It will be observed that in recent years, I have voted for the presidential candidate on the Democratic ticket, and this has been interpreted by many to mean that I am a member of the Democratic party. This relationship has been charged against me by Republican party leaders and yet never claimed by Democratic party leaders, for they know better. The Republicans used it with the hope of weakening my influence. . . .

As I have already stated, in the first four years of my citizenship I was a member of the Republican party. For years after in presidential elections I cast a protesting vote. I believed that the Republican party had fulfilled its mission, growing out of the Civil War, and so far as the Democratic party was concerned, it had no concept of the political and industrial problems of the times.

Anyone who will doubt the sincerity of the nonpartisan policy which I have endeavored to pursue may compare the platform declarations of the Democratic and Republican parties and judge for himself whether I was not justified as a labor man and—I hope I may say—as a forward-looking citizen, in casting my vote for a candidate nominated upon the Democratic platform. . . .

The first President of the United States whom I met personally was General U. S. Grant. At that time Grant was to me a hero of a great war for human freedom. I felt that the Republican party was still fulfilling the high purpose for which it had been brought into being and that I was making a kind of pilgrimage in going to see him upon a mission whose purpose was highly humanitarian. Later, at the time of the [attempt to corner the gold market] and the public scandal attending the financial crisis of 1873, my faith in the destiny of the Republican party was rudely shattered. The Workingmen's Union of New York and the New England Eight-Hour League paid my fare to Washington in order that I might present their position upon the eight-hour law. This law, signed by President Johnson, Grant endeavored to have enforced fairly without reduction in wages. After I had made my statement for my fellow workers and rose to leave, President Grant placed his hand on my shoulder and said, "You are not a very tall man, Mr. Gompers." I looked across into his eyes and replied, "Yes, but I am not the President of the United States."

Rutherford B. Hayes I met several times. . . . As soon as my name was mentioned to him he recognized me and spoke of the great problems with which I have to deal. . . . The conversation was exceedingly interesting and pleasant and he asked me to call upon him at the White House. I called upon President Hayes on two occasions during his term at the White House, discussing labor problems, industrial problems, and politics.

President Garfield I met when he was a member of Congress, but never in the White House. He was vividly impressed upon my mind in connection with a speech which he made on the railroad strike of 1877 in which he declared that the military ought to be called out to shoot workingmen down in the streets if that were necessary to restrain them from striking. I could not forget such an untempered declaration even after Garfield became President nor after he was shot. . . . I could not pretend to change my opinion of Garfield. He lingered for weeks. His body was . . . lying in state only a few blocks distant from where the Cigar Makers' convention met. . . . A motion was submitted that the convention adjourn for the day as a mark of respect to the dead President. I opposed that motion and I recited the wrongs of labor and declared that as representatives of labor we could not consistently express respect for a man whose counsel was ever against efforts to right our wrongs. My speech created something of a sensation and the newspapers declared me a dangerous man. However, the motion prevailed. . . .

With Chester A. Arthur . . . I had only chance meetings. He was a New York politician.

Grover Cleveland . . . was a typical representative of what was then called the business type—cold-blooded, methodical, in no way influenced by a weakness for humanity. . . . A few years after President Cleveland's retirement from public office . . . he became interested in the affairs of the National Civic Federation, the meetings of which he frequently attended. At these meetings he always manifested deep interest in the subjects discussed, and in truth I may say that he had softened a great deal in his manner and in the expression of his thoughts. I do know that he manifested a greater cordiality toward me than he had ever shown, either directly or indirectly, when he was in public office.

Ulysses S. Grant provoked ambivalent feelings. The Civil War made him a hero—the disheveled but hard-driving Union soldier who rose to supreme command and cornered Lee at Appomattox. President Grant, as Gompers notes here, was something else—a naive and ineffectual politician who did no credit to his high office. But Gompers approved of Grant's regard for the eight-hour day and of his commutation of the death penalty given two sailors for mutiny at sea.

Rutherford B. Hayes reached the White House by way of the disputed election of 1876, when a partisan electoral commission decided in his favor, and the South accepted the decision. Hayes paid this debt by ending Reconstruction. At a lunch he and Gompers attended, some guests began to abuse the unions. Gompers spoke up: "I . . . represent all the people you are condemning." Then President Hayes gave him the cordial reception mentioned on this page.

James A. Garfield won a military reputation in the Civil War and, although accused of accepting favors from firms seeking government contracts, managed to achieve the Presidency in 1880. He was assassinated by a demented office-seeker in 1881. Gompers frankly confessed antagonism for the dead President (see page 163), but added: "In later years I came to a better understanding of the respect due to an office that represents an ideal."

Gompers thought that Chester A. Arthur was merely a machine politician, and there is no doubt that President Hayes removed Arthur from a lucrative post as Collector of the Port of New York because he was a political spoilsman. Arthur became Vice-President largely by chance, and when he succeeded Garfield it was widely feared he would disgrace the Presidency. Instead, he took many federal jobs out of politics and proved to be an honest President.

During President McKinley's term I had as good opportunity to meet with him to discuss important matters as I have ever had with any President. . . . I had known Mr. McKinley for many years. When he came to Congress he was a . . . protectionist, and regardless of whether the fundamental principle is right or wrong or whether free trade is natural and protection artificial, so far as the cigarmaking industry is concerned, free trade would have meant the annihilation of the industry in the United States. But be that as it may, I was frequently drawn into contact with Congressman McKinley. That business relation in time developed into genuine friendship. He became Governor of Ohio and later was elected President. When he had under consideration the appointment of the Industrial Commission, he told me he wished to include my name. I appreciated the honor, [but preferred] to stay with the labor movement. The President tried to prevail upon me to change my decision, but I steadfastly declined.

Shortly afterwards, the Caledonian Club of Washington held its annual dinner. . . . There was a toast to the President of the United States . . . and [I] delivered an address extolling the qualities of Mr. McKinley and the great powers and opportunities which were in his keeping. On the following day I had a conference with the President. After greeting him, I related to him that I had the pleasure of responding to the toast in his honor the night before. He said, "I am confident that you made an excellent address and that you spoke kindly of me." I replied, "You had better ask others who heard me, for I would not dare to tell you all the mean things I said about you." With an assumed haughtiness he said: "Mr. Gompers, let me tell you an anecdote. Out in one of the mining countries there was a bully who cheated all with whom he came in contact. He lied, he swore, he killed, and finally he died with his boots on. Of course, the miners wanted to give that person, even though he was a brute, some religious service and they were at their wits' end how to do it, so they sent two of their men on horseback to a neighboring camp where they heard there was an old-time itinerant preacher prospecting for gold. They found their man and asked him whether he would not preach a sermon over the dead man's remains. He said he would like to know something about the characteristics of the man and they said: 'We can say nothing good for him. He is guilty of every crime on the calendar and had no conscience, no sympathy, no honor.' He said, 'All right.' They replied, 'You mean you are going over to preach the sermon over his remains in spite of what we said?' 'Oh, yes.' 'What will you say?' 'Well, I shall speak of the great times in which he lived.' " The point was splendidly made and we began talking of the speeches that he had made and those that I had made. He asked me if I had a stenographer take down my addresses. I said, "No, I have not the time to prepare them, nor the luxury of having a stenographer take them down." He said, "That is a good kind of a speech which one can deliver in regular order one day and the following evening begin from the other end and work toward the first part and then at another time begin in the middle and work both ways." . . .

His successor, Colonel Roosevelt, I also knew well. I broke through his reserve in our effort to secure the enactment of law by the Legislature of the state of New York, for the abolition of the tenement-house system of work. . . . When he became Police Commissioner of New York City, I again came in contact with him. Joe Barondess and I brought to his attention the brutality with which the police treated the striking garment workers. He went around with us to make an investigation and he found the representations made to him by us were well founded. Then he issued an order that fair treatment should be accorded to the strikers. . . .

When he became President after the assassination of President McKinley, I felt a strong inclination to go and express my personal gratification that he was now in a place where he could exert wide influence, but I restrained the impulse, partly because of my feeling for McKinley. In an accidental meeting shortly afterwards, President Roosevelt reproached me for not coming to see him, telling me there were a number of things he wanted to talk over with me. He urged me to come soon and frequently. It was necessary for me to go soon afterwards. . . . He said he wanted to read to me portions of the message [to Congress] he was preparing. He began reading the portion which had to do with anarchists and advocates of violence. I saw at once that Colonel Roosevelt had not appreciated the difference between making an official statement and the expression of a private citizen, so I interrupted him by saying, "Mr. President, I think you ought not to say that. You will be misinterpreted." The Colonel went on reading enthusiastically, interested in what he wanted to present. Again I interrupted, "But, Mr. President, that statement is wrong." This time a bit impatiently he began where he had left off. By this time I, too, was a bit impatient, so I leaned forward and said with all the force in my make-up, "Mr. President, you are absolutely wrong. You must not say that." Roosevelt then came to an abrupt stop because he realized I would not be swerved. We then discussed the statement and he agreed that I was right and made changes accordingly. He had written a statement that would have been permissible as a statement of opinion of a private citizen, but which would become ill-advised if not disastrous if uttered by the Chief Executive of the land.

I went to the White House frequently thereafter. I had a great admiration for the forceful personality of the man. . . . It was characteristic of Theodore Roosevelt that he disregarded red tape. He brought to the problems of the White House a realism that had never previously pervaded the executive offices. It was because he was vitally interested in realities that he captured the imaginations of the American people and became their great evangelist in a demand that the government should serve the people. It is entirely in keeping with the general character of the man that he should be the first President to use in an official message to Congress the term "organized labor."

He was always a forceful figure and interested in the human aspects of all questions. He could concentrate both physical and mental energy to a startling degree. A person with such qualities must necessarily be egotisti-

Grover Cleveland, the strongest President between Lincoln and Theodore Roosevelt, lived by his convictions—and made as many enemies as friends. He annoyed veterans by vetoing pension bills, silverites by opposing the Silver Purchase Act, the British by rejecting their Venezuela claims, and unions by sending troops to end the Pullman strike. Gompers, critical of the latter action, felt Cleveland had given "full support and backing to the Pullman Company" and had slighted labor.

William McKinley, the victor over Bryan in the 1896 campaign masterminded by Mark Hanna, stood for the gold standard, high tariffs, and American imperialism. The annexation of Hawaii, Guam, and the Philippines during his Administration marked the rise of America as a world power. Gompers—who considered McKinley "kind and gentle, willing to the best of his abilities and opportunities, a fine type of man"—was much distressed by his assassination in 1901.

Theodore Roosevelt, advocate of "the strenuous life," was a naturalist, historian, explorer, reformer, Rough Rider, and statesman. He took his "big stick" to the trusts, promoted American imperialism (the Panama Canal was his achievement), and won the Nobel Peace Prize for mediating the Russo-Japanese War. But T.R. lost his bid for a third term in the futile Bull Moose campaign of 1912. Gompers said: "Frequently, he talked very bad Holland Dutch to me."

William Howard Taft, Roosevelt's Secretary of War and a former Governor of the Philippines, succeeded T.R.—who thought that his own policies would continue. Gompers, however, "did not share that confidence, for I knew that Taft did not understand men as Roosevelt did." T.R. later reached the same conclusion. Taft subsequently became Chief Justice of the United States, maintaining a conservative position and upholding injunctions in labor disputes.

cal. He compelled attention by his strenuous activity, his passionate espousal of causes, and his enthusiasm for a constructive measure. He had a great influence upon those with whom he came in contact. I know of no instance when I had to wait to see him for more than a few minutes. I accepted him as a friend with brain, sympathy, and willingness to serve, and he believed in me and at times accepted my advice and acted upon it. Our relations were of the most cordial and confidential character. . . .

On one occasion I had a conference with President Roosevelt to interest him more effectively in the conditions and situation as they existed in Porto Rico. . . . I expected to have not more than fifteen minutes of the President's time. However, the interview was prolonged for over an hour and at its close he asked me whether I would not come to see him at six o'clock that evening. When I was ushered into the President's office, I found him attired in his tennis clothes and at his desk eating his dinner from a tray. He had just finished a game of tennis and had no time to dine with his family and keep his engagement with me. . . . The conference lasted until nearly midnight and resulted in the President deciding on taking action that would be helpful to the government and the people of Porto Rico. . . .

The first time I heard of William Howard Taft was in connection with the Phelan injunction case which came before his court. His name is associated in my mind with injunctions, so that in his presidential campaign I gave him the name of "Father of Injunctions." I met him first when he was Secretary of War and found him to be one of the most genial and likable men I have ever met. Repeatedly, I found myself wishing he had never entered the legal profession, for legal training, I believed, hampered a mind that was otherwise constructive and clear. I was afterwards confirmed in this opinion when I watched his services on the War Labor Board in the capacity where he was dealing with practical matters and production as a growing machine. In that capacity his decisions were constructive and his approach to every decision was guided by a fundamental desire to better human life. . . . When Mr. Taft was elected to the Presidency, he manifestly bore me no ill will for the part I played in the campaign. In truth, Mr. Taft is not a man who could bear ill will, particularly against a man acting in good conscience. His greetings were always cordial. He frequently called me "Sam" or "Hello, how are you, my old antagonist?" . . .

Near the close of Mr. Taft's term, Congress passed the bill creating the Department of Labor which awaited the President's consideration. Of course, he had the right to veto it or to allow it to die with the expiration of Congress. . . . We . . . argued and pleaded with him to sign the bill. . . . On March 4, the President went over to the Capitol and there was prevailed upon by Senator [Boies] Penrose and Senator [Henry Cabot] Lodge to sign the bill which he had been reluctant to do. Senator Penrose later told me that he told the President that both Mr. Lodge and he would have to bear the brunt of attack if the President refused to sign the bill or had allowed it to die without his signature. President Taft signed the bill.

Woodrow Wilson was not my choice for the presidential candidate for the Democratic party. I had never met him, but what I had heard of him was not calculated to predispose me in his favor. Certain of his earlier academic writings indicated that he did not understand labor problems. Rumors came to me that Mr. Wilson did not feel any too kindly to me. . . . Sometime in August 1912, I obtained from Governor Wilson the courtesy of a conference with him. . . . In that meeting I felt my prejudices disappearing before the sincerity and the obvious humanitarianism of the man. . . . I left Trenton feeling very much relieved. However [on] the issues which were of fundamental interest to organized labor I did not know what was the personal opinion of Mr. Wilson.

When the November election placed the Democratic party in control of both the executive and the legislative branches for the first time in many years, I felt that a test of the effectiveness of labor's political policy was then to be made. Either the Democratic party would have to make good its pledges or labor would have to change its political policy. . . . It became my duty to present several matters to the President. My respect for him grew into a feeling of well-nigh reverential admiration. I admired his keen, alert mentality, his beautiful English, the perfect enunciation and modulation of his speaking voice. There was that in his personal dignity that made me feel when the door swung open to admit him that a real President of the United States was entering. While he was President, he was every inch a man. I always enjoyed talking to him and always left stimulated by a wider vision and a keener determination to service. While I found that his mind was open, yet that did not mean that he yielded to all requests. . . .

When the Immigration Bill passed Congress in 1917, President Wilson vetoed it. Despite the fact that similar measures had been vetoed by the

Of all the Presidents he personally knew, Gompers' favorite by far was Woodrow Wilson. During Wilson's two terms, from 1913 to 1921, Gompers often cooperated enthusiastically with him. In this photograph, taken at the dedication of the new AFL headquarters building in Washington on July 4, 1916, a beaming Gompers is flanked by Woodrow Wilson (left) and Secretary of Labor William B. Wilson, a former miner who (though a member of President Wilson's Cabinet) was not related to the Chief Executive.

Warren Gamaliel Harding was probably America's worst President. A mediocre politician, hand-picked by party leaders at the Republican convention of 1920, Harding made "return to normalcy" his slogan. But he brought the "Ohio Gang" to Washington, and it made his regime a byword for corruption. Secretary of the Interior Albert B. Fall went to jail for the era's most infamous case of graft, Teapot Dome. Gompers accepted appointments from Harding until the latter's growing coolness to labor convinced him that "I could not, with any self-respect, request any further audience with the President."

three preceding Presidents, an attempt was made to repass the measure over President Wilson's veto. It was generally understood that the measure was termed labor legislation and that the A. F. of L. had taken the initiative in advocating the restrictive standards of the bill. Up until that time no legislation had been enacted contrary to the judgment of President Wilson. When the bill was repassed over his veto, the action was generally hailed as the victory of labor over the President. Despite this fact, President Wilson did not alter his attitude toward me or the labor movement, and . . . in wartime he vetoed the legislative, executive, and judicial appropriations bill because it contained the Borland Amendment increasing the hours of work of government employes from seven to eight. . . .

I have never known a man either within or without the White House with whom it was so satisfactory to cooperate upon big matters as President Wilson. He instinctively assumed that I would not present to him either in person or in writing any proposal which I did not think of first importance and in which I did not wholeheartedly believe myself. Therefore, any communication from me received personal and early consideration. There are no letters in my files which I value more highly than the inimitable ones which bear his signature. There was always something so personal in the wording or in the spirit that each seemed like a very special communication. When the European war came and war clouds began to gather over our own continent, I felt implicit trust in the leader of our country and I had reason to believe he had equal confidence in me. Not only did he manifest confidence in me, but [also] an understanding of the significance of the national group which I represented. . . . In addition to this, Mr. Wilson always made me feel that my advice to him upon matters in my personal experience was regarded as something valuable and useful. Those who worked with him confidentially during that period always treated me as a co-worker. . . .

I was proud of Woodrow Wilson throughout his period of service. It was a matter of personal gratification to me that he was our national representative during the period when America had to assume world leadership on many issues. He made mistakes, of course, but it is easy to criticize the mistakes of others. The fact remains that under most trying tests Woodrow Wilson was a President for whom we did not have to make excuses. . . . I believed wholeheartedly in his plan for a League of Nations. Understanding the influences at work at Paris, I knew only too well why it was impossible for him to secure a perfect treaty. To my mind we owed it as honest redemption of war pledges to accept the treaty under the League of Nations and begin the development of organized international relations. What I could do to support the President's policies, I did. The great tragedy of President Wilson's physical collapse made him plainly one of the war's victims, wounded more grievously than many who fell on the battlefield. . . .

President Harding I saw several times after he became President. I opposed him for the Presidency but when he was elected, he was my President as he was the President of every citizen of the country. I went to the

White House soon after his inauguration to take up matters which the [AFL] convention had directed me to present to him. After I had finished the business which was the purpose of the interview, he put his arm around my shoulder and taking me aside and extending his hand, which I gladly took, he said: "Mr. Gompers, I want your help. I want you to know that I do not believe you to be as black as you have been painted to me and I want to assure you that I am not as black as I have been painted to you." I found him cordial and he expressed the hope that I would come to him freely. I was glad to find that attitude, for I wanted to have the opportunity to give him information which I knew would help him in deciding policies aright. . . .

It was during the June 1921 convention of the American Federation of Labor that a resolution was adopted calling upon the President of the United States to invite other nations to meet at Washington for the purpose of agreeing upon terms for the reduction of armaments. That declaration was sent to President Harding. About a month later the President announced that invitations had gone abroad for such a conference. Whether this was a mere coincidence or not is more than I can say. The only purpose of my mentioning it is that about two months before the Washington Conference, I received from the President a commission appointing me as one of the Advisory Commission to the American delegation to the conference. He also appointed me as a member of the Conference on Unemployment and upon Agriculture. . . .

My first conference with Mr. Coolidge as President was on the afternoon of the first day of his arrival in Washington, after the death of President Harding. . . . I went to the Willard Hotel to consult Colonel Sherrill and to ascertain from him in which manner we could participate in the funeral procession and services. After leaving Colonel Sherrill's room, I ran into about fifty newspapermen, who immediately questioned me upon the purpose of my visit to Colonel Sherrill, which I explained. They asked me whether I was not going to call upon the President. I stated that that was not my intention and that I felt it would be indelicate to do so. However, they . . . said that President Coolidge was in a suite of rooms three doors away and that unless I paid my respects to him the deduction might be made that it was an intentional slight. Apprehensive that that might be true, I at once proceeded to the door where an attendant greeted me and asked me whether I had [come to call] upon the President. I gave him an affirmative answer. He retired from the room and in a few seconds returned and said the President would see me. I discussed a few important matters and when I requested an opportunity to see him again later, expecting that such a conference would take place a few weeks thereafter, Mr. Coolidge suggested the following Monday morning. . . .

The President asked me what in my judgment was the labor situation and what were the most important measures which were affecting labor. I enumerated a number, emphasizing three: child labor, the abuse of the injunctive writ in labor disputes, and immigration. He was interested and expressed full sympathy with the movement to safeguard child life from

Calvin Coolidge became President on Harding's death in 1923. He was a Vermont-born lawyer famous for his taciturnity. As Governor of Massachusetts, he put down the Boston police strike in 1919, wiring Gompers: "There is no right to strike against the public safety by anybody, anywhere, anytime." As President, he cleaned up the Harding mess, but otherwise pretty much let the nation drift, in accordance with his credo that "the chief business of the American people is business." Coolidge, reelected in 1924, rejected a third term with the laconic pronouncement: "I do not choose to run."

An essential part of the one-man task that Gompers managed to perform so effectively in building up the AFL was accomplished by means of the speaking tours he often made. Each of his appearances was publicized in advance by local notices such as this one, which was prepared by the Central Labor Union of Terre Haute, Indiana. On pages 188–189, Gompers mentions with obvious pride the fact that on three of his Indiana speaking engagements he drew larger crowds then Ethel Barrymore, Colonel Robert G. Ingersoll and John L. Sullivan. However, Gompers neglects to say that all three of his "rivals" charged substantial admission fees—while his talks were free!

exploitation and recalled the fact that as Governor he [had] signed the Child Labor Law of Massachusetts. He expressed himself as greatly concerned regarding the immigration problem and recognized that the standards of America should not be lowered by the influx of immigrants not easily assimilable.

## SLOW GROWTH OF THE AFL

*Emerson's thesis that an institution is but the lengthened shadow of a man assuredly applies to Gompers and the AFL. Perhaps no other American organization owes so much to a single human being. Gompers himself was short, even stubby—yet the shadow cast by the AFL long remained more truncated than his own.*

■ My job as the president of the A. F. of L. was coveted by no one in the early days. There was much work, little pay, and very little honor. . . . I became a seeker of men. I wanted to win them for a labor movement which was sound philosophically, competent economically, and inspiring spiritually. At times I was well-nigh consumed with zeal. . . . I was still writing all my letters by hand—a long toilsome process—and I press-copied them myself. . . . In 1889 I submitted to the executive council a proposal to buy a secondhand typewriter for fifty-five dollars, and after very careful consideration this purchase was authorized. Everybody in any way connected with the office learned to operate this machine, and finally we arrived at the period of development that justified our having a stenographer.

Many of those letters tell the story of the painstaking attention to seemingly unimportant details that contributed to the upbuilding of the Federation. I watched our local unions and gave them suggestions and advice. I fostered the organization of city centrals and state federations. I sent reminders to national officers urging them to pay per capita dues. In the case of national bodies which the Federation had fostered, local unions and members expected me to be a sort of fatherly supervisor of the organization. I wrote letters and talked to officials, diplomatically urging them to performance of duties and constructive policies. I got trade unions to put on their letterheads "affiliated to the American Federation of Labor" and thus helped advertise the name. All this work had to be done in such a way as to win men to the cause. The Federation had no compulsory authority—it was absolutely dependent upon voluntary cooperation.

Then there was the problem of establishing the custom of maintaining membership in the Federation. Unions wanted to come in and go out as best suited their temporary convenience. There was not then an understanding of the necessity for maintaining membership in local trade unions, to say nothing of understanding the value and the service that a national labor movement could render. Without warning and for only fancied grievance, organizations withdrew from the Federation. Sometimes a national organization would write that because no assistance was given

New York,     April 5,    1894.

Mr. Henry D. Lloyd,
    Winetka, Ill.

My Dear Mr.Lloyd:- I am in receipt of your favor of the 2nd.inst.together with the articles of Miss Willard and Miss Murrell,and of course

so. The columns of the "American Federationist" are open to you at any

and all times.

    Reciprocating your kind wishes and hopes for success,I am,
       Sincerely Yours

     *Saml Gompers.*    President.

      American Federation of Labor.

them in this or that trade difficulty, no further per capita tax would be paid. No consideration was given to the fact that the Federation was accomplishing everything possible within its means. Simply because they were not served at a particular time they were ready for the whole structure to fall. I had to reason with these organizations, both by letter and in person. Sometimes I was fighting single-handed to hold the line of federated organization. . . .

Legislative work demanded that I go to Washington occasionally. When I went and worked to the limit of my energy, I was increasingly conscious of the conviction that only a full-time Legislative Committee could protect labor's interests. Congressmen were not so much indifferent or hostile as they simply lacked knowledge of industrial problems and labor needs. It was not until there was an organized attempt to force Congress to oppose labor legislation that our legislative work became extremely difficult. . . .

The nineties brought no spectacular growth for the A. F. of L. There was steady progress, but it seemed painfully slow to my ardent hopes and boundless aspiration. I fairly yearned for a stronger labor movement in order that greater justice and opportunity might come into the lives of the world's workers. While we were sowing the seeds of trade unionism, we had to combat and supplant the forces of disintegration. The process was very like attempting to keep weeds out of a garden—the effort must be continuous or the weeds will choke the plants. . . .

Instinctively, I sought out those men for whom the trade union was a great ideal and those who were willing to spend and be spent in its service. Because I appealed to this side of their nature, I won groups of men to

As editor of the AFL's official publication, Gompers welcomed contributions from prominent journalists of the period—not the least of whom was Henry Demarest Lloyd. A native New Yorker and a graduate of Columbia Law School, Lloyd was on the staff of the Chicago *Tribune* from 1872 to 1885, and then was a nationally known free-lance writer until his death in 1903. A vigorous social reformer, Lloyd was a tireless and influential advocate of rights for trade unions, the individual consumer, and small business. Gompers wrote this particular letter in what was probably the busiest single year of Lloyd's life, for during 1894 he not only defended Eugene Debs's actions in the Pullman strike and ran unsuccessfully as a Populist candidate for Congress, but also published his most significant book, *Wealth Against Commonwealth,* a well-documented attack on industrial monopolies, notably on the methods then being used by the Standard Oil Company to eliminate virtually all its competition.

cooperation under Federation leadership. My method of appeal was very ingenuous. I loved men and liked to be with men. Indeed, I hated to be alone. Solitude had no joy or comfort for me. I wanted to share thought and action in order to get the fullest meaning out of them. A companion with the love of life in his heart added pleasure to the day's work. My life became an endless pilgrimage that carried me over the length and breadth of the country.

Between 1890 and 1900, obviously the primary thing to do first was sustained effort to gather into the folds of the Federation national labor organizations that were eligible to membership. . . . The following national organizations I helped to organize: barbers, boot and shoe workers, brewery workers, building service employes, carpenters, post-office clerks, retail clerks, electrical workers, steam and operating engineers, steel and copper plate engravers, federal employes, fire fighters, stationary firemen and oilers, garment workers, hod carriers, hotel and restaurant employes, meat cutters, musicians, oil field workers, painters, paper makers, powder and high-explosive workers, pulp and sulphite workers, quarry workers, street-railway men, stage employes, stove mounters, textile workers.

The United Garment Workers eked out a most precarious existence. . . . Time and time again the Federation loaned money to this organization. With the Garment Workers as with other organizations, after manifest inability to repay, these "loans" were finally canceled. Our Federation was poor. The organizations were poor. The wage earners were poor. No organization had a chance to grow if prospective members found they first had to pay off old debts before there was a chance to do constructive work. In that formative period I favored loaning money to needy organizations

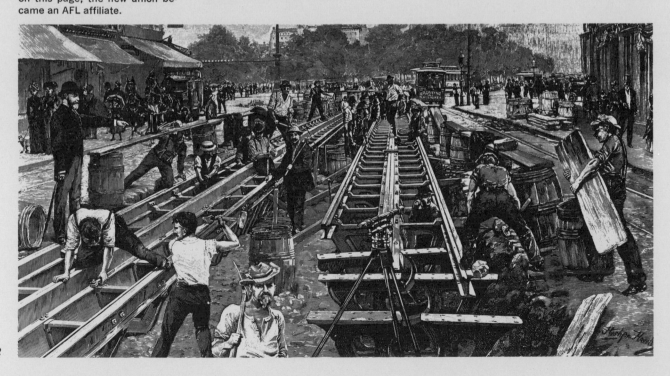

Workers lay cable along a new section of the Broadway streetcar line near New York's Union Square. In 1891, the year this drawing appeared in *Harper's Weekly*, the AFL resolved to bring the nation's streetcar workers together for the purpose "of forming the whole into one organization." In this the Federation set no mean task for itself: Two strong unions had been vying for dominance of the trade for years. At an 1892 conclave called by the AFL, one of the two unions agreed to a merger proposal, but the other stubbornly refused. Gompers, though disappointed, knew he would have to proceed with caution so that factional strife would not destroy both groups. It took two years for differences to be settled and a single union of streetcar workers to emerge. Then, as Gompers proudly notes on this page, the new union became an AFL affiliate.

and frequently held that writing off loans by changing them into donations was as necessary as bankruptcy laws to the business world.

Another organization which was a frequent pensioner and in which I had especial interest was the Miners. . . . In 1894 the United Mine Workers applied to the Executive Council for funds to keep the union alive. Although we had only $5,000, we contributed $1,000 to the organization and $500 to its journal. These are only instances of the sort of aid the Federation found it necessary to render in the early days.

Few organizations had sufficient funds to carry them through a critical emergency. They had to appeal for aid either from the Federation or from individual unions. The only way to build a Federation was to make it the agency for collective effort. Such an agency, when of a voluntary character, has to render service. Counsel and support constituted the service we offered. They have been of sufficient cohesive form to make of a rope of sand the strongest economic organization in the world.

*One thing Gompers wanted that "rope of sand" to provide was a living wage. Spelling out his famous slogan "More, more, more, now," he repeatedly hammered home—through speeches, editorials, and testimony to government commissions—his conviction that a living wage was no "benefit" but a birthright:*

■ To say that an industry does not admit, or will not allow, the payment of a living wage is a libel upon the human race. If this table is of any value, if a coat is of use to man, it is worth the payment of a living wage in its production. . . . The living wage I regard as one of the important contentions of labor. . . . A wage shall be paid to the laborer sufficient to maintain him and those dependent upon him in comparative comfort commensurate with his economic and social surroundings. . . .

Is there a limit to the employer's profits? Is not the rule "charge all the traffic will bear"? Where is the law of nature ordaining that employers shall have all the comforts and luxuries and the workmen the bare necessities, and not always even that? What is "too much"? . . . No industry, no country, has ever become great, or ever can become great, founded upon the poverty of its workers. . . .

The old theory that the selling price of an article shall determine the wages paid to the workmen is hollow, shallow, and unnatural. The order must be reversed and the first consideration in the selling price of an article must be a fair wage to labor. Wages must dominate prices, not prices dominate wages. It is a libel upon the human family to assert that in the production of an article for the use and benefit of man, a living wage can not be paid. . . . If an industrial reaction shall set in, would not a curtailment of the consuming power of the masses still further intensify the industrial depression?

*During the year (1894–1895) that followed Gompers' failure to be elected president of the AFL, he served as an organizer for the United Garment Workers. A good deal of the time was spent in the old Confederate states,*

W. E. B. Du Bois, who seldom viewed a situation the way Gompers did, was a sensitive intellectual whose Harvard doctoral dissertation on the slave trade became volume one of the Harvard Historical Studies. His fierce concern for Negro welfare continued during his teaching career, particularly at Atlanta University. In 1903 he clashed with Booker T. Washington, who wanted Negroes to concentrate on training for industrial jobs, while Du Bois believed in a "talented tenth" to assume leadership in a revolutionary era. Du Bois helped to found the National Association for the Advancement of Colored People (NAACP) in 1909, with himself as editor of its monthly, *The Crisis*. "The problem of the twentieth century," he said, "is the problem of the color line." But his leftist sympathies, rewarded by Russia's Lenin Peace Prize in 1959, alienated many Negroes who believed in integration into American society, and he had to leave the NAACP. He joined the Communist Party in 1961, lived as an expatriate in Ghana, and died in 1963 at the age of ninety-three.

*giving him a much more intimate view than he had previously experienced both of Negro segregation and of Jim Crow tactics in the South. Gompers made some efforts to help Negro workers, but his observations on the matter—including his flat rejection of "anything approaching social equality"—clearly indicate that he shared many of the anti-Negro prejudices of the period.*

■ I accepted the commission for the Garment Workers and started on a long trip through the Atlantic Coast states, the Gulf states, and up through Missouri and back to New York. That trip constituted my first real acquaintance with the South. It brought me face to face with facts which no intelligent person could ignore. Of course, I never entertained the thought of anything approaching social equality, but I did believe, and still to a very large extent believe, that equality of opportunity in the economic field should be accorded to colored workmen. At least, they ought to have the right to organize for their common protection and mutual interests, and every assistance should be given them by our labor movement in the furtherance of that purpose.

At the 1891 convention of the Federation held in Birmingham, we changed the hotel headquarters of the Federation in order that all delegates should be treated equally. There were several Negro delegates. It had been our pleasant custom to arrange an annual dinner as part of the convention program. This was turned into a reception in deference to local feeling. That Southern trip made me realize the difference between racial problems as theories and [as] practical situations.

*To some extent Gompers did try to eliminate the color line in labor matters. But he feared that Negro workers would merely let themselves be used as pawns of the employer in his effort to keep white workers in line, and that Negroes would willingly serve as scabs or strikebreakers to wreck efforts by member unions of the AFL to improve their pay or working conditions. Commenting on this possibility in 1897, Gompers declared that "if workmen are so lost to their own self-respect and interests as to turn the weight of their influence on the side of the capitalists as against that of the workers, these men are the enemies of progress, regardless of whether they be white or black, Caucasian or Mongolian." About this time, however, Negro draymen in New Orleans organized a union and tried to win a contract from their employers, who not only declined to negotiate a contract but would not even talk with the Negro spokesman. The AFL backed up these colored workers with a sympathy strike, and in 1899 Gompers testified as follows to the United States Industrial Commission in Washington:*

■ Organized labor of New Orleans went on a strike; every machinist went on a strike; every printer went on a strike; no paper made its appearance; the men working in the gashouses went on a strike and there was no illumination that night; the bakers went on a strike, and all other white workers went on a strike for the purpose of securing recognition of the colored workmen. . . . If there is any union of labor that says anything or takes any action [against] the colored man of the South, it is not because of his color; it is because he has, as an individual, or because they have generally in that trade, so conducted themselves as to be a continuous convenient whip placed in the hands of the employers to cow the white men and to compel them to accept abject conditions of labor.

*In 1900, in his report to the annual AFL convention that met at Louisville, Kentucky, Gompers elaborated further on the subject:*

■ Unless we shall give the Negro workers the opportunity to organize, and thus place them where they can protect and defend themselves against the rapacity and cupidity of their employers; unless we continue the policy of endeavoring to make friends of them, there can be no question but that they will not only be forced down in the economic scale and be used against any effort made by us for our economic and social advancement, but race prejudice will be made more bitter, to the injury of all.

*Despite these brave words, spoken in a former slave state, Gompers personally did much to formulate the rather suspicious AFL attitude toward Negro laborers. Unfortunately, many of the unions affiliated with the AFL have maintained this viewpoint ever since. In 1901, Gompers summed up both his positive and negative attitude on Negro workers as follows:*

The Knights of Labor claimed to be a basically non-discriminatory organization, treating its members equally regardless of race, religion, creed, or nationality. But Terence Powderly, who led the Knights for fourteen crucial years, shared some of Gompers' reticence in acknowledging the rights and status of Negroes. Indeed, Powderly leaned toward the "separate-but-equal" attitude. He once advised a fellow Knight to "organize a colored assembly in your city and turn all applicants of that kind over to them." And in 1886, just prior to a Knights of Labor convention in Richmond, he scotched plans that would have enabled a Negro delegate to introduce the principal speaker, Virginia's Governor Fitzhugh Lee. To Powderly, it seemed disrespectful for a Negro to introduce a Southern dignitary. So a compromise was worked out, the results of which can be seen in this contemporary drawing: The Negro delegate, Frank J. Farrell, is depicted introducing Powderly, who in turn is to introduce the bearded Governor Lee.

175

■ We have more than 700 volunteer organizers and a number of organizers under salary, among which are several who are devoting their time exclusively to the organization of the colored workers. This certainly should indicate not only our desire and interest, but also the work which is being accomplished. . . . The real difficulty in the matter is that the colored workers have allowed themselves to be used with too frequent telling effect by their employers as to injure the cause and interests of themselves as well as of the white workers. They have too often allowed themselves to be regarded as "cheap men," and all realize that "cheap men" are an impediment to the attainment of the workers' just rights, and the progress of civilization.

*These circumstances explain why—in Gompers' time and since—Negro workers have never composed more than a minute fraction of the AFL's membership—in brutal fact, a far smaller percentage of the AFL than Negroes represent in America's total population. Nevertheless, Gompers had a much higher opinion of Negroes than he did of Chinese. The first paragraph of the excerpt below tells of a visit he made to San Francisco in 1891; the second paragraph contains comments he made in the early 1900's; the last paragraph summarizes his views on Chinese immigration:*

■ I made a trip through Chinatown—not the especially prepared route for tourists. It was an awful experience with all its hideousness. I had read Dante's *Inferno*, but Chinatown seemed to me a greater horror with its reeking smells, the human wrecks, gambling, and mad licentiousness. The picture burned into my mind that night came to me vividly throughout future years when Chinese immigration was under consideration. The Cigar Makers took me to Chinese cigar factories. I had made an investigation of tenement-house cigar factories, but they were sanitary in comparison with the Chinese places, two or three stories underground. . . .

Never in the history of the world have Chinese gone to any country in any considerable numbers without one of two things occurring—first, that the Chinaman has dominated, or he has been driven out by force. The Chinaman is a cheap man. . . . The American people do not object to the Chinese because they are Chinese; they know from their own experience, as well as from the experience of ages of the people of other countries, that the Chinese coolies and laborers can not assimilate with our race; that their civilization, and ours as well, can not coexist; that the physical condition, the standard of life, the progress of our people will not only be endangered but undermined and destroyed. . . .

I did not believe that our national interests would be furthered by granting . . . unrestricted right to import cheap labor that could not be Americanized and could not be taught to render the same intelligent efficient service as was supplied by American workers. I did not believe that cheap labor contributed to national welfare and development. I gave much time and thought to immigration problems and to efforts to secure constructive immigration policies and the enforcement of the law excluding

Chinese. . . . Among the great economic and social problems which gripped me was Chinese coolie immigration to the United States. . . . It is my desire to state emphatically that I have no prejudice against the Chinese people. On the contrary, having some understanding of their history and the philosophy of their early sages, I have profound respect for the Chinese nation. I have always opposed Chinese immigration not only because of the effect of Chinese standards of life and work but because of the racial problem created when Chinese and white workers were brought into the close contact of living and working side by side.

*Gompers, though himself both an immigrant and a Jew, did not hold a consistently favorable outlook toward either his fellow immigrants or members of other minorities. He despised the fact that immigrant workers, most of them unskilled, were expanding America's work force, competing for jobs— at generally lower wages—with skilled workers who belonged to unions. He explained his feelings, in somewhat lofty terms, in a portion of his report to the AFL's 1891 convention:*

■ I view the immigrant problem not from the mere selfish standpoint of our own protection, but I am persuaded that it not only tends to destroy the independence, progress, and advancement of our people, but also is an efficient means by which the effete institutions of some of the European countries are perpetuated and thus economic, political, and social reforms postponed or avoided.

One immigrant who consistently displayed a more favorable attitude toward his fellow immigrants (see pages 94–95) than did Gompers was Joseph Keppler (above). He came to America from Austria in 1867 (four years after Gompers), became the principal artist of *Frank Leslie's Illustrated Weekly,* and later published the lusty humor weekly *Puck.* One of Keppler's own powerful cartoons for *Puck* appears at left: A Roman Catholic prelate blesses angry strikers as they toss stones at a worker who, having refused to strike, now lies injured in the street. Firmly Democratic in politics, Keppler aimed venom-tipped shafts at Republican leaders. He was prolabor, but he believed the advocates of violence were dragging down the cause of the workingman. A perfectionist whose standards of draftsmanship were unusually high, he advised one would-be cartoonist: "Draw cigarbox labels; they pay."

*Gompers' lack of sympathy for those who, like himself, were foreign-born resulted from the fact that he never considered himself a foreigner. He had immigrated as a lad—with English as his native tongue—and had learned a trade while still a teen-ager. Thus, with little difficulty, he had become assimilated. The immigrants he writes about in his memoirs were not so fortunate. Coming from vastly different cultures, they were unable to adjust so quickly to the radical change in environment or to the urgent need to find their place in America's "classless" but clearly stratified society.*

■ In my boyhood home in London, emigration to the New World was regarded as a very special opportunity for those who were able to make the journey. We heard that there was land in plenty for everyone, work in manifold abundance for everybody. . . . When I reached the New World, never for a moment did I think of myself as an alien. I spoke the same language as the citizens of the United States, though around about our little home in Attorney Street were to be heard many more different languages than could have been found in East Side London. Instinctively, I thought of those speaking other languages as the foreigners. As for myself, I felt identified with the people of my new home and it was without a question that I accepted American customs and American institutions and the American life. To my mind the foreigner was the one who did not identify himself with American life and purposes.

So when I went to work in David Hirsch's shop, I found myself surrounded by fellow workers who spoke little but German. However, I never thought of them as foreigners because they had identified themselves with the effort to work out the problems of our industry and participated in the common life of the city. But when the Bohemians began to come to New York in large numbers and allowed themselves to be used by the employers to build up the tenement-house factory system which threatened to submerge standards of life and work that we had established, I felt that those tenement workers were foreigners. The first step in Americanizing them was to bring them to conform to American standards of work which was a stepping-stone to American standards of life.

The next big industrial problem in immigration with which I came in contact resulted from the enormous influx of Jewish workers into New York in the eighties. As the volume of these workers increased, they could no longer be absorbed into existing industrial opportunities without disturbing the balances in industrial forces.

I became interested in the racial problem in organization. Beginning in the early eighties, the number of Jewish workers from Russia and other Eastern European countries greatly increased. Very few of the Jews who came had industrial training. Those who did were handicapped by not speaking English. Consequently, those immigrants crowded into any available employment where training and language offered the fewest obstacles. They were strangers in a new land. They had to provide subsistence for tomorrow in whatever opportunity it could be found. They crowded into unskilled callings and worked at starvation wages. They

IMPORTED. DUTY FREE,
by
TRUST, MONOPOLY & CO.
TO COMPETE WITH
AMERICAN LABOR.

Labor's rising hostility toward "imported" workers in American industry is reflected in this drawing of an unskilled man coming down a ship's gangplank. Labor was particularly incensed when immigrants were hired during depression years or were brought in as strikebreakers. A typical incident occurred in 1875, when an American coal-mine operator armed some Italian immigrants, ordering them to shoot any strikers who came near. The immigrants killed two men and were jailed for murder; the mine operator was let off with a mere five-dollar fine. Union pressure bore fruit in 1885: Congress passed the Alien Contract Act, which made it "unlawful for any person, company, partnership, or corporation . . . to assist or encourage the importation of any alien or aliens."

undermined standards and labor organizations, but they were under the urge of dire necessity. They were the products of decades of persecution. Even trades that had previously not been organized, under the need of protection against foreign workers, began to struggle to establish an agency to maintain definite standards.

We found it practically impossible to organize these Jewish workers in unions with other nationalities and, in fact, very hard to get a language by which we could give them an understanding of unionism. . . . Despite many difficulties, we organized several Hebrew trade unions. There was a racial emotionalism and aspiration that both helped and hindered unionism. The Jews were fairly ravenous for education and eager for personal advancement, so that all industrial work was merely a stepping-stone to professional or managerial positions. We formed unions of cap makers, chorus singers, cutters, cloak makers and others. Individual unions fluctuated sharply, but the union movement grew steadily. I gave a great deal of time to this work and finally assisted in organizing the United Hebrew Trades—a policy that was theoretically bad but practically necessary and has eminently justified itself.

By the beginning of the nineties, the racial problem in the labor movement was beginning to assume serious proportions. Our problem was part of the larger national problem, for the majority of immigrants no longer came from Western Europe, where language, customs, and industrial organization were similar to those of the United States, but from the countries of Eastern Europe where lower standards of life and work prevailed. As these immigrants flooded basic industries, they threatened to destroy our standards.

I approached the immigration problem with the somewhat mixed feelings of one who had been an immigrant himself. Grateful that no barriers prevented my coming to this new country, I have always felt that restricting opportunities for others is a grave responsibility; yet as the number of immigrants rapidly increased and the admixture of various races was too rapid for assimilation, I could not escape the conclusion that some way must be found to safeguard America. America is the product of the daring, the genius, the idealism of those who left homes and kindred to settle in the new land. It is an ideal typifying a haven and an opportunity. In the early days, boundless and undeveloped resources made possible and expedient a policy of stimulating immigration. It was not until industrialism developed and there were evidences that the newer immigration was not being assimilated that as a nation we began to consider policies of regulation. The labor movement was among the first organizations to urge such policies. Our first proposal was the contract labor measure under which we hoped to prevent employers from importing strikebreakers or workers to lower the standards by overcrowding what was termed the labor market.

As New York was the port of entry for a great majority of immigrants, it was there that we felt most keenly the seriousness of developing constructive immigration policies. It was my custom to keep in close touch

John McBride, the only man to unseat Gompers as president of the AFL, was a forceful Ohioan who at age nine went to work in the coal fields and eventually headed the United Mine Workers. Like Gompers, he came up the hard way, but he lacked his rival's canny approach to labor problems. Gompers knew the limits of the AFL presidency; McBride rashly tried to extend its powers. Gompers would use cajolery to bring restive unions into line; McBride, instead, would bully them. For example, he deeply offended the Brewery Workers by rejecting a request to answer criticism published in the *American Federationist*. When the union challenged the rejection, McBride hotly declared that the union chief had assigned "as reasons for the action . . . causes having no existence in fact, but which had their sources in your imagination and distorted brain." Stung by this retort, delegates from the brewers' union, who had once backed McBride, joined the slim majority that voted Gompers back into office in 1895.

with the affairs of the Immigration Bureau [in] New York City. I was able to give them information which it would have been difficult if not impossible for them to have secured otherwise. . . . The steel industry was among the first to inaugurate deliberately the practice of importing cheap labor in order to maintain low wages, thereby assuring a surplus of workers to replace those who became Americanized. . . . When I was in Pittsburgh at the headquarters of the Amalgamated Steel Association during a strike in the nineties, I met a young Italian, Saverio Merlino, unusually intelligent and alert and interested in the welfare of his fellow countrymen. I talked over the immigration situation with him and pointed out the necessity for safeguarding the welfare of American as well as Italian workers.

In addition to the difficulties which confronted all immigrants, the Italians had to combat a system under which they were exploited by their own fellow countrymen. Italians with some knowledge of American conditions and with some influence and financial backing would offer to secure for Italian immigrants employment under paternalistic supervision. These men were called *padrones*. They made contracts with employers in this country to supply labor. The padrone was to collect and pay wages to his group of workers and, of course, took his fee before distributing compensation to the immigrants. Vicious exploitation and the worst sort of graft resulted. As the majority of the Italian immigrants were illiterate, the padrone's grip was very strong. . . .

I realized that continual progress in organizing the wage earners of the country involved the education and Americanization of the hordes of immigrants coming through our ports of entry. I did not believe that our national interests would be furthered by granting to the trusts unrestricted right to import cheap labor that could not be Americanized and could not be taught to render the same intelligent, efficient service as was supplied by American workers. I did not believe that cheap labor contributed to national welfare and development.

## ARBITRATION—AND ANGLING FOR VOTES

*Gompers took great pains on many occasions to emphasize that he never—no, never—did anything to affect the outcome of an AFL election or to win votes for himself. His friends found this assertion amusing, since Gompers hated to lose out on anything, especially anything that directly concerned him, and was exceedingly adept at the discreet wire-pulling that would bring victory either to himself or a cause he favored. In 1895 he was anxious to accomplish two goals —his return to the AFL presidency he had lost to John McBride the year before, and defeat of compulsory arbitration, a principle that McBride had strongly favored. The first paragraph below is from a letter Gompers wrote in 1895 to George Perkins, head of the Cigar Makers' Union, who had begun to line up votes for him and was resoundingly successful in this effort. The rest of the excerpt is from Gompers' memoirs, written many years later, and provides some ironic contrasts with what actually occurred.*

■ I am frank to say to you that I should esteem it a pleasure to be again the president of the Federation. . . . The movement as I have often said has become part of my very self, my yearnings, hopes—everything. . . . I fall entirely into your way of thinking on this matter. . . . If you can show to a number of delegates that in the interest of our cause they ought to vote for me, I am sure that you will do so and I shall appreciate your action beyond measure. Heretofore I even forbade that but . . . I now can see my error, more especially in view of what I am reliably informed [my opponent, John McBride] . . . is doing. . . .

The Federation convention at the end of 1895 was held in New York City. During that year . . . President McBride had publicly and consistently advocated compulsory arbitration "as a settlement of all labor troubles." To this policy the trade-union movement was emphatically and decidedly opposed. McBride's position on this question alienated a large number of trade unionists from him.

I had not the slightest idea of again being a candidate for the presidency of the Federation. With the work which I had done during the year, including newspaper and magazine articles, my income was larger than the salary which the Federation paid its president. I had not deviated from my principles; on the contrary, I had large opportunities of service in the cause of labor and, in addition, I had the privilege of being more at home. But I was nonetheless, as much as anyone, opposed to allowing compulsory arbitration to constitute one of the tenets of the American labor movement and, in fact, prepared a resolution which I introduced in the convention emphasizing our Federation's opposition to compulsory arbitration which, by the way, the convention adopted. However, during the early days of the New York convention, a number of representative men came to me and urged my acceptance of the candidacy for the presidency of the American Federation of Labor. I expostulated with them against their proposal. They finally prevailed upon me, stating that there was no one who stood so unequivocally against compulsion, and that I was, therefore, necessarily the logical candidate in making the contest. Finally, I yielded, and at the convention was elected to the presidency over McBride who had occupied that position one year.

Acceptance of the call to further official duty meant something of the nature of sacrifice to both my family and me. When I went west to take charge of the Indianapolis office, January 1, 1896, I did not feel enough permanency in the relationship to warrant the expense of moving my family to that city. . . . When I reached Indianapolis, I found the . . . work had dwindled distressingly. . . . There was one stenographer who apologized when I began dictating the mail, explaining she had had no dictation for considerable time. . . . McBride was as genial a man as I have ever known and had a most winning voice, but he shrank from hard work. Federation work was always of secondary importance to him. . . . I planned to concentrate first upon organizing channels of communication from my office and began working with intense energy to recover the ground lost by the Federation during the previous year. Since I had no home obligations

The labor philosophy expressed by Gompers on these pages was keenly challenged by one of his most vociferous rivals, William D. Haywood. Called "Big Bill" because of his height and girth, Haywood was a free-thinking radical whose one aim in life, he said, was to liberate the workingman from the tyranny of machines and their owners. Blinded in one eye by a childhood accident, he accepted violence like a scarred warhorse. Strikes, protest demonstrations, riots, prison cells—all knew his presence as he pursued his cause. Born in Utah in 1869, he went to work at fifteen in the Nevada metal mines, and early became a disgruntled unionist. He played a key role in organizing the Industrial Workers of the World, and himself became the IWW's rallying voice. He aimed the Wobblies' "One Big Union" appeal toward unskilled workers and against the "pure and simple" trade unionism Gompers personified. Haywood was a dazzling orator whose following was as loyal when he was in jail as when he was on the podium. For years he was the hope of the downtrodden, but rank-and-file Wobblies turned against him in 1921, when he fled to Russia. He had jumped bail after being convicted on charges of interfering with America's war effort in 1918. He left behind a faction-torn movement that vitiated itself in resisting a Communist takeover. Big Bill himself died in Russia in 1928.

I worked unrestricted by normal customs. As a result, along in January I became very ill. I never suffered more acute misery in my life. There was not a portion of my body in which I could take comfort. After I had been ill for several weeks, Mrs. Gompers became too anxious to stay in New York and came on to Indianapolis where she nursed me until I was able to move around again.

One of the first letters I wrote after assuming direction at Indianapolis was to my friend Jack O'Sullivan, and in it I told him of my hopes and expectations to do better work than ever I had done in all my life. Within a few days afterwards the news of my serious illness was telegraphed over the country and I received a letter from Jack in which he said: "And this is what you call giving the best that is in you, you mean the worst. If you are about to peg out you should do it quickly, turn up your toes, and not keep an anxious public waiting to hear of your finality. . . ."

This letter proved to be the turning point which visibly marked my starting on the road to recovery. Probably, my intense enjoyment and hearty laughter brought a readjustment of the internal mechanism. At any rate, I was shortly again in the office taking up the work of correspondence and travel. Mrs. Gompers returned to the family in New York and I was again left to devote all of my time to the Federation. . . .

In developing a human organization like the Federation, office work could only supplement personal contacts and the spoken message, and before long I found myself spending fully half my time in traveling. Organization was spurred on by contact and both oral and printed appeals and argument.

The reports of the year's work I carried to Cincinnati for the approval or disapproval of those whom I had served, wondering a bit what their verdict would be and half hoping to be released from the responsibility of office. The convention was interesting although turbulent. . . . The result was the complete justification for my course by unanimously reelecting me to office. . . . The convention moved Federation headquarters to Washington, D.C.

*Gompers' contempt for compulsory arbitration, which had helped propel him back into the AFL presidency, was hardly modified by the passing of time; he campaigned vigorously against that concept for most of his life in labor. Here are his remarks on the subject at the AFL's 1900 convention:*

■ It is submitted that the very terms, "arbitration" and "compulsory," stand in direct opposition to each other. Arbitration implies the voluntary action of two parties of diverse interests submitting to disinterested parties the question in dispute, or likely to come into dispute. Compulsion by any process, and particularly by the power of government, is repugnant to the principle as well as the policy of arbitration. If organized labor should fail to appreciate the danger involved in the proposed schemes of so-called compulsory arbitration, and consent to enactment of a law providing for its enforcement, there would be reintroduced the denial of the right of the workmen to strike in defense of their interests, and the enforcement by government of specific personal service and labor. In other words, under a law based upon compulsory arbitration, if an award were made against labor, no matter how unfair or unjust, and brought about by any means, no matter how questionable, we would be compelled to work or to suffer the state penalty, which might be either mulcting in damages, or going to jail; not one scintilla of distinction, not one jot removed from slavery.

It is strange how much men desire to compel other men to do by law. What we aim to achieve is freedom through organization. Arbitration is only possible when voluntary. It never can be successfully carried out unless the parties to a dispute or controversy are equals, or nearly equals, in power to protect and defend themselves, or to inflict injury upon the other.

The more thoroughly the workers are organized in their local and national unions, and federated by common bond, policy, and polity, the better shall we be able to avert strikes and lockouts, secure conciliation, and if necessary, arbitration; but it must be voluntary arbitration, or there should be no arbitration at all.

It is our aim to avoid strikes; but I trust that the day will never come when the workers of our country will have so far lost their manhood and independence as to refuse to strike, regardless of the provocation, or to surrender their right to strike. We seek to prevent strikes, but we realize that the best means by which they can be averted is to be the better prepared for them. We endeavor to prevent strikes; but there are some conditions far worse than strikes, and among them is a demoralized, degraded and debased manhood.

*Gompers also opposed the enactment of any law that would impose mandatory restrictions on workers. Thus he harshly criticized proposed legislation calling for the delay of a strike until a public inquiry—and an evaluation—could be made. His feelings are summed up in excerpts from editorials he wrote for the* American Federationist *in 1913 and 1916:*

■ Laws must not invade personal rights and liberty. . . . The free man's ownership of himself involves his labor power. In fact the only difference between a free man and a slave is the right to sell or withhold his labor power. This precious right must be cherished and guarded against all invasions. . . . When any workmen or number of workmen are compelled by law to work one month, one week, one day, or one hour against their own volition, then there has ensued and been established slavery. . . .

Compulsory investigation legislation is identical in principle with compulsory arbitration; the difference is only one of degree. Compulsory arbitration makes strikes illegal and strikers criminal for all time instead of for a definite period. . . . Under either, men who refuse to work for any reason, who refuse to perform involuntary servitude, may be fined and imprisoned. . . . Stripped of all sophistry and all verbiage, compulsory investigation or compulsory arbitration resolve themselves into compulsory service.

## A FIGHTER FOR FREE EDUCATION

Hamilton Holt, later renowned as an educator, was a journalist when Gompers met him at the Social Reform Club. After graduating from Yale and studying sociology and economics at Columbia, Holt edited *The Independent,* a national weekly, from 1897 to 1921. Holt served with the League of Nations Non-Partisan Association, the World Federalists, and the Woodrow Wilson Foundation. From 1925 he was president of Rollins College, Florida, where he reduced the number of examinations, replaced crowded lectures with informal seminars, and allowed students a voice in the hiring of professors. The American Association of University Professors criticized him, but he stuck to his principle that education needed new methods to bring faculty and students together. "I have never met a student I didn't get something valuable from," he said. Holt retired from Rollins in 1949, two years before his death.

*Gompers believed in the fundamental importance of education to the advancement of democracy, and he was convinced that free public education provided the key to the general enlightenment of working men and women. The first paragraph below is from a speech he made to the National Educational Association in 1916, and the remainder is from editorials he wrote on the subject:*

■ Education is an attitude toward life—an ability to see and understand problems and to utilize information and forces for the best solution of our problems. New information and wider knowledge make possible the maintenance of this attitude as long as life shall last. . . . The noblest mission of the schools is to teach the worth of a man or a woman, to teach the value of the individual and his life. This teaching must be supplemented with practical knowledge that enables each to realize his fullest possibilities. Education must be founded on truths that break down insidious and unjustified distinctions between the kinds of work by which individuals express themselves. . . . An education that glorifies the creative ability of the individual—his labor—is injecting a revolutionary idea into all our philosophy of life. Such a plan of education will bring into the spirit of our nation a force that will make for larger freedom, for greater progress and effectiveness. It will be in direct opposition to that education which promotes docility, submissiveness, conformity. It will make possible for each to stamp his life work with all of the artistic imagery of which his nature is capable. . . .

The whole problem of progress is fundamentally educational in character. The problems of today and the future will tax the ability of our citizens even though equipped with the best education which our schools can afford. Within our republic every individual should possess the rudiments of education with which he can train himself to a higher education, if denied other opportunities and assistance. To withhold opportunities for education for the least among our people is a crime committed against our republic. . . .

The whole purpose of education is to develop the best men and women to be the most high-minded, resourceful, and effective citizens of our republic. Upon the citizens depend the destiny of the nation and the contributions to institutions of liberty and progress. Citizens under a democratic government must be able and competent to express and maintain their ideals.

*Gompers was what Thomas Jefferson would have termed a true natural aristocrat who rose to the top by diligent application of his own talents. His memoirs reflect a lifelong regret that his own formal education had been limited; as he put it: "My desire to assist in promoting agencies for continuous education is an outgrowth of my own difficulties." His detailed description of the several aspects of education that immediately and deeply concerned him ex-*

*presses not only his genuine enthusiasm for the subject but also his frequent tendency to lavish undue praise when assessing the achievements of the labor movement:*

■ It would be difficult to overestimate the educational work which has been done within the trade-union movement. That was an undertaking in organization—or creation if you please. . . . We began with chaos and worked toward orderly thinking. In those days, terms, theories, methods, were unstandardized. Thought on labor problems was a miscellaneous conglomeration. All who had interest to contribute met on the same forum and we talked and worked together. No lines of orthodoxy were drawn. . . . This grew out of experience crystallized through conference, friendly discussion, debate both written and oral. In those days I frequently wrote out my conclusion on a subject after many discussions. That process helped me to crystallize my own thought. While working in the shop, if any thought came to me as a result of reading or any current of thought, I would stop and make a memorandum on slips of paper which I kept for this purpose. It was good that piecework prevailed in my trade, for I doubt if on any other basis any employer would have had patience with my notebook habit.

Looking back upon that work with a perspective that indicates relationships, I can see that we were developing the discipline of the trade-union movement, a discipline that has been more influential in educating millions of Americans who work for wages than any other single agency. It is an education that reaches millions of the citizens and their families. It makes for stability in industrial life, as well as in all other relations. We do not always realize that some of the most vital problems are those of the work life. Any agency that gives light upon these problems is performing an educational function of first-order importance. The trade union has been a constructive agency in adult education, focusing attention on the human element in many big social issues and problems. It has performed what is truly public service in interpreting social and industrial problems. Since the labor movement is a voluntary institution, it depends upon educational methods to attain its ends. I take great pride in having helped to develop this understanding and method of the American trade union.

I have also been associated with organizations for more formal educational work. One of the first of these was the Ethical Culture Society which was founded by Felix Adler, a brilliant young thinker. . . . I joined this little group. . . . We were trying to work out ethical standards that would have meaning in the affairs of everyday life—that was what appealed to me. . . .

A somewhat different organization was the Social Reform Club of New York City, which was an outgrowth of the Henry George movement. The club was composed of trade unionists and others interested in the improvement of the conditions of wage earners. It represented a genuine effort of all interested in the labor movement from various approaches, to unite in practical work. It was a nonpartisan body, desirous of helping the public

Jacob A. Riis, who worked with Gompers on social reform, came to America from Denmark in 1870. As an outstanding reporter and photographer, he helped to clean up noisome tenements. Personally and politically closer to Theodore Roosevelt than was Gompers, Riis wrote a campaign biography of T. R. in 1904. In turn, T. R. called Riis "New York's most useful citizen" and, after his death in 1914, "the ideal American citizen." New York City contains many memorials to him.

Gompers rejoiced at finding, in the Ethical Culture Society, a philosophy that made morality rather than theology the key to the good life. Its guiding genius, Felix Adler (above), put duty to man ahead of duty to God and "deed over creed." The son of a rabbi, Adler came to New York from Germany as a young boy. He founded his group in 1876, opened one of America's first free public kindergartens, and publicized his concepts in books that have remained influential.

*185*

The Social Reform Club, which Gompers discusses on this page, attracted William S. Rainsford (above), an Irishman who became an Episcopal minister and who preached the social gospel. When he came to St. George's Church in New York in 1883, Rainsford demanded open pews, full authority, and a fund of $10,000 a year for parish work. Vestryman J. P. Morgan replied, "Done!" And Rainsford stayed until 1906, by which time he had increased the congregation to four thousand. He and Morgan got along (except for one falling-out over the size of the vestry) despite Morgan's distaste for Rainsford's liberal theology. Doubting the Last Judgment, Rainsford told one Town Hall audience: "Banish the supernatural!" He guided his church into social work, called for higher wages and better working conditions, founded trade schools and summer camps, and supported birth control. But in 1907 he prompted Morgan, a director of the Metropolitan Opera, to force the withdrawal of *Salome,* which he considered licentious. Rainsford was also a big-game hunter; he shot bears in the West and lions in Africa, and arranged Theodore Roosevelt's notable 1909 safari. Rainsford was still shooting pheasant in 1932, only a year before his death.

to understand the union label, trade-union activity, and social reforms. The club constituted a common center for the consideration of the next step or steps in social reform. It was the regulation that wage earners should constitute fifty percent of the club. I served on the Advisory Board with Lyman Abbott, Felix Adler, Wm. Dean Howells . . . and Albert Shaw. Among those most active in this work were Ernest O. Crosby . . . W. S. Rainsford . . . Hamilton Holt, Father Thomas J. Ducey, Jacob Riis. . . . I early advocated in the Social Reform Club a plan for providing free evening lecture courses in the various schools, when not otherwise in use. We helped secure the law enacted in 1888 which authorized provision for the employment of competent lecturers to deliver addresses on physical sciences and other subjects in schools in the evenings for the benefit of working men and women. We hoped to make schools civic centers or public forums. . . .

It took considerable of a fight to open the schools for the use of the community. However, we interested the New York Board of Trade in the project and nominal approval was secured. Then the Social Reform Club appointed a committee of which I was a member to see that the plan was carried out. We succeeded in demonstrating the benefits of such courses in such a convincing way that the Board of Education extended plans until courses were given in all the schools upon various subjects, natural sciences, mechanics, labor, political theory, sociology, art, economics, literature, etc. . . . The club took an active part in shaping public opinion on Employers' Liability and Workmen's Compensation. . . .

Within my lifetime has come a change in the "dismal science," economics. It is abandoning the practice of basing its theories upon abstractions and "economic man" and has been substituting individuals at real work. In this change, labor problems have found a place in college and university studies. With the increase of such courses, invitations to address classes and groups of college students have increased steadily. There is hardly an important college or university to which I have not accepted at least one invitation. To many that were close by . . . I have gone as frequently as other duties would permit. I have always felt that if the labor movement were understood it would find sympathetic support. College-trained students generally find places of control in the outside world; hence, I have felt that organized labor ought to do all within its power to help to educate this group. For this reason I have been glad to respond to approaches from individual students and professors. . . . I have made it a special point to see that Federation literature was furnished to college libraries.

Somewhere in the nineties I received an invitation from Professor Jeremiah Jenks to deliver a lecture to his students on some phase of the labor movement. Professor Jenks was teaching economics in Cornell University. Later, I was asked to deliver a series on the history and the philosophy of the labor movement. The lectures were delivered after the regular hours for university classes, late in the afternoon. The result was very gratifying. Attendance, of course, was voluntary, but during the week attendance grew steadily from about four hundred to approximately fifteen hundred on the closing day. At the close of the course there was opportunity for questions and answers. A reflection of Professor Jenks expressed at that time has often recurred to me as I have faced similar student groups. "Mr. Gompers," he said, "you cannot imagine now what this service will mean. These young men will become employers of large numbers of people, members of boards of directors, superintendents, engineers, foremen, and master mechanics, and what you have presented to them will in some degree modify their thinking and administrative decisions."

*Despite his devotion to his family and his absorption in complex labor affairs, Gompers found time to indulge his passion for the stage—especially, grand opera. He not only enjoyed going to the theater but also being with theater people—actors as well as singers—and from what he has written, it would seem that, reciprocally, his favorite performers very much enjoyed being with him. The passage ends with a moving tribute to his daughter Sadie.*

■ My father and every one of my paternal ancestors were passionately fond of music. When we were still living in London and I was a mere child, I remember that my father frequently borrowed money in order to go to the Italian opera. He had an excellent tenor voice, and even until a year or so before his death at the age of ninety-two, he frequently sang the old-time ballads which were favorites of his, and his voice rang out clear and strong.

In the London house where we lived in Fort Street the Lellyveld family that lived on the third floor all had good voices. The boys of the family, who were approximately my age, sang with their father and an uncle who lived near by. The boys often asked me to join them in singing songs in which we arranged ourselves for a quartette, and now and then one of us sang solo parts. I never had a tenor voice and after thirteen my voice developed into a pretty fair baritone and then bass. I sang at home and in any company which we had or in which I happened to be. My emotional nature exceeded my power of expression in the early days. All that was repressed found release in music. . . .

The Italian operas have always been my favorites because of their distinctively lyric quality. The first Wagnerian I heard was *Die Walküre* and I found myself so irritated with some of the orchestral parts that I could not enjoy the power of the music. . . . Later . . . I caught the genius of Wagner's instrumentation and the daring of his composition and I thoroughly enjoyed the opera. However, the Italian opera never lost first place in my preferences. But I loved them all—*William Tell, Tristan and Isolde, La Tosca, Norma,* and even *Cavalleria Rusticana.* These greatest operas sung by the most superb artists—I heard them all: Wachtel, the great German tenor with his extraordinary power and range; Scotti, my favorite baritone; Jean de Reszke; and the incomparable Caruso. Later, I met many of them as my work widened my sphere of contacts.

Although Gompers disliked ethnic divisions in the labor movement, he appreciated the work of Abraham Cahan (above), whom he termed "father, counselor, and spiritual advisor" of the Jewish immigrants on the Lower East Side. Cahan, fleeing the Czarist police, arrived in New York in 1882, attended grade school as an adult to learn English, and became a journalist. He helped to found the *Jewish Daily Forward* and became its editor in 1902. By substituting human interest for arid socialist polemics, he raised the circulation to 225,000, highest for a Yiddish newspaper. The colorful Bundle of Letters page was the result of his editorial plea: "Send us your life stories." Supporting labor, he attacked low wages and sweatshops. However, during a garment strike in 1913, the *Forward* urged a settlement, and its windows were smashed by angry strikers who thought the newspaper was betraying their interests. Cahan came out and told them: "It's like a husband who comes home angry. . . . Will he go into any other house to smash the dishes? No, he goes to his own home. This is your home, for the *Forward* is your paper." The strikers then cheered for him. Cahan continued to defend the cause of labor until his death in 1951.

He was short and stout, and it took him years to refine his Neapolitan accent. But to opera lovers the tenor voice of the age was undeniably Enrico Caruso's. From his Metropolitan Opera debut in 1903, when he was thirty, until his death in 1921, he dazzled New Yorkers by singing more than thirty leading roles, among which was the passionate Don José in *Carmen* (above). He hardly looked the part, but the soprano Lotte Lehmann wrote of one of these performances: "His complete abandonment . . . communicated itself to his audience, breathless under his spell." He was not only gifted musically; he was also an accomplished caricaturist. When he was restless he would sketch whoever happened to be nearby, capturing both likeness and personality in revealing strokes. Gompers and others numbered among their prized possessions the caricatures that Caruso had dashed off during rehearsals and interviews.

I spoke at many meetings at night and it was my custom never to eat a meal before speaking. After my meetings usually some of my pals went with me to a restaurant where we could enjoy a meal with the gratifying consciousness of having completed the day's work. Many singers and actors had the same habit, and as the number of restaurants serving at that hour were somewhat restricted, I met many of them as we had our early morning meal. There was an Italian restaurant to which I sometimes went which Caruso habitually patronized. The restaurant served spaghetti à la Caruso which I often enjoyed while talking with Caruso. No king was ever treated more royally than was Caruso by the Italians in America. Brignoli, the lyric tenor, I knew also. His voice was liquid music though he was like a totem pole on the stage. Bonci, a younger tenor, sang with Sembrich in her farewell appearance. One night they were singing *La Bohème*, an opera that I loved. The music was glorious. At the end of the first act my friend came to me and said: "There is a boxing match tonight that is worth seeing. Let's get out of this damned music and see something real." In loyalty to my friend I left grand opera for the prizefight. However, I can enjoy both.

Though superficially there seems to be a wide chasm between a grand opera singer and a labor leader, yet in the last analysis we both are ministering to the souls of men and we have to understand and sympathize with their deepest experiences if we would interpret them to themselves. Beauty in life is found in widely different languages and aspects. Beauty is only the establishment of relations of harmony so that the soul may express itself. But as between grand opera and the crude raw materials and emotions of human life which have been part of my daily experience for years, the wonder and the beauty of art is overshadowed by the glory of that in which I have participated. I have known acute suffering of mind and body, but if I had the power and the opportunity I would not change my life lest I lose something of completeness of vision and understanding. Life has never been tame for me. I have natural safeguards against getting into ruts because I cannot work without the inspiration of feeling. This personal characteristic keeps my mind alert to human and dramatic values of happenings—a faculty that serves me in timing speech and deed. It has also made me keenly appreciative of drama as interpreted on the stage.

Only difference in rhythm and range of tone distinguishes the opera from the drama in which I also find joy and inspiration. The great actors, like the great singers, I saw first from the gallery. Edwin Booth, E. L. Davenport, Lawrence Barrett, Mary McVicar I saw in Shakespearian rôles. This group had an interesting practice of exchanging characters which added interest. Eleonora Duse, Richard Mansfield, Henry Irving, Ellen Terry, Mary Anderson are among the great actors who thrilled me with their fine understanding of human nature.

Now and then whimsical fate brought me into competition with some of my friends of the dramatic and lecture world. I remember one night after I had spoken in a town in Indiana, I was in a restaurant getting my dinner after my meeting when Ethel Barrymore entered. She requested me to come over to her table where we talked. She had played to a small house while I had had a large crowd.

When Colonel Ingersoll and I spoke in Hammond, Indiana, on the same night, he spoke to an almost empty house. It was a pity, for the lecture was an excellent one—I had heard it the night before. Ingersoll told me that in the future he would avoid engagements competing with my mass meetings. A bit later I was amused to see in Elwood, Indiana, where I was speaking, notices of John L. Sullivan's management that the boxing match would take place after my mass meeting. . . .

After the organization of the Metropolitan Grand Opera Company and the completion of that Opera House in 1883, the production of operas was more beautiful, but also more expensive. . . . A personal friend of mine who was connected with the management always pressed complimentary tickets upon me and hospitably gave me admission to the stage. He said that there was no reason why I should take from my meager earnings to pay for an opera ticket when that small amount would never be felt by the millionaires who took care of the deficit. . . .

Sometimes when my work detained me past the hour for the beginning of the opera, I went back of the stage and listened from the wings. This habit gave me the opportunity of meeting many of the singers who are most genuinely democratic. Enrico Caruso was a favorite of mine and I came to know him quite well. I heard him in practically all of his rôles. I have stood in the wings listening to him sing some of the marvelous passages in that golden voice of his throbbing with human emotion. I remember hearing him singing *La Bohème* as though his very heart would break and with tears coursing down his cheeks. In the last scene the passion of the music affected him so deeply that it was necessary for the stage aids to help him to his feet, and yet within a moment he came off the stage laughing like a schoolboy and joking with everyone along the way.

Caruso was very clever with a pencil and frequently made sketches of bystanding persons. The sketch was usually a caricature or in some way exaggerating the person's characteristic that had happened to catch his mood. One evening as he stood by me talking in his dressing room he drew out a pencil and rapidly began to sketch me. After he finished he signed it and gave it to me [see page 110]. . . .

Many of the actors came to know me very well and never fail to let me know when they are in Washington. In my emotional life I have often felt very close to these people, only their art is used for the stage and mine is used as a weapon in the fight for humanity. Many of them told me their troubles, so that there were few things about relations between actors and managers that I did not know. Just before I left for Amsterdam to attend the reorganization of the International Federation of Trade Unions in 1919, I had a conference with Francis Wilson, George Arliss, and others of the Actors' Equity Association who told me the actors were on the verge of open revolt. From the ship bulletin on the return trip I learned that the strike was on.

Though an aristocrat of the theater, Ethel Barrymore joined the actors' strike Gompers describes here, giving benefit performances to enrich the strike fund and publicly stating that managers were unfair. "I shall never forget [how] the strike ended," she wrote in her memoirs. She "was up all night waiting for the lawyers, managers, and players to get the papers ready . . . to sign. When we left the room about three o'clock in the morning, the strike was over . . . and we all went back to work." For her, "back to work" meant a succession of starring roles in plays and films that ended with her death, at eighty, in 1959. More than one photographer captured the rare beauty of her youth (above), but it was Caruso, in a caricature (below), who conveyed her jaunty animation.

When the *George Washington* reached dock in New York, August 26, the first message that reached me was to come immediately to the actors' meeting in Lexington Avenue Theater. For nine days we had been on the water, eating army chow which made us realize one of the daily hardships of army life. I had promised myself a good meal as soon as we reached New York and did not eat luncheon, our last meal, on the boat. As between my promised "civilian" luncheon and the actors' request there was no choice and I went immediately. It was about five when I entered the theater where Wilson was explaining my absence to about twenty-five hundred striking actors. Someone remarked I must be fatigued, but I replied that I was only hungry.

I have never had a more rousing greeting or more enthusiastic cheers than came from that temperamental crowd. We humans are all alike under our skins; a ditchdigger and actor tackled the problem of getting a living wage in the same way. . . .

When I had the opportunity to spend an evening at home I always liked to have some kind of music. My daughter Sadie sometimes sang at home, but I was never impressed with her singing. One time [when] I had come home from a business trip, my wife informed me that the music teacher in the Washington public schools offered to give Sadie private tuition in singing and music without charge. For more than a year this instruction went on. Sadie's music improved very much and then for the first time I realized that she had a voice. I then made arrangements with Dr. Bischoff, the blind organist and great musician of the First Congregational Church of Washington, and put my little girl under his tuition for nearly four years. After Dr. Bischoff died, Professor Paul Savage, who had his studio in the Carnegie Institute of New York, was recommended to me. For nearly three years he taught her, even having her as one of about one dozen

One reason for Gompers' devotion to his daughter, Sadie, was that she closely resembled her mother—not only in looks (as is evident in this family portrait of 1915), but also in good-natured temperament. A newspaper article on her death in 1918 noted that her father "always carried her picture with him, and whenever he spoke of her his voice thrilled with the deepest affection." The article added that Sadie had "had a reputation well established as a talented concert singer . . . [She] had also appeared in vaudeville with success, making her debut in Springfield. . . . On that occasion she sang before a big delegation of labor men. She was exceedingly attractive . . . and of a lovable disposition that endeared her to a large circle of friends."

pupils whom he taught in the summer months in one of the lake villages of New Hampshire. . . . Professor Savage and Mrs. Savage, who was a great concert singer, had two interesting summer seasons.

The lessons under Professor Savage required Sadie going from Washington to New York twice each week, all of which bore very heavily upon my purse. If I could possibly arrange it I intended for her to remain with him as long as there was promise of a vocal education. Later, after two seasons, she sang in vaudeville, principally houses of the Keith circuit, and then was given an opportunity on the concert stage. She finally decided to give up her professional career. In her prolonged tours her mother accompanied her and as a consequence I practically had no home. I had no home while on the road and when I returned the house was empty. Sadie finally decided that the first duty of her mother was to be with me and inasmuch as she declined to travel alone, she came home and sacrificed her possible future career to be with us. She was a comely young woman and refused many offers of marriage for the same reason. Our home was happy, mirthful, and musical. To the extent of our means we had parties at home. People of a musical turn of mind would come to us. There was scarcely an evening in which I did not have a musical treat. This lasted until we entered the World War. After Sadie passed away, a victim of the "flu," there was no music. The song which was peculiarly Sadie's because she sang it from her heart was "The Rosary"—a song to which I cannot listen now.

## LADIES' MAN, FAMILY MAN

*He frequented burlesque houses; he savored being with showgirls; seldom did an attractive woman in the vicinity escape his scrutiny. Yet Sam Gompers was a ladies' man in a courtly rather than a pursuing sense. He idealized womankind in the dual role of wife and mother. In 1905, a woman's magazine asked him to answer the question, "Should the wife contribute to the family support?" Here is the heart of his reply:*

■ I have no hesitation in answering, positively and absolutely, "No." . . . I contend that the wife or mother, attending to the duties of the home, makes the greatest contribution to the support of the family. The honor, glory, and happiness that comes from a beloved wife and the holiness of motherhood are a contribution to the support and future welfare of the family that our common humanity does not yet fully appreciate. . . . There is no reason why all the opportunities for the development of the best that women can do should be denied her, either in the home or elsewhere. I entertain no doubt but that from the constant better opportunity resultant from the larger earning power of the husband, the wife will, apart from performing her natural household duties, perform that work which is most pleasurable for her, contributing to the beautifying of her home and surroundings. In our time, and at least in our country, generally

Though Gompers had mixed feelings about women in industry, he would have given wholehearted approval to the ladylike protest of these pickets of the early 1900's —with their hats, gloves, feathers, and furs. The first strike by women in America occurred in a Pawtucket, Rhode Island, textile mill in 1824, and though the impetus for improvement had begun then, gains for women were slow to come. A survey made in 1841 disclosed that some women worked as long as sixteen hours a day—for as little as $1.56 a week. Despite tireless efforts for reform, a major breakthrough did not occur until 1908, when the Supreme Court sustained the right of a state to limit the female workday to ten hours. During the next nine years the struggle was largely won: Forty-one states passed or improved maximum-hour laws for women, twelve states set up women's minimum wage laws, and five states declared it illegal for women to work at night.

speaking, there is no necessity for the wife contributing to the support of the family by working—that is, working . . . by wage labor. In our country, rich and fertile as any in the world, producing wealth in such prodigious proportions, the wife as a wage earner is a disadvantage economically considered, and socially is unnecessary.

*During most of Gompers' active career, American women were struggling to get the vote; not until 1920 did the woman suffrage amendment to the Constitution finally permit them to cast ballots in a presidential election. He gave strong support to their efforts, but he was quite realistic in predicting that their getting the ballot would not in itself be a universal panacea. In this as in other matters, he was a pragmatist rather than a dreamer, certain that suffrage as such would not solve all the problems of women in industry. Likewise, he feared that a minimum wage scale for women would set a ceiling on their pay instead of a floor—and that men as well as women might then be forced to work for this minimum. The following is drawn from statements he made between 1914 and 1916:*

■ The right to vote does not mean that women will necessarily have work. Equal suffrage does not necessarily mean equal pay for equal work. These industrial problems women will work out only when through organization they have industrial power and influence that will enable them to secure higher wages, shorter hours, and better working conditions. The relations

between suffrage and industrial betterment must not be confused. It is a matter of justice that there should be equal pay for equal work. The ballot will help but will not necessarily bring this about. It will result only from the intelligent self-interested activity on the part of the women. . . .

There is no difference in the industrial problems and difficulties which confront women from those which confront men. The fundamental principles which underlie all efforts of women to establish their rights and industrial justice are those which underlie efforts of men. Men and women united can work out a general plan for the economic welfare of all, and together they can enforce their demands and ideals. Divided in their efforts, or working along separate plans, there must be some degree of conflict and wasted activity. . . .

I apprehend that once the state is allowed to fix a minimum rate, the state would also take the right to compel men and women to work at that rate. . . . The attempts of the government to establish wages at which workmen may work, according to the teachings of history, will result in a long era of industrial slavery. . . . In my judgment the proposal to establish by law a minimum wage for women, though well meant, is a curb upon the rights, the natural development and the opportunity for development of the women employed in the industries of our country.

*In writing his autobiography some years later, Gompers discussed in greater detail all the foregoing aspects of women's rights and waxed eloquent about the "remarkable women" he had been privileged to know, both in the labor movement and outside it:*

■ Nothing has been more essential to the sustained progress of the labor movement than the conscious and unconscious cooperation of the womenfolk of union men. My daily observation taught me the meaning of the sacrifices made by the wives of men who have devoted themselves to the labor movement. Not only did the wife share privations and actual want, but she lived the spiritual sacrifice of being helpmate to a man who gives an absorbing cause first demand on his life. I have often said that labor leaders ought not to marry—but I did not follow that advice. Neither my wife nor my daughters ever made a murmur against the hardships of our life, which included even hunger.

There have been within the labor movement, in addition to those who sustained this sort of auxiliary relationship to the labor movement, wonderful women trade unionists, for the labor movement, like all primary human movements, is neither male nor female—it is the instrumentality of unity. So I have never felt that there was properly a sex phase to the fundamentals of trade unionism. Trade unionism is to protect all who work for wages, whether male or female. . . .

Devotion to trade unionism leads to interest in movements for freedom in all relations of life; consequently, I was early interested in the movement for equal suffrage. Equal rights for all brought me logically to endorse the women's struggle for equal political and legal rights. At that early day, the

Two quite different—but equally characteristic—aspects of Victoria Woodhull's colorful career are illustrated by these two pictures. Opposite, she stands sedately presenting the case for woman suffrage to the House Judiciary Committee in 1871. Elizabeth Cady Stanton (page 194) accepted her as a worthy recruit to the suffragette ranks, but neither Gompers nor many other early backers of woman suffrage supported Victoria when she tried to dramatize the cause by running for President. Instead of reaching the White House, she became notorious for her advocacy of free love, which prompted Thomas Nast to draw her as a female devil (above) in a cartoon titled "Get thee behind me, Mrs. Satan!" The crusading Harriet Beecher Stowe, author of *Uncle Tom's Cabin*, called Victoria "a snake" who deserved "a good clip with a shovel," while Gompers said she was confusing the suffrage movement with "wild ideas." In 1877, Victoria moved to England, where she married—for the third time— most respectably and lived to a ripe old age.

Elizabeth Cady Stanton spent most of her life laboring for women's rights. She had the word "obey" deleted from her marriage service, bore seven children, and in 1848 boldly paraphrased the Declaration of Independence in her Declaration of Sentiments: "We hold these truths to be self-evident, that all men and women are created equal. . . . The history of mankind is a history of repeated injuries and usurpations on the part of man toward woman." When Mrs. Stanton called for equal voting rights, co-worker Lucretia Mott is said to have protested, in Quaker idiom: "Oh, Lizzie, if thou demand that, thou wilt make us look ridiculous." But Mrs. Stanton did demand it, and persuaded the suffragettes to follow her. She became head of the woman suffrage group in 1869. In 1892 she joined Gompers and other freethinkers in attempting to establish a secularist organization—she blamed the subjugation of women mainly on the teachings of the Bible, which she attacked in a number of publications. Equal suffrage remained her primary concern, but she died in 1902 and did not see the ratification of the Nineteenth Amendment in 1920.

cause was at the height of its greatest unpopularity. I was one of the early advocates of woman's suffrage. . . . In 1891 I secured the signature of over 229,000 organized workmen to a petition which I presented to Congress asking for the Susan B. Anthony constitutional amendment providing suffrage for women equally with men. Dr. Frances Dickinson of Chicago was in charge of the campaign. I had met her when in Chicago and I also came to know very well the group of big-hearted women living at Hull-House, headed by Jane Addams. During the long campaign of education necessary to make woman's suffrage the law of the land, I helped continuously in such ways as I could. I not only spoke for the cause, but I worked actively for it until women became generally organized in associations through which they were then able to conduct their own fight. In later years I found myself in harmony with the suffrage movement as led by Mrs. Carrie Chapman Catt, and it was a source of considerable gratification to me to cooperate with her from time to time until the equal suffrage amendment was finally passed.

The injustice done to women through industry which the labor movement seeks to correct, together with the constructive purpose of labor unionism, early attracted the understanding and sympathy of many thoughtful women who offered their services to the labor movement before a similar drift was apparent among men. . . .

Women were not employed in all industries when I first entered the industrial field, but I was accustomed to thinking of women as industrial employes from daily seeing them employed in the cigar industry. . . . I did not see how the welfare of wage earners could be most effectively promoted in an industry where the men were organized and the women unorganized. I firmly believed that the problem was economic and that the development and organization of the economic power of women wage earners were essential to the permanent economic betterment of all.

While the large number of women were advocating equal suffrage, but few of them devoted any attention or activity to a movement in which I was deeply interested—that is, the movement to secure to women and girls equal pay with men and boys who were engaged in the same work. It was one of the principles for which I strongly contended within the labor movement. In my own trade I have championed that principle in practice; and by precept and example [in] many other trade unions in the industries in which large numbers of women were employed, equal payment with men has been carried into effect.

I believed, and as time goes on, I have become more fully convinced, that political equality without some degree of industrial independence would be more of a fantasy than a practical reality. Insofar as was within my power, I endeavored to help women workers to understand principles and methods of economic power and self-help. In 1885 I helped to prepare a call . . . urging all women workers to unite in trade unions. . . .

It was the beginning of the twentieth century when the Women's Trade Union League was launched—a somewhat different type of working-women's organization—for the purpose of organizing women into trade unions. As before, the leaders in this movement were largely social workers. I was in sympathy with the movement and gave it my cordial cooperation because I hoped it would lead to genuine trade-union work. . . . I defended the movement against the dubious and tried to contribute counsel for its guidance. Under the leadership of Jane Addams and Mary McDowell, the movement became of national importance. The tendency has been steadily toward the domination of trade-union influence. I have attended many of its regular conventions which were really national conferences on women in industry. . . .

To these efforts of women to help women, interested women of means contributed funds. This sort of subsidizing created a problem of control— whether wage-earning women or those interested in wage-earning women should guide the movement. I had to be on guard constantly to help maintain the balance for trade unionism. It is hard for those who have not been a factor in real production enterprises to appreciate the nature and the self-efficiency of economic power. A trade-union movement is inherently a self-dependent movement. The friendly outsider may contribute advice and assistance, but there is no opportunity for him to play a conspicuous part. . . . I remember vividly a typical problem that arose— Should the women's society employ an office assistant or accept the services of some of the wealthy women who were able and willing to give their time? My reply was very blunt: "If you need office assistance, that should be had from girls you choose and pay, and whom you can criticize and dismiss if necessary. If the rich ladies wish to share the burden, let them give you money." . . .

As I have for years been an advocate of equality of compensation irrespective of sex, it is a matter of gratification to me that the International Labor Commission, of which I was chairman, recommended to the Peace Commissioners [at Paris in 1919] that principle, and there was incorporated in the peace treaty draft: "Equal pay should be given to women and to men for work of equal value in quality and quantity." Regardless of any other effect, that action has embedded the principle in international thinking in such a way that it cannot be dislodged. The practical achieving of this principle must rest primarily with women themselves.

*Having himself been sent out by his family to earn a living when he was a ten-year-old, Gompers was, not surprisingly, an implacable foe of the exploitation of children. For more than forty years he wrote and spoke passionately on the subject of child labor, which he considered "a menace to our civilization." In 1919 he said that the nineteenth century "was noted for many remarkable discoveries," then added: "Our present century will be noted for much greater and more significant advance, the importance of the discovery of child nurture, the value of childhood, the science of raising and training children as a serious proposition." It may be doubted whether this area of human affairs has actually been improved as much and as rapidly as Gompers hoped, but at least there have been heartwarming advances in the fight against exploitation of children in factories, shops, and farms, which he so gallantly pioneered:*

Carrie Chapman Catt was the leader of the second generation of suffragettes. She refused to marry her second husband until he signed an agreement allowing her to have time off for campaigning. In 1900, she followed Mrs. Stanton and Miss Anthony as head of the movement, a post she held when women finally won the constitutional right to vote in 1920. Looking back, she remarked: "To get the word 'male' . . . out of the Constitution cost the women of the country fifty-two years of pauseless campaign." In 1920 she founded the National League of Women Voters to educate those of her sex to "use their new freedom." She also headed the International Woman Suffrage Alliance, supported the League of Nations Association after World War I, and gave the United Nations similar backing after World War II. Preoccupied with peace (she joined Jane Addams in founding the Women's Peace Party in 1915), Mrs. Catt nevertheless supported American participation in both conflicts. World War II seemed to her a just war, for she had organized American protest against German anti-Semitism in 1933. She died in 1947.

Gompers' heartfelt concern for "the significance and the importance of the child," which he expressed so eloquently, also included a deep love for his own small grandchildren. Here is an affectionate message he sent to his granddaughter May Gompers from Atlantic City. The picture on the front of the card showed bathers on the beach near the "new Steeplechase and Steel Pier."

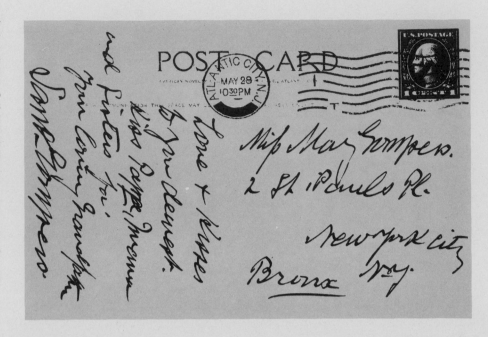

■ Of all the ills that mankind suffers from . . . the one that seems to me to rise to horrible proportions is that of child labor. . . .

Our centers of industry, with their mills, factories and workshops, are teeming with young and innocent children, bending their weary forms with long hours of daily drudgery, with pinched and wan cheeks, and emaciated frames, dwarfed both physically and mentally, and frequently driven to premature decay and death. The innocent smile of youthful happiness is soon transformed into wrinkles and other evidences of early decay. The life's blood of the youth of our land is too frequently sapped at the foundation. The hope of a perpetuity of free institutions is endangered when the rising generation is robbed of the opportunity to enjoy the healthful recreations of the playgrounds or the mental improvements of the schoolhouse. . . .

The humane work inaugurated and conducted by the labor movement to eliminate child labor in the industrial and commercial affairs of our country has borne good fruit and is destined to bring still better results. In the early history of labor's efforts to obtain this end, we were met by the bitterest and most relentless antagonism. Our motives were aspersed and our efforts ridiculed just as are now the demands which organized labor makes upon society in its claims for the present and for the immediate future. Today there is not an institution in our country, political, commercial, financial or religious, but which is committed in some way to the abolition of child labor. . . .

Every plan for national conservation and development must be based upon appreciation of the significance and the importance of the child—the child of the poor man as well as the child of the wealthy. There is wrapped up in every child born into the world an infinite potentiality. Into what a child may develop no one can say, but we all know well that the development is conditioned upon assuring to that child the protection and conditions that make for healthful physical development and opportunities for developing its mental powers. . . .

Child labor is a wicked practice—one totally abhorrent to all ideals of intelligence and devoid of heart understanding. There is nothing in later life that can ever compensate a neglected or abused child for the losses which were a part of its childhood. As the human body, the human mind, and the human personality develop they remain fundamentally unchanged. There is a time to grow and a time to develop which never returns. The fundamental problems which confront our nation are those of child labor and education. . . .

The most precious heritage of a nation is its children. This truth is scarcely yet fully realized. One of the greatest dangers to the health and patriotic life of a country has been the exploitation of our helpless children. Children are the wards of the nation, the responsibility of which can not and must not be shifted. . . . When the young heads, hearts, and minds are trained in an intelligent, scientific, and humane course, the era of the industrial slaughter of the innocents will have been obliterated, and they will in their innocence be preserved, cultured, and developed in their fullest mental, moral, and social welfare. Due to the patient and persistent efforts of the men and women in the great army of organized labor, the dawn of the emancipation of children from the workshop, in all its forms, is now clearly discernible.

*Not until he reached middle age could Gompers afford the kind of home he had always wanted for his family—"a home with four separate walls that were not attached to anyone else's walls . . . a real house surrounded by trees and grounds where flowers could grow and where I could watch the birds and hear them sing." In his early years he occupied a great many different dwellings, each as dreary as the next, but, as his memoirs indicate, he was fond not only of them but of the family life he enjoyed within them:*

■ By training and by instinct I have a profound reverence for the home and for the ties of blood relationship. As is true of the poor, my love of home was based upon sentiment. Though the room or rooms that I called home from time to time contained nothing materially restful or attractive there was always there the spirit of love and mutual concern. The first home that I remember was practically but one room.

After my coming to New York with father and mother . . . we moved frequently, seeking some little improvement in comfort or rent. All the little apartments of the poor were very much alike—we couldn't afford the individuality of beauty. Our little home nests were poor—usually two or three rooms with windows open to daylight in perhaps one room. Our apartment in Sheriff Street was a typical three-room home. The largest, the front room, was a combined kitchen, dining room, and sitting room with two front windows. There were two small bedrooms back, which had windows opening into the hall. We got water from a common hydrant in

Idealist, pragmatist, and effective social reformer, Jane Addams presided over America's most famous settlement house while she and Gompers were allies promoting woman suffrage and labor unions. Sedately reared, college educated, and widely traveled, she came to Chicago in 1889 and, aided by Ellen Starr, founded Hull-House in a slum area. Miss Addams kept the door of Hull-House open to all. She served free meals, went into the slums on errands of mercy, and pressed the authorities to assist the immigrants with clinics, garbage collections, and labor laws. Able volunteers assisted her, making the settlement a center of reformist movements. She opposed American imperialism in 1898, campaigned for Theodore Roosevelt in 1912, and declared her pacifism in 1914. In 1915, she helped found the Women's International League for Peace and Freedom, which remained one of her chief concerns thereafter. Her wartime service with Herbert Hoover's Food Administration did not prevent her from being blacklisted by the Daughters of the American Revolution, but it was one reason why she received the Nobel Peace Prize in 1931.

the yard and carried it upstairs. The toilet was in the yard also. It was not until we moved out to Sixty-ninth Street and Second Avenue in the late eighties that we knew anything of the comfort of water in the house or bathroom convenience. Conveniences that make water easily usable in the families of the poor have a beneficent value that few can appreciate who have not lived through the privations and hardships of those old days. Of course, I was away from home a great part of the time. I worked during the day in the factory and my evenings, Sundays, and whatever spare time might come were given with few reservations to the cause of labor. My wife acquiesced without question in whatever sacrifice was entailed by this service. Upon her fell the management of our little home, the expenditure of family funds, and the care of our children. There were many of our little ones that never grew up. Poverty and East Side homes are responsible for thousands of child graves. Our home on Sixty-ninth Street was only a few blocks from Jones' Woods and picnic grounds frequently used by the various organizations of labor, and sometimes the boys, Sam, Henry, Abe, Al, and I would go there and play ball together on Sunday mornings. These were rare outings which we all enjoyed.

Our little family group lived together happily. We lived our life without useless discontent because of the things we didn't have and without contention among ourselves. Parental force was unknown. . . . The brief hours I had at home were very happy. Mother usually had a baby in her arms. Many an hour she sang lullabies and crooned cradle songs in her soft musical voice that soothed baby and all of us. She was Mother Gompers to her family and all in need. Many a time she sat up all night with a sick friend or neighbor. As my work grew to embrace a wider field in the labor world, she became Mother Gompers to the whole labor movement. It was a title earned by her sympathy and by actual physical suffering that life might come to a great cause.

During this time I was giving more and more time to the labor movement, while still supporting my family by my trade. I could stand almost any hardship. Loss of a meal or a night's sleep did not make any changes in my day's work. I never got tired and never gave any thought to my body for it never demanded my attention. . . . I did not know I had a stomach, for there was never an ache or an ailment. A friend of mine once said to me, "You remind me of the tugs in the New York harbor—all machinery."

We wanted our children to have opportunities denied us, and sent them to school as long as we could. Sam, Jr., our eldest, had to leave school when only fourteen to earn his bit in a printshop. This change came when we were living uptown. To get to work at 7:30, he had to leave home about 6:30 for, of course, we couldn't afford streetcar fare at all times. He worked from 7:30 in the morning until 6 at night, so I rarely saw him except on Sundays.

All my succeeding homes were rooms or apartments or some segment of larger buildings until I came to live in Washington. Washington in 1897 was not a large city and the separate home was the rule. Of course, my salary limited my choice. My first home was a little six-room house on H Street, Northeast. There we lived for a number of years until my son Al married. As we planned to have him and his wife with us, we needed more room. We bought a house in a row on First Street, Northwest.

My son Sam had been living in Washington for a number of years and was employed in the Government Printing Office. He had married a daughter of my old friend Dampf. My Abe remained in New York where he was employed in a clothing concern. Rose was married and living in New York. She had two children then. Henry, Al, and Sadie were all living at home. My mother, who lived with us many years in New York, had died suddenly while I was on a trip in the West. She had grown quite old and helpless before she passed away, but my wife was always kind and gentle with her and accepted the additional care without a murmur. With mother's death, father moved around, living with first one of his children and then with another. He came to Washington and stayed with us in our home for quite a long time. He was living with us when my Rose died and we brought home her two children. We kept them until her husband married again. Father worked as long as he was physically able, but in later years, after his eyes failed him, he lived in Boston with my sister Bella. I never failed to see him when I went to Boston and every month I sent him a check—often a small one, for my salary was small in those days and the requirements of my own family numerous. . . .

My Dear Son!—
Just a little respite from work, worry or pain and I take advantage of it to, first, acknowledge the receipt of your recent letter and second to say to you that I

for me and give my love to Mother and the Children. and for for yourself accept the kindest feeling and best wishes of
your dear Father
Sam Gompers.

Here are the opening and closing lines of a letter, written from Louisville in 1895, that typifies many missives Gompers sent to members of his family during the frequent absences from home that his AFL work required of him. The "pain" he mentions was caused by a sudden illness on this particular trip. In the body of the letter he wrote: "I am doing the best I can to take care of myself. . . . The intensity and persistency with which I have striven have at last told on me. They have made the inroads on my constitution, which I fear will never be as strong again as it was of yore. I think however that I am now on the road to recovery. You can imagine how I suffered when I tell you that I lost 22 pounds in six days. In the past week I have again gained 12 pounds. . . . I long to be home and see all those who are near and dear to my heart." Gompers was then forty-five; he retained his tremendous energy—along with surprisingly good health—for the next twenty years of his life.

At all times our home was open to friends and all felt free to come informally. Labor men and other friends came to my home when they could not reach me at my office. Many an important conference has taken place unexpectedly at our breakfast table. I was in the habit of taking groups of friends home to dinner where we could thrash out our problems with comfort. My family had been brought up in the labor movement, enjoyed meeting labor men, and [was] interested in labor problems. In administering household affairs, my wife and family scrupulously observed trade union principles in all their dealings.

## THE WAY HE OPERATED

*Scattered through Gompers' memoirs are numerous examples of his dealings with widely differing people and situations and of his humorous appreciation of human conduct. Excerpts given here include his encounters with the noted newspaper editor Charles Dana of the New York* Sun, *the British labor leader John Burns, and the conservative Republican Senator Mark Hanna of Ohio. Following these anecdotes, Gompers tells why he bought his first dress suit and discusses his attitude toward pessimism.*

■ In the early formative period of the Federation I knew personally the great majority of the members of local unions. This personal acquaintance and contact [was] of primary importance in mobilizing wage earners in support of trade unionism. There is nothing I like better than to meet people and feel that good comradeship that comes from mutual understanding and liking. There is no other one factor to which my ability to secure cooperation in the work of the labor movement can be attributed more than friendly good-comradeship and ability to meet men on their own level. I feel equally at ease with the ditchdigger, the skilled artisan, the businessman, the employer, the professional man, men of science, men in public life from aldermen up to Cabinet members and even the President of the United States, provided they are genuinely human in their attitude toward life. I love life and enjoy living. I have always rebelled at conventionalities that merely repressed, and hated hypocrisy. Many a time over a mug of beer or a drink of whiskey I won men for the cause of trade unionism when I had failed in every other way. I have never taken a drink during any part of the day until my whole day's work was done—and often that was not done until far into the night. As I seldom made prepared speeches and as I knew my stomach and brain did not function best at the same time, I never ate prior to the making of my address. Often I sat through luncheons, dinners, and banquets without touching food. Not infrequently it was a real hardship to abstain, but I put my work first. . . .

There had long been Cuban cigarmakers in New York City and some of these were [friends of mine helping to free Cuba from Spain in the 1890's]. In that work . . . I met Charles A. Dana whom I came to know very well. As I had long admired Dana's editorial work, I counted it a privilege to be associated with him in the movement. . . . He had a wonderful ability to attract people to his leadership and a sustained virility and incisiveness of expression that made the numerous Dana stories so delightful. One became almost a legend—Dana's office cat. This vigorous, well-nourished animal Dana declared lived on manuscript. The cat was especially fond of inferior articles, but if such were not available its appetite could be appeased on various degrees of mediocrity. That cat was accredited with consuming editorials and articles that would otherwise have lowered the standards of the New York *Sun*, and many an anxious inquiry from persons who had submitted articles met the urbane reply, "We are very sorry but our office cat was beyond control and your manuscript was the only one available." No goat in all the world ever had so rapacious an appetite as the *Sun*'s office cat. . . .

I was early familiar with the leaders of the British labor movement . . . among them John Burns, Ben Tillett, James Sexton, and Tom Mann. . . . In 1894 there was established between the Federation and the British Trades Union Congress the custom of exchanging fraternal delegates annually, which constituted a powerful influence making for better understanding and friendliness between the labor movements of the two most important English-speaking countries. . . . David Holmes and John Burns were the first fraternal delegates from the British Trades Union Congress to our Denver convention in 1894. David Holmes was a sturdy, intelligent trade unionist, and a most congenial companion, and made many friends; John Burns, able, alert, assumed an air of superiority and the latter caused somewhat of a coldness between him and some of our men. He was hypercritical of everything he saw in the United States except the Library of Congress in Washington. . . . The Lexow Committee, a committee of investigation into the corruption of the police force of New York City, was meeting, and Burns being a member of the London County Council, I was sure that the investigation in progress would interest him. . . . We went to the Council Chamber where the hearing was on and . . . Burns became engaged in conversation with some person whom I seemed hazily to recognize, but I did not attempt to interfere. The plainclothesman drew me aside and informed me that the stranger was a bunco steerer and would surely wheedle some money out of Mr. Burns unless he was protected. He had no authority to interfere with the man because he could not press the charge against him. I turned rather abruptly and saw Mr. Burns in the act of handing two golden sovereigns and a ten-dollar bill to this stranger. Quick as a flash I put my hand over the outstretched hand of the bunco man, got the money, held it in my hand for a moment, much to the consternation of the bunco man and John Burns. I threatened the man that unless he quit at once I would have him arrested on the charge of fraud. I said that by my side was an officer of the police department to take him into custody upon my charge at once. He fled as if he were already pursued. Then I turned to Mr. Burns and handed the money to him, informing him of the character of the man and that he would have been swindled had I not interposed. Much to my surprise Mr. Burns was not at all pleased;

John Burns, Britain's "Man with the Red Flag," played an important pioneering role in his nation's labor movement. But as noted here, Gompers rather disliked him. Born into a working-class family and compelled to go to work at the age of ten, Burns became a fiery Socialist with a program for "the revolution." He advocated forceful actions and was a leader of the dock strike of 1889, which nearly paralyzed Britain's economy. He entered Parliament as a radical member in 1892. Appointed to a relatively minor Cabinet post in 1905, Burns told the Prime Minister: "This is the most popular thing you have done!" Reminded of his saying that no man was worth more than £500 a year (some $2,500 then), and that he himself was now making much more, Burns replied airily: "Oh, I just took the rate for the job." These observations reveal the egotism that often isolated him from his colleagues. He resigned from the government in 1914 as a protest against the war, and never held another major office.

indeed, he manifested anger at my intervention and later said that he would rather have been swindled out of the money than to be humiliated in his own estimation. . . .

Mark Hanna [was] an outstanding employer . . . who stood for the principle of collective bargaining before [most employers] would accept it. . . . One day a strike broke out among the men who were employed in the Hanna Blast Furnaces in Buffalo. Within a very few minutes after the information of the strike came to me, I had a telephone call. [Senator Hanna] complained very strongly about the men striking. . . . He said that if the fires went out it would mean that the molten metal would solidify and then neither the furnaces nor the metal would be of any further use. I called his attention to the causes of the strike—that is, that the superintendents and the foremen were in league with each other and they had required men to pay from ten to fifty dollars for securing employment and that when the men had paid this money either in advance or in installments, within a short time after the payment was made they were discharged and new men employed who were also required to make the identical payments. . . . The Senator was astounded and would not accept my statement as true. I answered that if he would have two or three of his superintendents and foremen in his office the following morning I would see to it that a few of the men who were the victims would be there also and . . . added that if he would carry this plan out I would advise the men by telephone to return to work immediately and I felt confident that they would do as I requested. . . . The conference was held the following morning in the Senator's office. The Senator was astounded when the true situation was disclosed and at once peremptorily discharged all the men who were responsible for the scheme. . . .

Newspaper magnate William Randolph Hearst heartily disliked Mark Hanna. All the Hearst papers, but especially the New York *Journal,* attacked the Senator on every conceivable charge—and on some that were quite inconceivable as well. A *Journal* cartoonist, Homer C. Davenport, waged the most relentless vendetta, always putting dollar signs on Hanna's clothes to symbolize his alleged greed and corruption. Later Davenport told Gompers how sorry he was for having caricatured the Senator so unfairly. The cartoon on this page was titled "Mr. Hanna's Stand on the Labor Question." The one opposite shows President McKinley as a mere puppet in the hand of his fellow Ohioan.

The Senator asked me to stay after all the others had gone and he said, "Sam, I didn't know that any such thing could exist in any plant and much less in a plant which I owned. I am glad you brought it to my attention. If it can be stopped in any way, I will stop it. But," said he, "these men in striking blast furnaces acted so undiplomatically." I replied, "Yes, that is true, Senator, very undiplomatic, but we don't raise diplomats on thirteen, fourteen, or fifteen cents an hour." My reply changed his entire mood. It hit him just right. He leaned back in his chair and laughed more heartily than I had ever seen him.

The man who was chiefly responsible for the general opinion of Hanna was Homer Davenport, the cartoonist. Davenport came to see me at my office a short time before [Hanna's] death. He discussed with me many things of interest and importance. Among the things he mentioned was regret which he felt for two acts of his professional career as a cartoonist: one, his misrepresentation of labor; and the other, his caricature of Senator Hanna as the man with the dollar mark, and added, "I placed a suit of clothes with the dollar mark on the wrong man." . . .

One of the first invitations that came to me from the Brahmins of big business was to speak at the banquet of the New York Board of Trade and Transportation in 1902. . . . I was to respond to "Labor is Always Honorable; To the Laborers Always Honor Is Due." I wrote a simple statement of the meaning of the trade-union movement. In addressing a group usually classed as labor's enemies, I felt the responsibility of an ambassador to seek to bring about better understanding between two contending forces. An amusing but illuminating sidelight on my new undertaking was a personal problem—should I wear a dress suit? I talked the problem over with my secretary who, like every real secretary, was an emergency institu-

Andrew Furuseth, of whom Gompers speaks glowingly on page 204, was a Norwegian sailor who came to America in 1880 and dedicated himself to the welfare of merchant seamen. His crowning effort resulted in passage of the Seamen's Act of 1915. "Cold to men while on fire for man" is how a writer described him, for he was inclined to be aloof in personal relationships. Gompers was among his few close friends. The two men thought alike, sharing a similar regard for "pure and simple" unionism. Furuseth represented the seamen's union at every AFL convention from 1893 to 1936. He died in 1938.

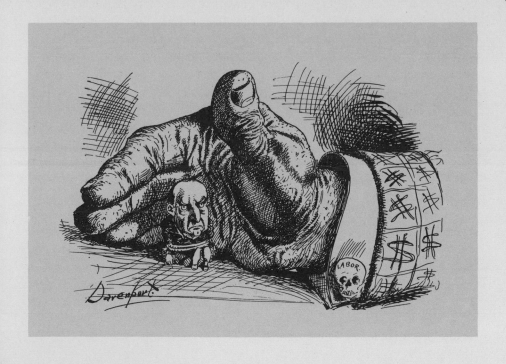

tion. Finally, I concluded that nonconformity to conventions would only make me conspicuous and would not help my cause. . . .

Though I have had to know many of the ulterior forces of life, I have never become pessimistic nor indeed have I found that avowed pessimists really disbelieved in human virtue and honor. Two of the outstanding figures of a pessimistic type I have known were a shopmate in the cigar factory, M. Wagenhousen, and the other [labor official] Andrew Furuseth. Wagenhousen vowed that there is no honest man in the world. I remember how most of us used to gibe him about that feeling and when sometimes a really decent, honest fellow passed away we would ask Wagenhousen— "Well, how about him?" He would say, "Well, he didn't live long enough to be dishonest." And yet I know of no more kindly disposed man than this pessimist and he too was sometimes imposed upon because he trusted people. Andrew Furuseth always sees the worst side of any situation, economic, political, or social, but in intelligence and in courage he has been one of the most constructive and thoughtful men it has been my pleasure and honor to meet and know. So far as I am concerned there is no pessimism in my makeup. I have always taken into consideration the fact of the struggles of life and the painstaking sacrifices which may be necessary in order to achieve any worthy object. . . . I have always made the best fight that I could for the attainment of any specific purpose and ideal in the cause of labor, freedom, and justice, and in the back of my head I have invariably held the possibility of failure so that I was buoyant, energetic, enthusiastic in the pursuit of my purpose, anxious for victory, but never woefully crestfallen.

*One of the most dismal situations Gompers ever encountered was the great depression of the 1890's. In the fall of 1893, the AFL met in Chicago and he recalled: "When the session of the convention ended for the day, there were hundreds of homeless, workless men seeking refuge in the corridors. . . . We had to walk down the stairs very carefully for we had to pick our way over men who were lying on the steps and on the floor with only newspapers for protection. It was a scene that burned into my mind." In New York that same year, Gompers roused men to fury by the agonized protest he here describes. In 1896 he wrote the editorial cited in the final paragraph below:*

■ At that great mass meeting of the unemployed I [attacked] the conditions, misery, and poverty by which we were surrounded and of which I was at times one of the victims. . . . I rendered with the most dramatic inflections I could command the following lines:

> "Oh, that a poor man's son as has been said,
> Became a convict to earn his bread,
> That a poor man's daughter to earn a crust
> Became a victim of some rich man's lust.
> Oh, angels shut thine eyes,
> Let conflagration illumine the outraged skies!
> Let red Nemesis burn the hellish clan
> And chaos end the slavery of man!"

The state of mind of the audience, nearly half of whom were unemployed, was such that at the conclusion of my address I doubt if there was one person who was not on his feet, cheering and shouting his approval. It was a wild scene [with everyone] in an ugly frame of mind. I could not imagine the lengths to which, under the influence due to their own misery and my harangue, they might have gone. . . . The world is filled with the cry that there is nothing wrong at the foundation of society. . . . Nature is generous in her bountiful gifts, man is a willing worker, genius has made it possible to make the laborer's productivity manifoldly greater than his progenitor's. . . . Yet . . . misery, heart-rending misery, abounds. . . . Those employed, overworked and underpaid, while the rest—the "superfluous" balance—may, through lack of opportunity to find work at all, go down step by step to the verge and abyss of misery, demoralization, and despair. Modern society answers these conditions with erecting more jails and almshouses, the police club or the military force. . . . The workers are organizing. . . . No! It will not ever be thus.

Henry Clay Frick revealed his love of art and money when he said: "Railroads are the Rembrandts of investment." Related to the Overholt whiskey distillers, Frick had enough money to buy into the Pennsylvania coalfields, where he was called "the Coke King." His biggest customer, Andrew Carnegie, proposed merging their coke and steel companies—Frick became general manager of the combine in 1889. Three years later, while Carnegie was in Europe, Frick dealt ruthlessly with the Homestead strike (see pages 49–50), which helped precipitate the social unrest described on this page. Frick himself was wounded by a would-be assassin who invaded his office, but he exulted over breaking the strike. Carnegie, however, disliked his tactics; bad feeling developed and Carnegie finally ousted Frick in 1899. Frick died in 1919. His plush New York mansion is now a gallery for discriminating art lovers who come to view the old masters in the priceless Frick Collection.

## DUELING WITH THE SPINY LEFT WING

*Increasingly convinced that socialism could never solve America's economic problems, Gompers fought recurrent Socialist efforts to take over the AFL. At first his rebuffs of the Socialists were mild in tone. But as the years wore on and his patience wore thin, he turned harsh and denunciatory. These five paragraphs are dated, successively, 1891, 1896, 1898, 1903, and 1905:*

Although Morris Hillquit furiously challenged Gompers' negativism toward socialism, he did believe that Socialists should cooperate with such organizations as the AFL—an attitude that more radical Socialists disavowed. Hillquit was born in Russia in 1869 and emigrated to New York in 1886. He had some early schooling, but the bulk of his education came, he said, from discussions held with other immigrant intellectuals on the rooftops of Lower East Side tenements. One of his first jobs was a four-dollar-a-week clerkship in the Socialist Labor Party office. He subsequently maintained simultaneous careers as a lawyer, author, and active Socialist. He also dabbled in politics. In 1917 he ran for mayor of New York and drew 22 percent of the vote, which was remarkable, as he had campaigned on an antiwar platform at a time when pro-World War I sentiment was strong. He ran for Congress unsuccessfully five times and attempted the mayorality again—in 1932—the year before he died. Hillquit hewed to leftist precepts but was not a doctrinaire Socialist. Significantly, he felt at first that the Bolshevik revolution "has vindicated the claims of international socialism as a living and driving force." But he later wrote ruefully: "The Soviet government has been the greatest disaster and calamity that has ever occurred to the Socialist party."

■ We do not antagonize the Socialist Labor Party. I deny that any one had given utterance to a word that could be so construed, but we ask that the trade unions be let alone. . . . I say to you . . . that the man who would accuse me or charge me of being an anti-Socialist simply says what he does not know anything about, he does not know Sam Gompers. I say here broadly and openly that there is not a noble hope that a Socialist may have that I do not hold as my ideal. . . . But our methods are different. . . . Working people are in too great a need of immediate improvement in their condition to . . . devote their entire energies to an end however beautiful to contemplate. I maintain further that the achievement of present practical improvement for the toilers places them on so much vantage ground gained and renders them more capable to deal with the various problems it is their mission to solve. The way out of the wage system is through higher wages. . . .

We note that the work of union wrecking is being taken up by [members] of the so-called Socialist Party of New York. . . . In following out their program of destruction they have attacked first one union and then another. Nothing was sacred. Achievement or failure, fair conditions or foul—everything was alike so long as they could either rule the union or crush it. The fact that the workers would become an easy prey to the . . . greed of the capitalists was nothing to these union wreckers. . . .

By their deeds shall you know them rather than by their honeyed and smooth words, with which they seek to . . . capture our movement as a tail to their political party kite. . . . I propose to succinctly call attention to the difference between the mask and the real face of the Socialists who . . . have done all they could to mistreat this organization and the wage earners in the trade unions. . . . They have besmirched the name of labor and sought to destroy our organization; they have attacked the honor, fidelity, manliness, and principles of the men who have tried to stand by the workers in their natural struggle for bettering the conditions of today. . . .

I want to tell you Socialists that I have studied your philosophy [and] your standard works, both in English and German—have not only read them, but studied them. I have heard your orators and watched the work of your movement the world over . . . for thirty years; have been closely associated with many of you, and know how you think and what you propose. I know, too, what you have up your sleeve. . . . I am not only at variance with your doctrines, but with your philosophy. . . .

The Socialists have called another convention to smash the American trade union movement. This is the sixth "concentrated" effort in this direction in the past decade. . . . So these trade-union smashers and rammers from without, and the borers from within, are again joining hands; a pleasant sight of the pirates and the kangaroos hugging each other in glee over their prospective prey.

*At home and abroad, Gompers continued to show hostility, and his Socialist opponents amply reciprocated. In the first paragraph below, Gompers records a clash with the noted American journalist Lincoln Steffens at the 1908*

*Democratic national convention. The remainder of the excerpt is his account of triumphing over the Socialists at the September 1918 Inter-Allied Labor Conference in London. At a conference the previous February, European Socialists had succeeded in getting a resolution adopted that would probably have allowed Germany to escape defeat in World War I. Gompers got this resolution altered.*

■ Lincoln Steffens . . . said: "I have a piece of information which, with regret, I feel I ought to deliver to you. The Committee on Platform has agreed to include labor's declarations and I am very sorry." I asked him the reason of his regret. He said, "Well, you know I am a Socialist and this will simply mean the taking away of a large number of votes of the Socialist party." I answered, "Don't you realize that the inclusion of these proposals in the platform is in the interests of the masses of the people and will make for freedom and justice?" He said, "Well, I am less interested in that." . . .

At the conference I said: "Socialism holds nothing but unhappiness for the human race. It destroys personal initiative, wipes out national pride—the hearthstone of a people's culture—and finally it plays into the hands of the autocrats. One has only to watch its ravages on the human soul—the soul without a country—to know that socialism is the fad of fanatics, the sophistry of so-called intelligentsia, and it has no place in the hearts of those who would secure and fight for freedom and preserve democracy." . . . Just before the close of the session I remarked how strange it was not to hear the word "labor" used in such a conference and . . . submitted that wage earners should be called wage earners and not Socialists. . . .

The report of the committee on war aims embodied the proposals of the American delegation and was satisfactory to me except the proposal for a labor conference in which all belligerent countries would be represented and a criticism of governments withholding passports from persons wishing to attend such conferences. I stated my objections emphatically. . . . I was accused, after the American program had been adopted in every detail, of running the A. F. of L. steamroller over the conference. To this I replied that if five Americans unacquainted with European parliamentary procedure could put their program through a meeting of over seventy-four delegates familiar with these tactics, call it what they might, we were entitled to the victory won.

As a result of this conference, labor and Socialist representatives were pledged to return to their homes and devote their entire efforts to assist their respective governments in winning the war until such time as the Central Powers occupied no foot of invaded territory and their military machine was no longer a menace. Three days after the conference of September 17–21, 1918, had adjourned, [American] Ambassador [Walter Hines] Page told me [in the London] Embassy that he had received word that the printed proceedings of this conference, which proved that the American trade union movement had completely broken down the German propaganda, had been delivered and placed on the desks in Berlin and in

Arthur Henderson, who led the British delegation at the conference described here, mingled pacifism, Methodist preaching, and Labor party politics. Although he endorsed the British decision to go to war in 1914 and served in the wartime cabinets of Asquith and Lloyd George, he went so far in backing an abortive international peace congress in 1917 that Lloyd George ousted him as a hindrance to the war effort. Woodrow Wilson feared that Henderson would become Prime Minister and make peace with Germany while the Allies were at bay on the battlefield. Henderson joined the first two Labor governments as Home Secretary (1924) and Foreign Secretary (1929–1931), despite his belief that Prime Minister Ramsay MacDonald was subordinating socialism to the honors of Britain's highest office. Chairman of the League of Nations disarmament conference in 1932, Henderson said: "If the people want disarmament, they can have it." His judgment was faulty—big-power rivalries ruined the planning of the pacifists. But his efforts in behalf of international amity won him the Nobel Peace Prize in 1934. On one of his last public appearances before his death in 1935, he spoke by radio from London during the Washington ceremonies honoring Jane Addams—the most complex broadcast to that date, it also included Paris, Moscow, and Tokyo.

Vienna. Mr. Page also stated that it would be impossible to calculate the influence this would have upon the German government and people and he was convinced that the last hope of Germany for a negotiated peace had been destroyed by the declarations of the London conference. . . . When the [conference records reached] Berlin and Vienna, the last hope of weakening Allied morale was gone and it became evident that the policy of the American Federation of Labor had superseded that of the February conference.

*Gompers also took a stern view of labor sympathizers from outside the movement who tried periodically to impose their outlook. He spelled out his distrust and dislike of these intellectual do-gooders and middle-class reformers rather baldly in editorials he wrote for the* American Federationist *between 1900 and 1918:*

■ We court the sympathetic aid of all, but we resent the attempt on the part of anyone not a wage worker to try to formulate the policy of the trade union movement. . . . It is better that we may err and learn by experience to avoid errors in the future than to have men whose interests are not identical with those of wage workers direct the affairs of any of our labor organizations. . . . That from the counsel of many comes wisdom has long been recognized; and this wisdom is much more far-reaching in its influence for good than the supposed "superior" intelligence of either the professoriat, the businessman, the theorists, the self-seekers, or the camp followers. . . . Friendly constructive criticism is always welcome from any source, but the attempt to bulldoze or dominate the labor movement by others than the workers themselves will be resisted and resented. . . . American workers insist that . . . they work out their own problems in their own way. . . .

The labor movement must be guarded not only against enemies but [also against] its misguided friends. It is a movement of wage earners, for wage earners, by wage earners, and it may not be amiss to warn even the well intentioned, the so-called "intellectuals," the "saviors of labor" who would dominate the labor movement with their panaceas or destroy it, that they had better watch out. . . . The labor movement does not discount the service to civilization rendered by intellectual ability, but . . . information gained in the college lecture room or in doctrinaire discussions is not a substitute for the knowledge gained through solving labor problems in the shop, in the mill, or in the mine. Intellectuals usually suspend their labor programs from skyhooks. . . .

Many a plain, unschooled toiler in the ranks has an understanding of industrial conditions and forces that makes him an authority in that field. Though their terms may not be as nicely discriminating as those of the more conventional "economist," yet they know the realities of economics, what is practical, and what is merely theoretical and speculative. Culture does not consist wholly of book learning but is an attitude of mind, alert and aware of tendencies, able and willing to discern the real from the

Lincoln Steffens was often at odds with Gompers (see page 207) but was outstanding among the muckraking journalists who attacked glaring evils of American life early in the twentieth century. Born in San Francisco and educated in Europe, he was known as New York's "gentleman reporter." After working on newspapers he received a roving commission from S. S. McClure, who wanted hard-hitting articles for *McClure's Magazine.* Steffens went to a number of cities, dug into the rank subsoil of civic corruption, discovered the facts, and turned out the pieces later collected in his book *The Shame of the Cities* (1904), a landmark in the history of exposé literature. His subject was municipal government, which he found to be largely in the hands of politicians working in concert with tycoons to pillage the public. He named names, noted deals, and captured local conditions in mordant phrases (Philadelphia was "Corrupt and Contented," Chicago "Half Free and Fighting On"). Steffens realized that democracy itself was on trial: "The spirit of graft . . . is the American spirit." His books had helped to change that spirit by the time of his death in 1936.

false, the enduring from the ephemeral. Nor would we discredit the work of the colleges, universities, or social workers, nor undervalue the constructive work done by these agencies in helping to establish a more sympathetic, democratic understanding of social and industrial problems among all the people. It is because we deprecate any action or policy that detracts from the value of that work, that we deplore the assumption of censorship and arrogance on the part of any. . . . The workers are not bugs to be examined under the lenses of a microscope by the "intellectuals" on a sociological slumming tour.

*Gompers strongly opposed compulsory government health insurance. When sickness insurance was proposed in several states in 1916, he called it "repugnant to a free-born citizen [and] at variance with our concepts of voluntary institutions and of freedom for individuals." The same year, he declared:*

■ Upon the honor of a man, and realizing the responsibility of my words, I would rather help in the inauguration of a revolution against compulsory insurance and the regulation than submit. . . . I am heartsore, ill, and sad when any, the least of my fellows, is hurt in any way. And sore and saddened as I am by the illness, the killing and maiming of so many of my fellow workers, I would rather see that go on for years and years, minimized and mitigated by the organized labor movement, than give up one jot of the freedom of the workers to strive and struggle for their own emancipation through their own efforts.

*"Some people say," Sam Gompers once jovially observed, "that I have a genius for organization, and some philosopher has said that a successful organizer requires the lowest type of intellectuality." Whatever the type or quality of intellect or genius required, he assuredly possessed masterful techniques for running an operation, for bypassing or otherwise negating opposition to him, and for firmly establishing organizational patterns of the type he preferred. If he disliked an order given to him by the vote of an AFL convention, he often simply ignored it—and he had enough power in the Federation to make his defiance stick. In 1899 his colleague Joseph Bauer wrote that a clause in the AFL constitution prevented effective action. Gompers answered:*

■ Dear Sir and Brother: At a railroad station a young man was about to enter a car on the train. Seeing the conductor, he asked him whether he could smoke his cigar in that car. The conductor peremptorily said, "No," when the young man retorted: "Why, I saw a man coming out of that car smoking a dirty old pipe." The conductor replied: "Well, he did not ask me." Your letter of the 7th to hand, and I make this private reply. Fraternally yours, Samuel Gompers.

*There was an ambivalence to Gompers' regard for power. Publicly, and in his writings, he maintained that as AFL president he was merely an instrument responding to the will of the workingman. But privately he was a shrewd*

"You can do business with anyone," said J. P. Morgan, "but you can only sail with a gentleman." Morgan had vast experience in both worlds—and coined the famous saying that if you have to ask how much it costs to own a yacht, you should never own one! He became a power in American finance after the Civil War, and in 1895 organized the formidable J. P. Morgan and Company on Wall Street. With a genius for ending competition by forming combines, he arranged mergers of railroads, of shipping firms, and of manufacturing companies, his greatest triumph being the United States Steel Corporation, which he formed to buy out the Carnegie Steel Company in 1901. In the great anthracite strike of 1902, Gompers backed the union in its proposal that "the entire controversy" be submitted to Morgan; even though Morgan had large investments in anthracite, Gompers said that "the miners had confidence in his fairness." Morgan's wealth allowed him to live on the princely scale dictated by his tastes. He owned splendid yachts, decorated his sumptuous home with European art treasures, and built the Morgan Library to house his great collection of books and manuscripts. His benefactions ranged from the Metropolitan Museum of Art to the Harvard Medical School. As a vestryman of St. George's Church in New York, he built the "Memorial House" for use by parish workers under his and Gompers' mutual friend, Rector Rainsford (page 186).

*manipulator, using careful committee appointments and tight control of conventions to keep AFL policymaking close to his own wishes. Concerning politics, he insisted that neither he nor any member of his executive council should endorse candidates for public office—yet various candidates received personal letters from him to use at their discretion. For Gompers, political nonalignment was a position to which he could retreat, as he often did, when he was unsure of a candidate or fearful of antagonizing the other side. In 1896, his endorsement was earnestly sought by Democratic presidential candidate William Jennings Bryan, who advocated free silver. "I was for free silver, not the Democratic party," Gompers wrote, and he remained on the periphery of the contest. As the following passage from his memoirs indicates, he apparently believed this stand to be consistent with previous actions, but it was not.*

■ Throughout the campaign I refused to let the labor movement be annexed by a political party, and I refused to lead them into a policy from which it would take decades to recover. I was attacked by the silver people, but I refused to yield my responsibility to the American labor movement. In Colorado, feeling was intense. Every effort was made to force me from my nonpartisan stand. My reply to W. H. Milburn of the Denver *Evening Post*, who protested against my attitude, may be of interest as it expresses a lifetime principle: "You say that if I value my position as 'leader' of the common people I should lead them now. This betrays what a poor conception you have of the fundamental principles of our labor movement. Your idea seems to be that an executive officer of an organization should be their 'leader.' You do not seem to understand that a leader implies followers, and that where there are leaders and followers, there are dupers and duped. You do not know that our movement is based upon the recognition of the sovereignty of the workers; that when they declare for a purpose, they're presumed to mean what they say, and to act in accordance with it; that they require their executive officer not to lead them, but to execute their will."

## BOYCOTTS AND FREE SPEECH

*The workers of America not only learned to strike and picket for their rights but also developed the boycott to emphasize unfair working conditions and the inequities committed by some employers. Here are examples of what Gompers said on the subject between 1891 and 1910:*

■ Workmen have a right to say that they will not patronize those who are unfriendly to them and those who support their adversaries. This is all that boycotting implies. There is no aggression here, no criminal purpose. . . . The boycott is a very powerful weapon in the hands of wage workers, but . . . an unjust or inconsiderate boycott does more to injure the cause of labor than a hundred victories achieved through its agency. Whenever an application has been submitted to headquarters an investigation was instituted and the concern complained against given an opportunity to state its version of the matters in dispute. In no case has a concern been placed upon our "We Don't Patronize" list until it has had an opportunity to be heard in its own defense. . . . Labor claims the right to suspend dealings with any and all who refuse to support what it considers its legitimate demand. . . . The right of any man to do with his patronage what he pleases must be recognized. . . . The organized wage worker moves by two cardinal moral principles. The first is: His right, if he is a free man, to dispose of his labor power as he wills. The second is: His right, if he is not a slave, to dispose of his purchasing power as he chooses. And what is the right of one man is the right of many.

*The most crucial test of the boycott's effectiveness—and legality—as a retaliatory tool of labor came in the Buck's Stove & Range case (see pages 68–70). No other episode in Sam Gompers' long life was as stormy and dramatic—or more significant. When the AFL boycotted this St. Louis company, that organization struck back. Gompers' memoirs tell the story:*

■ The company secured an injunction from the court [enjoining] all reference to the dispute in circulars, letters, or the spoken or printed word. It enjoined even our attorneys from discussing the principles involved. Of course, as president of the A. F. of L., I could not ignore the terms of the

The Buck's Stove & Range case added to Gompers' notoriety just as age and hearty living padded his silhouette. By the early 1900's his stature was such that any event affecting workers elicited his response. At left is part of his draft of a press statement on the panic of 1907. In mid-October some errant stock-market speculation had set off a frenzy in New York financial circles. Investors and depositors began selling stock, calling loans, and withdrawing funds. To curb the panic's spread, J. P. Morgan persuaded New York's top financiers to pool enough money to keep all but the weakest institutions from failing. A crisis was reached—and met—on November 2, the day Gompers, in this statement, described the "financial flurry" of the previous fortnight as "a Gamblers' Panic" and urged employers "not to attempt false measures of supposed relief by wage reductions." Business felt the effects of the panic for some time, but, due to Morgan's intervention, the "financial flurry" ended a few days after Gompers' statement was written.

211

The jail sentence he received but never served—for defying a court injunction in the Buck's Stove & Range case—made Gompers more than ever sensitive to injustices against trade unionists. Below is the final paragraph of a letter he wrote to the head of the United Mine Workers in 1910. In it he requested confirmation of a report that mine operators were exerting vicious reprisals on union members in a coalfield near Pittsburgh. A union organizer had apprised Gompers of harassment "by sheriff's deputies, hired thugs, and . . . Pennsylvania's standing disgrace, the State Constabulary." The organizer stated that more than a dozen miners had been "shot down in cold blood by the operators' hirelings," and added: "Despite these deplorable conditions the miners are gallantly contending for their rights, for free speech, for trade organization, and for the abolition of conditions in the mines that has meant for them nothing less than serfdom." Gompers ended this letter with a hasty postscript that asked, "What about the arrest yesterday in the Pittsburgh Dist. of 80 organizers of the U.M.W.'s under the Sherman Antitrust law?" It had been his contention for twenty years that the Sherman Act was being used as a weapon against labor. His concern would be relieved, finally, in 1914 when the Sherman Act was modified by the Clayton Act, hailed by Gompers as "Labor's Magna Charta."

injunction. It was absolutely essential to report the history of the case, including the injunction, to the following convention of the Federation, and this report, as well as the other evidence, was used in the contempt proceedings showing the violation of the terms of the injunction. This I held was manifestly in violation of the constitutional guarantees involving the right of free speech and free press. . . . Abuse of the injunctive writ had grown in frequency, until it had become the paramount issue in labor problems. It was at my suggestion that the Federation determined to select a particularly flagrant injunctive abuse to make a test case. Soon after that course was determined, the Buck's Stove & Range Company instituted injunction proceedings against the A. F. of L. This case was selected as it contained practically every phase of the abuse we wished to remedy. . . . I refused even to consider suggestions that I should restrict my discussion of economic issues or place limits to my freedom of speech—written or spoken. When the injunction was made permanent, I continued to exercise the freedom which I knew was my right. Since the Federation had made this injunction a test case, upon me rested responsibility for leadership in this campaign. That implied making plain labor's grievances and suggested remedies. It was impossible for me to obey the injunction and perform my duties. It was impossible for me to be true to my ideals of American principles and . . . recognize a judicial order subversive to them. I [was] determined to maintain my rights as an American citizen and continued to discuss . . . the controversy between labor and the Buck's Stove & Range Company and the principles involved in the misuse of the injunctive writ. . . . Contempt proceedings were instituted against . . . me in the court of Judge Wright. . . . Being a "martyr" for a cause is a bitter-sweet experience. There are moments of humiliation as well as periods of exaltation. The hour which I spent in Judge Wright's court listening to him read his opinion and pronounce sentence upon us was one which burned itself into my very soul. . . .

I appreciate the fact that you are exceedingly busy and yet if you can find time to give me any information as to the above, that is, as to its accuracy, or any other facts in connection therewith, it would be greatly appreciated and would be helpful.

Thanking you in advance, I am,

Fraternally yours,

_Sam'l Gompers_

President,
American Federation of Labor.

P.S. What about the arrest yesterday in the Pittsburg Dist. of 80 Organizers of the U.M.W. of A. under the Sherman Antitrust law? S.G.

Before pronouncing sentence the judge asked me if I had any reason to present why sentence should not be pronounced against me. My reply was: "Your Honor, I am not conscious at any time during my life of having violated any law. . . . I would not consciously violate a law now or at any time. . . . It is not possible that under the circumstances in which I am before Your Honor this morning, and after listening to the opinion you have rendered, to either calmly or appropriately express that which I have in mind to say. But, sir, I may . . . say this, that the freedom of speech and the freedom of the press have not been granted to the people in order that they may say the things which please, and which are based upon accepted thought, but the right to say the things which displease, the right to say the things which may convey the new and yet unexpected thoughts, the right to say things, even though they do a wrong, for one can not be guilty of giving utterance to any expression which may do a wrong if he is by an injunction enjoined from so saying. It then will devolve upon a judge upon the bench to determine in advance a man's right to express his opinion in speech and in print. . . .

"I may say, Your Honor, that this is a struggle of the working people of our country, a struggle for rights. . . . It is a struggle of ages, a struggle of the men of labor to throw off some of the burdens which have been heaped upon them, to abolish some of the wrongs which they have too long borne, and to secure some of the rights too long denied. If men must suffer because they dare speak for the masses of our country [or] because they have raised their voices to meet the bitter antagonism of sordid greed, which would even grind the children into the dust to coin dollars, and meeting with the same bitter antagonism that we do in every effort we make before the Courts, before the Legislatures of our states, or before the Congress of our country, if men must urge this gradual rational development then they must bear the consequences.

"That which Your Honor has quoted and criticized and denounced in us, in the exercise of our duties to our fellows in our own country, is now the statute law of Great Britain. . . . If in monarchical England these rights can be accorded to the working people, these subjects of the monarch, they ought not be denied to the—theoretically at least—free citizens of a republic. In this struggle . . . better men have suffered than I. . . . But if I can not discuss grave problems, great questions in which the people of our country are interested, if a speech made by me on the public rostrum during a political campaign after the close of the taking of testimony in this case, if the speeches in furtherance of great principle, of a great right, are to be held against me, I shall not only have to but I shall be willing to bear the consequences. I say this to you, Your Honor, I would not have you to believe me to be a man of defiant character, in disposition, in conduct. Those who know me . . . know that that is not my makeup; but in the pursuit of honest convictions, conscious of having violated no law, and in furtherance of the common interests of my fellow men, I shall not only have to, but be willing to, submit to whatever sentence Your Honor may impose." . . .

Elbert Henry Gary—"Judge Gary" to his business associates—left an Illinois farm to serve briefly with the Union army during the Civil War. He taught school, studied law, and became a corporation lawyer, county judge, and head of the Chicago Bar Association. Abandoning the law for the presidency of Federal Steel in 1898, he was in a strategic position to assist J. P. Morgan in organizing United States Steel. Gary was chairman of its board from 1903 until his death in 1927. An ardent Methodist, Gary took a high ethical tone—"Moral principles [are] the basis of all business success"—yet he often used very sharp business practices. He opposed all efforts to unionize the giant steel corporation, an intransigence that provoked the AFL into the steel strike of 1919. By refusing to meet labor spokesmen, by importing strikebreakers, and by demanding troops, Gary forced the violent showdown that ended in union capitulation. Gary, Indiana, is named after him.

Richard Olney brought into President Cleveland's Cabinet the violent temper that had caused him to disown his daughter for a marriage of which he disapproved. Although a scion of an old Massachusetts family, a graduate of Harvard Law School, and a corporation lawyer, he was little known nationally when Cleveland named him Attorney General in 1893. Olney supported the use of injunctions as heartily as Gompers opposed it. Gompers rightly saw him as the villain of the Pullman strike of 1894, for Olney had urged the President impetuously forward in using the injunction and the army against the strikers. Olney was appointed Secretary of State in 1895, becoming Cleveland's right-hand man. At the State Department, Olney took a characteristically lofty attitude toward Britain during the 1895 dispute over the boundary between Venezuela and British Guiana. He was behind the Cleveland message to London that virtually threatened war. However, when this dispute was settled by arbitration, Olney negotiated an Anglo-American treaty calling for universal arbitration of such cases (the Senate rejected it). Olney left office with Cleveland in 1897, resumed his law practice, and died in 1917.

The case [was] doggedly contested through every stage up to the highest judicial authority. For seven long years we were either presenting briefs or awaiting court decisions. The litigation was expensive and absorbed money, time, and energy that were needed for constructive work. In that period I was several times seriously ill. It was hard to reconcile myself to the thought that if the end should come, a blot would rest upon my name which no amount of explanation could completely remove. The shadow of that prison harassed my wife, my father, my children, for seven years.

When finally the U. S. Supreme Court came to pass upon our case, it evaded the fundamental issues and declared the case outlawed by the statute of limitations. However, because of the discussion growing out of the case and because judicial perversion had solidified labor's forces in the political field, we were able to press for remedial legislation. . . .

I entered into this case with my eyes wide open. There were two points of advantage in having the fundamental questions brought before the court and the public. We hoped to obtain a decision from the courts that would sustain labor's contention that the issuance of injunctions in a dispute over labor relations was unwarranted and unconstitutional. We hoped that the issue would attract countrywide interest and concentrate the thought of the people upon the principles involved; that if we failed to gain a favorable decision from the court, the subject would become an issue of paramount importance in the political campaign, and finally, as a cumulative result, we would obtain from Congress the legislation establishing justice denied us by the courts. . . . An opportunity came to me and I felt that it would be cowardice did I attempt to avoid it or evade it.

*While under the shadow of the injunction, and later the threat of a jail sentence, Gompers defied the courts and continued to make public statements such as these:*

■ With all due respect to the court it is impossible for us to see how we can comply with all the terms of this injunction. . . . We would be recreant to our duty did we not do all in our power to point out to the people the serious invasion of their liberties which has taken place. That this has been done by judge-made injunction and not by statute law makes the menace all the greater. . . . What hope can our people entertain for reform at the hands of the lawmaking bodies for any evils unless the freedom of the press and of speech be maintained at all hazards? . . . So long as I retain my health and my sanity, I am going to speak upon any subject on God's green earth. . . . I am not likely to surrender . . . the freedom of speech and the freedom of the press, and let the consequences be what they may . . . I shall discuss the merits of the Buck's Stove and Range Company injunction. . . . If the injunction is strictly construed and enforced, I am in contempt of court again for telling you that, but . . . I can't help it. I must discuss it. I will explode if I don't, and I don't want to go to jail, but I prefer that to exploding. . . . I am enjoined from telling you I won't buy a Buck's stove or range. But I won't buy one just the same. I am enjoined from telling you there is no law compelling you to buy one; but there isn't such a law. Because of this case I . . . may have to go to jail. There is no fun in going to jail, and I don't want to go, for no man would feel more keenly the sting of having his liberty restrained. But the whole world would be a narrow cage were I denied the freedom of speech. . . . Jail or no jail, I'm going to discuss the principles of it. . . . If they must have their pound of flesh they may have it, but they won't find any yellow streaks in it.

*On various occasions, Gompers did demonstrate a solid belief in the thorniest aspect of honest-to-goodness freedom of speech—namely, when other people were disagreeing with him. The first paragraph below is from a passionate, and successful, speech he made at the 1907 AFL convention to restore the Brewery Workers' Union charter, which had been canceled earlier in the year over his heated objection. The second paragraph illustrates Gompers' insistence that, though the idea was anathema to him, every worker did have the right not to join a union.*

■ [I do] not believe in the revocation of charters as a remedy for the grievances that come up in the labor movement. I am not asking the favor of the Brewery Workers . . . because I want to [add] that I believe the Brewery Workers are wrong; and this conclusion does not come because they believe or do not believe in a philosophy of the trade union movement I do, or because they and I are at variance on that question. My judgment on trade union affairs is not formed on whether a man differs or agrees on any economic or philosophical proposition. . . .

There may be here and there a worker who for certain reasons unexplainable to us does not join a union of labor. This is his right no matter how morally wrong he may be. It is his legal right and no one can or dare question his exercise of that legal right.

*One of the most trying and, for Gompers, humiliating events of his career came after a bomb killed a score of people and wrecked the building that housed the Los Angeles* Times. *In April 1911, two officials of the Bridge and Structural Iron Workers' Union, James B. and John J. McNamara, were arrested and charged with the crime. They denied it, and Gompers backed them to the hilt. Clarence Darrow, the greatest defense lawyer in American judicial history, was retained on the McNamara brothers' behalf. But James McNamara ultimately confided to Darrow that, in an attempt to scare the newspaper's antilabor publisher, Harrison Gray Otis, he had set off a small explosion in an alley alongside the plant. That explosion, in turn, had ignited gas lines and barrels of volatile ink. Darrow realized he could never get the McNamaras acquitted, even though they had not intended to destroy the building or take any lives. So with their concurrence—and to prevent their execution—Darrow made a secret deal with the prosecution. In return for changing their pleas to guilty, the brothers were sentenced to jail. The McNamaras' confession was announced on December 1, 1911, a date Gompers never forgot. Later he wrote:*

■ For many years General Harrison Gray Otis, the owner of the Los Angeles *Times*, had been one of the most bitter enemies of organized labor. Our most obviously constructive policies appeared in his eyes as diabolical schemes to undermine the rights of employers. . . . The explosion which wrecked the *Times* building and destroyed human life was a terrible happening which I felt as deeply as did any other citizen. I knew of nothing that connected the catastrophe with organized labor. Without doubt, Otis incurred the resentment of the working people and the overwhelming condemnation of all our people. That such a resentment would ever be manifested in the destruction of the *Times* building and the death of a number of employes, not only did I not know, but certainly I did not expect or even imagine. . . .

I never met or knew James McNamara; indeed, I had never heard of him until after the arrest. I had met [John] McNamara only occasionally, but I had been assured of his intense devotion to organization and the mission of the trade union movement. Nothing of his habits and conduct indicated that he could be guilty of a crime. He was a devoted, practicing Catholic who stood in good repute with the Church and with all who came in contact with him.

The representatives of labor . . . had tentatively engaged the services of Clarence Darrow. . . . They had already made a public appeal for funds and wanted me to take over the administration and receipt of the funds and their distribution for defense purposes. I approved the plan. . . . While labor was marshaling its resources to get before the public an understanding of the underlying forces in the "open-shop" fight, one of the most influential men in the United States, Theodore Roosevelt, published an editorial which was one of the most unfair declarations I had ever seen. The whole tone of that editorial, entitled "Murder is Murder," was an insidious indictment of organized labor for standing by fellow workers [before] the courts had had an opportunity to produce evidence. I replied to Colonel Roosevelt most vigorously [and] quoted a statement which J. J. McNamara sent me, which said: "That I am innocent of any infraction of the law in word or deed needs no emphasis from me, for the truth is mighty and will prevail right speedily; and for it I shall be content to wait." . . . I could not understand why [Colonel Roosevelt] would write an editorial of that sort. . . . No one was denying that murder was murder, but we were trying to protect the McNamaras from being branded with the ignominy of murder until a fair trial had taken place. . . . But Colonel Roosevelt was too vigorous an actor always to wait for the verdict of mature consideration. Probably his picturesqueness as a public man was due in considerable measure to his impetuousness. . . .

Late in the summer of 1911 it was necessary for me to make a trip to the Pacific Coast. In California I went to see the McNamara brothers in the Los Angeles jail. . . . John J. took my hand and said, "I want to assure you that we are innocent of the crime with which we are charged." This was the message I carried to the labor movement and upon which reassurance we continued to base our plans to help them. . . . When the trial opened, the

McNamara brothers pleaded not guilty. On December 1, I was on my way from Washington to New York. . . . Two newspapermen came on board the train to tell me that the McNamara brothers that afternoon had pleaded guilty. . . . The McNamara brothers had insistently informed me of their absolute innocence of any crime or wrongdoing. Now that they had pleaded guilty I had no other alternative or desire than to believe them guilty.

*Gompers sincerely hated the use of violence in labor disputes. When asked why the McNamaras had kept him "in ignorance," he answered: "We want to know ourselves. We, who were willing to give our encouragement, our pennies, our faith, why were we not told the truth from the beginning? We had a right to know. . . . If they were guilty . . . and if they had told me so, I would have said to them to plead guilty. I believe in truth. . . . I do not believe in violence. Labor does not need violence." In 1921, John McNamara was released from jail and attended the AFL convention. He tried to shake hands with Gompers, saying: "All we ask now, my brother and I, is that we do not stand condemned in the eyes of labor forever." Refusing the proffered hand, Gompers replied:*

■ If you had told me in confidence that you were guilty, I would not have betrayed you, and you know it. But you should not have risked the prestige of the entire labor movement. . . . The last time I took your hand, you assured me of your innocence. After that, you betrayed yourself and labor. I can only say this: I will not attack you and your brother.

*The surge of industry in the late nineteenth century and commensurate rise in the number of industrial combines—called "trusts," then—created widespread concern. It was feared these corporate giants might become too powerful politically (to the point of dictating to government) as well as economically (to the detriment of farmers and small businessmen). Gompers' attitude fluctuated. At times he said trusts were a positive good, at other times that they were inevitable, and, often with resignation, that they were too strong to be broken. But his view of government efforts to regulate trusts was better focused and forthrightly stated: He was against any such effort. He was irrefutably opposed to the Sherman Anti-Trust Act, passed in 1890, having the foresight to suppose that in court cases, if this law were cited, labor unions might be considered illegal combinations in restraint of trade. His long battle to modify the Sherman Act—and thus safeguard the authority of labor unions—is chronicled in his autobiography:*

■ As I was in Washington when the Sherman bill was under final consideration, I endeavored to have labor organizations specifically excluded from its provisions. . . . Though there was a fundamental difference between trusts and trade unions seeking to better conditions of life and work for wage earners, I felt premonitions that we would be the field to which the judiciary would turn for atonement for failure to curb trusts. My premonitions were justified when suit was brought against the New Orleans

John Sherman badly wanted to be President (unlike his brother, General William Tecumseh Sherman, who roundly proclaimed that he would not run if nominated nor serve if elected). While John never reached the White House, he did serve his country for nearly half a century after Ohio voters elected him to the House in 1854. Specializing in finance as a Senator (1861–1877), Sherman favored Civil War greenbacks and supported a mint-reform bill that briefly halted the coinage of silver. His fiscal expertise made him President Hayes's obvious choice as Secretary of the Treasury in 1877, but four years later he was back in the Senate. In 1890 he sponsored two bills that still bear his name. The Sherman Silver Purchase Act restored the coinage of silver at parity with gold: President Cleveland brought about its repeal in 1893. The Sherman Anti-Trust Act declared monopolies acting "in restraint of trade" to be illegal. This law is still on the books, used by the government to maintain competition. Sherman's eminence made him a power in the Republican party, and during the 1880's he entertained real hopes for the presidential nomination. McKinley appointed him Secretary of State, but he resigned in 1898 in protest against the Spanish-American War, and died two years later.

Central Body under the Sherman Anti-Trust Act (February 11, 1891). That action would be justified only under a commodity theory of labor—the very thought of which is revolting. The humblest of human beings possesses the mystery of personality that infinitely transcends the material products of human skill. . . .

As the years went by, the scope and frequency of injunctions issued in labor disputes increased until the practice became a grave handicap in the necessary work of trade unions. Then we undertook to secure legislation to define the use of injunctions. . . . That was no child's work, for I was pitted against some of the ablest lawyers of the country. The issue rested upon a philosophy that few lawyers had grasped. In fact, at that time there were comparatively few labor men who were able to present a statement of our contentions. Since the issue was forced into politics, it was necessary to explain it to the American electorate in an appeal for support. . . . Despite our activity none of our bills in Congress were passed. . . .

It takes fortitude to continue hammering away at a project year after year, even though there is no visible giving way of opposition under your hardest blows. It takes straight thinking to resist all proposals to accept modification that sacrifices principle. For a long time the only results from our efforts were academic discussions. Finally, there came an opportunity. . . . The inauguration of Woodrow Wilson [in 1913] was accompanied by Democratic control of both houses. It was a situation fraught with great possibilities. . . . Personally, I felt that the trade union movement, and I as

His scraggly hair escaping from beneath his skullcap, Gompers points accusingly at a representation of a potbellied Congress and cries, "You big loafer!" in a newspaper cartoon of 1920. That was an election year, and labor's demands were being ignored. The congressional figure in the cartoon wears a beaver top hat, long a symbol of political razzle-dazzle. A similar hat is worn by Champ Clark (above), who was Speaker of the House in the Wilson years, when passage of such laws as the Clayton Act delighted labor. Born in Missouri and trained as a lawyer, Clark was elected to Congress in 1892 and, except for one term out of office, remained there until 1921, the year he died. In 1910 he led a congressional faction that tried to curb the Speaker's powers, which were being exploited by the archconservative Joe Cannon. Though his efforts failed, Clark became Speaker in 1911 after the Democrats had won control of the House. Gompers wrote of Clark that "a more intrepid friend of labor never occupied [the Speakership]."

president of the Federation, had considerable at stake. If the Administration fulfilled its pledges in good faith, the political policies which I helped to inaugurate would have proved themselves. The Administration recognized that labor had been an effective agency in taking the political control out of the hands of reactionaries. . . .

When in 1914 Congress undertook the revision of antitrust law, Arthur Holder, our legislative committeeman, suggested we attempt to have labor sections included in the law instead of attempting to have separate bills passed. The suggestion was adopted. The antitrust measure was sponsored in the House by Congressman [Henry De L.] Clayton of Alabama and we had a number of conferences with him. . . . On the day when the labor sections of the act were to come up for discussion in the Senate, I went to the Capitol early and took a seat in the gallery. . . . I must confess that I felt a measure of sincere gratification as I realized that the justice of our cause was about to prevail despite the tireless opposition of vested interests. . . . When the debate began, I sat tense through the long hours that followed. . . . The debate was keen and illuminating. It was evident that each speaker realized the importance and significance of the matters under consideration. When the labor measures were finally adopted by the Senate, my emotion well-nigh overcame me. It was a great hour for labor, when there was enacted into the law of our republic a basic fundamental declaration upon which humanitarian endeavor could be based.

The law contained this section from which we hoped to secure protection from perversion of antitrust law: "That the labor of a human being is not a commodity or article of commerce. Nothing contained in the antitrust laws shall be construed to forbid the existence and operation of labor, agricultural, or horticultural organizations, instituted for the purposes of mutual help and not having capital stock or conducted for profit, or to forbid or restrain individual members of such organizations from lawfully carrying out the legitimate objects thereof, nor shall such organizations or the members thereof be held or construed to be illegal combinations or conspiracies in restraint of trade under the antitrust laws."

The Clayton Anti-Trust Law was signed by President Wilson, October 15, 1914 [and] I received the pen with which the President signed the law. . . . President Wilson . . . said: "Justice has been done to the laborer. His labor is no longer to be regarded as if it were merely an inanimate object of commerce disconnected with the fortunes and happiness of a living human being to be dealt with as an object of sale and barter. But that, great as it is, is hardly more than the natural and inevitable corollary of a law whose object is individual freedom and initiative as against any kind of private domination."

Of course, I, as everyone else, knew the effectiveness of the measure depended upon judicial action and interpretation. . . . The purpose of Congress was plain. Sections 6 and 20 were intended as a guarantee of industrial rights to workingmen engaged in a conflict to establish better conditions of work. They constitute the charter of industrial freedom or, as I called it, "Labor's Magna Charta."

just written to Mr. Henry Grasser, Secretary Hair Spinners' Union #14543, Chicago, Ill., notifying them that their wage scale has been approved by the Executive Council.

Please continue to assist the union in securing the enforcement of their scale.

With kind regards, and hoping to hear from you whenever convenient, I am,

Yours fraternally,

*Sam Gompers.*

President
American Federation of Labor.

Gompers was sixty-seven in 1917 when he wrote this letter to inform an AFL organizer in Chicago that the executive council had approved a wage scale set by the Hair Spinners' Union. He was still in command of Federation affairs then, but age was beginning to sap his vigor. The size and clumsiness of his signature suggests that his coordination was impaired—and that writing by hand had become an effort.

## THE WORLD WAR AND AFTER

*Gompers' thoughts on war changed radically during the course of his life. In 1887 he published an article denouncing war and militarism for being as evil as capitalism itself. When Austria began the World War by invading Serbia, Gompers condemned "this unnatural, unjustified and unholy war . . . for the glory . . . of an effete royalty." But by 1916 he had changed his tune. The first paragraph below quotes his 1887 article; the second is drawn from public statements he made in 1916—months before the United States itself entered the fray on the side of the Allies.*

■ The capitalistic, no less than the aristocratic, class is responsible for the stupid and wicked policy that has turned many of the fairest lands of the world into huge military camps, and has deluged every continent in blood for the aggrandizement of their own countries, and to force upon the conquered people the products which their makers cannot consume in consequence of the lowness of their wages. . . . To the working people it is of very little consequence whether the United States have a fleet of ironclads . . . but it is of very great importance that . . . we in this generation, by means of our trade unions, have challenged the capitalistic policy, and we will not cease our efforts until all workers, regardless of creed, color, or nationality, are united in the fraternal bond of one grand federation, making war and robbery forever impossible. . . .

If I could stop the present conflict by the raising of a finger I would not raise the finger, because I feel that something must be determined by this war: that is, whether the rule of the future is to be of autocracy and militarism or of democracy, liberty, and humanity. . . . Resistance to injustice and tyranny and low ideals is inseparable from a virile fighting quality that has given purpose and force to ennobling causes to all nations. . . . Though we may realize the brutality of war, though we may know the value of life, yet we know equally well what would be the effects upon the lives and the minds of men who would lose their rights, who would accept denial of justice rather than hazard their physical safety. The progress of all the ages has come as the result of protests against wrongs and existing conditions and through assertion of rights and effective demands for justice. Our own freedom and republican form of government have been achieved by resistance to tyranny and insistence upon rights. Freedom and democracy dare not be synonymous with weakness. . . . Rights carry with them obligation—duty. It is the duty of those who live under free institutions at least to maintain them unimpaired.

*In 1918, with the war nearing its climax, Gompers led an AFL delegation to Europe. John Frey and other associates helped him spread a kind of "Gompers Gospel" on labor among workers in factories, soldiers at the front, diplomats, politicians, generals, and members of royalty. Britain's commander on the Western Front, Sir Douglas Haig, made an especially favorable impression. Gompers, no knight himself, had one unfortunate chink in his armor: He could be deluded by people in high places who treated him cordially and with whom he did not have extended contact. Few, if any, of those who really knew Haig ever described him as Gompers did.*

■ The purposes of our mission . . . were twofold: to carry the message of the spirit and purposes of war work in the United States, thereby bringing hope and encouragement to hearten the war-weary soldiers and civilians to further service, and to see what had been accomplished on the military fronts. It was a most positive acknowledgment of the essential service that labor was giving to war work that we were given opportunities to see everything that was being done. We saw every phase of military activity when the final campaign was gathering momentum. . . .

It had been arranged that I was to meet General Haig. . . . The General was a wonderful man, a kindly gentleman; he impressed me as a soldier and a man. It was October 2, 1918, immediately after the battle of the Canal du Nord while General Haig was making a battlefield inspection with the object of assisting the several Engineering Corps in throwing bridges across the canal which would enable him to move his army with the necessary artillery to prepare for the final battle of Cambrai. He kept us with him several hours. The midday meal was an illustration of the General's delightful personality and democratic manner. At this point the battlefield was covered with dead horses, dead bodies, shattered trees. . . . We had our lunch seated on the ground, Sir Douglas Haig placing his large hamper between his knees and examining its contents in much the same manner as a customary picnicker. . . . While we ate, the shells were screaming over our heads and dropping in the fields about. . . . There flew over us numberless aeroplanes . . . bringing news of battles. About fifty feet from us a great white tarpaulin about twenty-five-feet square was spread on the

It was often said that John P. Frey "wore the mantle of Gompers," for he was as conservative as the AFL chief, as passionately devoted to craft unionism, and as stubbornly opposed to any transgression by labor into politics. Though he had had little formal schooling, he was nicknamed "Doctor Frey," for he wrote many books and for years lectured on economics at the University of Chicago. He had gone to work as a nine-year-old and at seventeen was apprenticed as an iron molder. In 1893, when he was scarcely twenty-two, he was elected president of an iron molders' local he had helped organize in Worcester, Massachusetts. He became secretary-treasurer of the AFL's metal trades department in 1927 and later its president. In 1940, while World War II raged in Europe, Frey told a convention of metal workers to "guard against being swayed" from their objectives by any governmental appeal to patriotism. "We must hew to our scheme, which is the protection of workers and the pure trade union and democratic method," he said. Less than a year later, however, he remarked that "the situation has become more urgent" and joined other metal trades union representatives in adopting a wartime no-strike policy. Frey, it seemed, wore "the mantle of Gompers" in more ways than one.

ground and this was the target at which the aviators, observers, and messengers while flying would throw small heavy cartons containing their written messages. On two occasions during the luncheon, squads of cavalry passed close by us, the first one coming from the battlefield, covered with sweat, blood and wounds of strife, and worn out. Seeing the squadron approach, Sir Douglas left us, met the head of the column, spoke to the officer in command, stood at salute while it passed, and spoke a few words to the officer in the rear. . . . Returning, he bade us adieu, mounted his horse and, attended by his aides, dashed away. He was as true a knight as ever lived in the days of chivalry.

*Long before war came to open America's eyes to the world beyond her borders, Gompers had been attuned to labor problems in such far-flung places as Cuba, Puerto Rico, Mexico, Germany, and Britain. And because of his unvarying mistrust of the precepts of socialism, he had been warily observing the Socialist ferment in Russia. After the second 1917 Russian revolution and the triumph of the Bolsheviks—advocates of communism led by Nikolai Lenin and Leon Trotsky—Gompers took pen in hand and, in articles composed in 1919, denounced Russia's new regime in terms as condemnatory as any he ever employed during his long life:*

■ Russia stands before our gaze like a flaming torch of warning. A thing called Bolshevism has reared its ugly head in that sad and sorry land. Bolshevism is a theory, the chief tenet of which is the "dictatorship of the proletariat." Leaving out of consideration for the moment the story of murder and devastation that has marched with the theory into practice, we must set down the theory itself as abhorrent to a world that loves democracy. . . . There is no group of men on earth fit to dictate to the rest of the world. It is this central idea of Bolshevism that makes the whole of it outcast in the minds of sane men [and] an enemy to our civilization. . . . Were there an American Federation of Labor in Russia there could have been no Bolshevism. Were there no organized labor movement in America devoted to the ideals of liberty and right and justice and unshaken in its faith in progress through the orderly processes of democracy, there would be Bolshevism in America. If there should be in America any great denial of the just aspirations of the working people as voiced by their organized movement there would be a dangerous flow toward Bolshevism. . . .

American labor views with heavy heart the terrible curse of Bolshevism forced by the gun and bayonet on the people of Russia, and sincerely hopes for the success of their brave and valiant fight to eradicate it forever from their sore-ridden land. No more monstrous or degrading government ever was set up anywhere in the world. Its entire existence has been one of terrorism, tyranny, and brutal slaying of those who are seeking for a just government. For the Bolsheviks have proved more tyrannous than ever were the Czar and his brutal officials. . . . The wage earners of America . . . desire of all things that the people of Russia will free themselves from this yoke of oppression.

Haig, so warmly praised by Gompers in this excerpt, was a Scot who attended Sandhurst (the British West Point) and then saw service in India and Africa. He became head of all the British forces in France in 1915 and directed great battles, such as the Somme (1916) and Passchendaele (1917). When Gompers visited him, he was preparing for the final drive past Cambrai. Haig, who never underestimated himself, often criticized his Allied colleagues, especially John J. Pershing, whom he termed "obstinate and stupid" for insisting on an independent American army. But Haig himself came under fire in Britain because of the fearfully high casualties his troops suffered on the battlefield. Churchill wrote: "Haig's mind . . . was . . . orthodox and conventional. He does not appear to have had any original ideas." Lloyd George forced his retirement in 1919.

*Ratification of the Eighteenth Amendment to the Constitution (in 1919), outlawing the manufacture, sale and transportation of "intoxicating liquors," was the culmination of a prohibition movement that had been gathering steam for many years. Gompers consistently had been its foe. In 1918, when a wartime ban on the sale of alcoholic beverages to men in uniform was being sought, an indignant Gompers told an advocate of this step:*

■ What have you been doing? Sold out to the so-called "social hygienists" and prohibition fanatics, long-haired men and short-haired women? You shall not make the war an opportunity for these complacent so-called "reformers" to accomplish their nefarious work! When have fighting men been preached to on the beneficence of continence? The millenium has not arrived, and until it does your pronouncements of yesterday will not be accepted! Real men will be men! And you employ this subtle propaganda in an appeal to the fathers and mothers of young men to foist prohibition upon the men and women of our country without their consent!

*The AFL overwhelmingly voted that beer of a 2.75 percent alcoholic content should be exempt from prohibition, and Federation delegates demonstrated in Washington "for the legal right of the workingman to drink a glass of beer after his day's labor." But Congress decided that any drink with more than .50 percent of alcohol was intoxicating. The entire amendment was repealed in 1933, but stringent prohibition was still on the lawbooks at the time Gompers died. He had pleaded in vain that Americans should at least have the right to drink light wines and beer, stating:*

■ I know what a glass of beer meant to me in the midday, in the factory full of dust, full of foul air. . . . Take the man who works in any industrial establishment for eight or nine hours or more a day; how welcome a glass of beer is to him cannot be known except to those who have had the industrial experience.

*Miss Florence Thorne (see page 80) worked closely with Gompers in the preparation of his lengthy autobiography during the years 1919 to 1923, taking dictation, doing research, and trying to duplicate his thinking and manner of expression as she set words down on paper. Since his eyesight was almost gone, she drafted much of the book for him, but—as she pointed out emphatically after its publication—every word of the final manuscript was read to Gompers for his approval or revision. And the autobiography bears the inimitable stamp of his personality. As the following passage indicates, he looked back, often wistfully but rarely impartially, at the events he had witnessed, at a world whose destiny he had helped to shape. From the vantage point of his advanced age, even the war was viewed in romantic terms.*

■ Through the transitional war period and the industrial storms of the past years, the labor movement emerged intact, stronger than at our entrance into the war. The past years . . . have demonstrated again the de-

Wearing a stovepipe hat and ill-fitting clothes, while carrying an umbrella to stay "dry," this cartoon creation by Rollin Kirby epitomizes the dour negativism of Prohibition. Gompers' vigorous defense of man's right to drink, as expressed on this page, no doubt amused his associates, aware of his frequent tippling. But, in truth, Gompers' antipathy to Prohibition was based on a belief that workers should pursue whatever relaxing endeavor they particularly enjoyed, so long as no one was harmed by it. When Prohibition permitted only "near beer," Gompers endorsed the quip: "Whoever named this 'near beer' was a very poor judge of distance."

Place Card at Luncheon given to the King & Queen Mr Samuel Gompers of Belgium. Washington DC. Och 30: 1919

Prince of Wales Dinner Honorable Samuel Gompers Nov 1 1919 Place Card Waldorf-Astoria Hotel New York City

Gompers' role as a labor states-man, which he played to the hilt in the last decade of his life, sometimes brought him into the presence of royalty. Here are two place cards bearing his name, zestfully annotated as to time, place, and nature of event. The card directly above marked his place at a 1919 luncheon for the King and Queen of Belgium, held in Washington during an interna-tional labor conference. The other card is from a dinner to honor Britain's Prince of Wales, which was held the same year at the Waldorf-Astoria Hotel in New York.

pendability of voluntary institutions assuring individual initiative. They reveal that genuine growth and progress do not come from above or the outside . . . but from the educational self-imposed discipline of the life process and are manifest in self-revealing work.

Whether the situation was of my own choosing or not, I have tried to be of service. I have my dreams as to what ought to exist in industry—a dream coordination of all in production, with unrestricted opportunity assured to all to devote mind and skill to production and distribution in the service of human needs. I yearn to have workers in industry know what a marvel-ously satisfying thing it is to feel that one is creating something. . . .

I have no overwhelming conceit of the value or the importance of what I have recorded in this book, nor do I wish to underestimate it. . . . Over-modesty is after all in itself a species of vanity. So I have in these pages written a faithful record of what I have seen and done with such comment as seemed necessary for clear understanding of the subjects and facts with which I have dealt. . . . What I have not included may be as important or more so than what these pages contain. So much which exists in the ar-chives of the labor movement and elsewhere for the time being baffles gathering and research. Perhaps if life, time, and opportunity afford, I may again attempt to devote myself to further presentation of facts of life and work. This I say without fear of dispute or refutation, that the World War changed me only in one respect. That is, when the war demonstrated that pacifism, in which I believed and which I faithfully advocated, was a vain hope I realized that the struggle in defense of right and freedom must ever be maintained at all hazard. In all other things, I have steadily held to the faith and struggled for the right of all humanity to freedom, justice, and democracy; for full enfranchisement of the wage earners of our country and our time not only politically but industrially; and to secure individual and social justice for all and opportunity for spiritual development. Labor must have the opportunity of free and untrammeled self-development that the toilers may find their places with absolute equality with all the citizens of our country regardless of their situation. Before the war I ardently advocated these principles. During the war I fought for them; since the war and so long as life shall remain with me I expect to devote whatever ability and all of the energy that is within me to the establishment,

maintenance, and perpetuation of this [gloriously memorable] ideal.

Thrice since Armistice Day I have looked death in the face very closely. But my seventy-third birthday . . . found me as usual at my desk, doing the work that I love best—work that is such a privilege to do that I sometimes feel selfish because of my opportunity to do so much. Frequently, there comes over me a feeling like liquid fire—it just courses through my veins—a yearning to work. The first thought that comes to my brain is a desire to do something, to do some work, to be of some service. I do not value the labor movement only for its ability to give higher wages, better clothes, and better homes—its ultimate goal is to be found in the progressively evolving life possibilities of those who work. There are such wonderful possibilities in the life of each man and woman! No human being is unimportant. My inspiration comes in opening opportunities that all alike may be free to live life to the fullest. The work of the labor movement does not grow less, for it has its roots in vital needs. That gives it the same intrinsic power to interest that life holds, and to me the two are inseparable. I hope to keep on with my work until I go out into the silence.

*In 1924, the last year of his life, Gompers became gravely ill and nearly died. While recuperating, he wrote the AFL executive council: "It is easy to say, 'Don't do any work; rest; dismiss work from your mind; relax; play.' But to me that is not rest; that is punishment. And so my physicians decided that it is good for me, and that work in a reasonably moderate degree shall not be denied me." The following excerpts from articles and reports Gompers wrote in his last fifteen months show his continuing concern for the future of labor:*

This cartoon of 1921 shows Gompers about to fend off John L. Lewis of the United Mine Workers, one of his few major rivals for the AFL presidency after McBride. Gompers won this contest by nearly 2 to 1, but Lewis' strength continued to rise. A proponent of industrial unionism—as opposed to AFL craft unionism—Lewis became chairman of the CIO while it was still part of the AFL, and president when it became independent in 1938. In uniting the dissidents and refusing to capitulate to the AFL, Lewis, as CIO chief, passed his first test of strength. But he failed his second. In 1940 he opposed President Roosevelt's bid for a third term and thought he could swing the deciding "labor vote" to Wendell Willkie. He even stated that, if Roosevelt were elected, "I will accept the result as being a vote of no confidence and will resign as [CIO] president." Roosevelt won overwhelmingly, and Lewis duly quit his CIO office.

225

"Labor is safe under his leadership; capital has nothing to fear" was how one newspaper reacted when William Green became AFL president upon the death of Gompers. In a press statement Green declared that he would "adhere to those fundamental principles of trade unionism so ably championed by Mr. Gompers." As president, Green stuck to his conservative guns through the depression of the 1930's and the Second World War—in fact, until his death at seventy-nine in 1952. He came to the AFL through the United Mine Workers. As a boy in rural Ohio he had hoped to become a minister but instead followed his Welsh-born father into the coalpits. Rising to prominence in the miners' union, he became eighth vice-president of the AFL in 1913, when Gompers decided that miners should be represented on the executive council. The two men were of similar mind on many issues but of wholly different natures. Green was sedate, generally humorless, and a teetotaler as well. Moreover, he lacked Gompers' steadfastness of purpose. In 1917 Green had said he believed in "organization of men by industry rather than by craft," but the AFL remained firmly committed to unionism by craft, even after he became its president.

■ I am confident and all labor is confident that when management with the help of labor succeeds in releasing itself from the shortsighted, selfish and unintelligent control of what we may well call financial oligarchy, most of the present restrictions of output will disappear and most of the dispute between employers and workers will be avoided. Future welfare demands cooperation between management, labor and engineers for the release of all industry from a senseless, wasteful, unsocial, and brutalizing control of powerful high finance. . . . We commit ourselves to greater efforts in the organization of all workers; we urge upon all useful persons the imperative need [for] organization, and finally the coming together in working bodies of all organizations through the representatives who shall speak for organic groupings. . . . We urge . . . a greater consciousness of purpose and . . . its rapid fulfillment because the needs of the time make it imperative. . . .

The road to democracy in industry is not a road that labor alone can travel. Democracy in industry implies and involves the participation of every useful element in industry. . . . Too frequently, labor is still compelled to fight for the simplest rights . . . for the very ABC of industrial freedom. . . . Labor is ready to move forward as rapidly as . . . industry. . . . But while reactionary and Bourbon employers stand across the pathway, labor must meet conditions as they are. This is what it will do.

*To the AFL's 1924 convention, held in El Paso, Texas, Gompers brought a speech that, carefully and thoughtfully prepared, summed up his entire union career. A tribute to the history and accomplishments of the American Federation of Labor, it was at the same time a painful personal farewell. He knew this would be his last convention. To conserve his strength and the strain on his emotions, he asked that the speech be read aloud by William Green, secretary of the United Mine Workers and the man destined to succeed Gompers as Federation president. With Gompers seated on the platform, Green delivered the speech at the opening session:*

■ Forty-four years ago in the city of Pittsburgh a group of labor men met to bring to fruition an effort extending over a period of years—to organize a national labor movement. We were a group of labor men with little experience in a national labor movement. We had to find our problems and devise ways of meeting them. There was little to guide us. The majority of us had a standing in our local trade unions and in our national trade organizations, but we had not joined hands with the representatives of other trade organizations in an effort to make the labor movement a force in the determination of national policies. . . . Industrialism growing out of constantly increasing invention of machinery, application of mechanical power which necessitated the factory system and the substitution of new materials for old, was making the need of economic protection for the workers increasingly imperative. Those of us who had opportunity to observe tendencies felt the responsibility to our fellow workers to make the effort for protection and for future progress.

There were but few paid trade union officials in those days, but after the day's work was done, those with the vision and spirit of service gave the evening hours and holidays to the cause of betterment of their fellow workers. More frequently than not the office of a trade union official was carried in his pocket and its code of laws in his heart and mind; benefits, even strike assistance, were irregular and undependable if provided at all; union dues and union rules varied from city to city, if not from shop to shop. The present trade union movement was then in the making—aye, had hardly begun. But the men who constituted that Pittsburgh labor congress in 1881 were as brainy and resourceful a group as ever gathered; they were men who knew the joy and inspiration of service that entailed sacrifice. Service in the early trade union movement meant to become a marked man whom employers were reluctant to hire and who was discharged first; whose family must forego the comforts and often the necessaries of life; upon whose children the handicap attaching to the name of a "labor agitator" fell. These very conditions of service in the labor movement assured the cause selected men of unusual qualities. They were men of self-respect and character.

When the Pittsburgh labor congress set itself the task of planning an organization, it studied the British Trades Union Congress, drafted a similar plan and organized the Federation of Trades and Labor Unions of the United States and Canada. In our optimism we thought we had settled our economic problems and that we needed only to consider the field of labor legislation. We elected as our executive a legislative committee, but provided no salaries, no permanent office, no full-time representatives. From year to year we met, accomplishing a little but keeping alive the thought of national organization and calling attention to the needs of the workers, until there came a crucial contest in which the existence of trade

The bust that appears on page 89 was begun in 1919 when Gompers sat for the London sculptor Frederick Louis Roslyn after being an American adviser at the Paris Peace Conference. The bust, now at AFL-CIO headquarters in Washington, was the only tangible result of Gompers' trip abroad that year. Trade union principles that had made him the most influential labor figure in America were either dismissed or rejected by European labor leaders. "At no time have I ever worked harder or against such tremendous odds," Gompers reported. "Time and again I felt that the situation . . . was impossible and that no constructive results could be secured." Even so, he remained with the conference because he felt his withdrawal "would react to the detriment of President Wilson."

A highly attractive music teacher by the name of Gertrude Annesley Gleaves Neuscheler became Gompers' second wife in April 1921, less than a year after his first wife, Sophia, died. The new Mrs. Gompers was a divorcee, a Gentile, and—of perhaps greater relevance—thirty-three years her husband's junior. What prompted her to marry him has been the subject of conjecture, but it is certain that she had little concern for his happiness. Although she gave her own brother and sister free access to Gompers' home, no member of his family was allowed through the door. Gompers retaliated by leaving her just one dollar in his will. When the document was probated, she in turn charged that his children had influenced the writing of the will. They denied the charge, offering to produce witnesses to attest to Gompers' soundness of mind at the time the will was written—and she withdrew her case.

unions was threatened. Then the trade unions sent out the warning of danger and . . . a message to rouse labor. Again in 1886 a national labor conference was called [and] resulted in the formation of our present American Federation of Labor with which the old Federation of Trades and Labor Unions was merged. This new federation recognized only the trade union card as a credential and proposed to deal primarily with economic problems. It was an organization that had no power and no authority except of a voluntary character. It was a voluntary coming together of unions with common needs and common aims. That feeling of mutuality has been a stronger bond of union than could be welded by any autocratic authority. Guided by voluntary principles our Federation has grown from a weakling into the strongest . . . labor movement of all the world.

So long as we have held fast to voluntary principles and have been actuated and inspired by the spirit of service, we have sustained our forward progress and we have made our labor movement something to be respected and accorded a place in the councils of our Republic. Where we have blundered into trying to force a policy or a decision, even though wise and right, we have impeded, if not interrupted, the realization of our own aims. But the very success of our organization has brought additional and serious dangers. Office in the labor movement now offers opportunity for something in addition to service—it offers opportunity for the self-seeker who sees an instrumentality for personal advancement. . . .

Men and women of our American trade union movement, I feel that I have earned the right to talk plainly with you. As the only delegate to that first Pittsburgh convention who has stayed with the problems of our movement through to the present hour, as one who with clean hands and with singleness of purpose has tried to serve the labor movement honorably and in a spirit of consecration to the cause of humanity, I want to urge devotion to the fundamentals of human liberty—the principles of voluntarism. No lasting gain has ever come from compulsion. If we seek to force, we but tear apart that which, united, is invincible. There is no way whereby our labor movement may be assured sustained progress in determining its policies and its plans other than sincere democratic deliberation until a unanimous decision is reached. This may seem a cumbrous, slow method to the impatient, but [it means] constructive development.

Our movement has found these voluntary principles the secure foundation upon which the workers of all America make united effort, for our voluntary cooperation has ignored lines of political division separating the United States and Canada, because economically we are a unit. Because we refused to be bound by arbitrary restrictions or expedients we have fostered cohesive forces which give play to the finer and more constructive faculties of the peoples of both countries. We are eager to join in an international labor movement based upon the same principles of voluntarism. We are willing to cooperate if we can be assured a basis that will enable us to maintain our integrity—a condition necessary for our own virility and continued progress. Understanding, patience, high-minded service, the compelling power of voluntarism have in America made what was but a rope of sand, a united, purposeful, integrated organization, potent for human welfare, material and spiritual. I have been with this movement since the beginning, for I have been given the privilege of service that has been accorded but few. Nor would that privilege have continued open to me had not service to the cause been my guiding purpose.

Events of recent months made me keenly aware that the time is not far distant when I must lay down my trust for others to carry forward. When one comes to close grips with the eternal things, there comes a new sense of relative values and the less worthy things lose significance. As I review the events of my sixty years of contact with the labor movement and as I survey the problems of today and study the opportunities of the future, I want to say to you, men and women of the American labor movement, do not reject the cornerstone upon which labor's structure has been builded— but base your all upon voluntary principles and illumine your every problem by consecrated devotion to that highest of all purposes—human well-being in the fullest, widest, deepest sense. We have tried and proved these principles in economic, political, social, and international relations. They have been tried and not found wanting. Where we have tried other ways, we have failed.

A very striking illustration is emphasized by circumstances connected with the present location of our convention. For years, force and selfish interests dominated relations across this international border, but the labor movement brought to an acute and difficult situation the spirit of patience and the desire of service, and a transformation has been brought which gives us courage and conviction for wider application of the same principles. As we move upward to higher levels, a wider vision of service and responsibility will unfold itself. Let us keep the faith. There is no other way.

Drawn by horses and surrounded by an honor guard, Gompers' flag-draped casket is taken from Washington's Union Station to AFL headquarters. It remained there an entire day, in a room filled with flowers, while crowds of mourners filed past. At nightfall the casket was returned to the funeral train and taken to New York. On December 17, 1924, Gompers' body lay in state at the Elks' Lodge where the service was to be held. The next day, at the hour of the funeral, activity in the United States Senate halted while eulogies to Gompers were read. In plants and factories across the land, workers stopped what they were doing to pay tribute to their departed chief. In 1950, on the hundredth anniversary of Gompers' birth, the Post Office issued a three-cent commemorative stamp that bore his likeness (above).

# CHRONOLOGY

PERSONAL LIFE                                PUBLIC LIFE

## 1850–1881

### The Young Worker

**1850** Born in London, January 27.
**1856** Enters Jewish Free School.
**1860** Works as apprentice shoemaker, then as apprentice cigarmaker.
**1863** Comes with family to America, settling in New York; begins joining and forming organizations.
**1867** Marries Sophia Julian.
**1878** After a brief withdrawal from union affairs to devote himself more to family, he plunges deeply into labor activities.

**1864** Joins Cigar Makers' Union Local No. 15, in New York City.
**1871** Marches with 25,000 others to demand eight-hour workday.
**1875** Helps to reorganize Local 15 as Local 144 of Cigar Makers' International, and becomes its president.
**1877** Attends first union convention.
**1877–78** Plays major role in cigarmakers' strike, establishing reputation as union leader.
**1881** Attends the National Labor Congress; helps to set up FTLU.

## 1882–1892

### Early AFL Struggles

**1882** Oldest son, Samuel, is forced to leave school to help support the Gompers family.
**1884** Misses annual Federation convention—the only one he did not attend in forty-four years—because of serious illnesses of wife and two children.
**1888** The family moves into its first home with inside water and a bathroom.

**1882–86** Conflict between Gompers and Socialist factions temporarily splits the cigarmakers.
**1883** His lobbying in Albany achieves a law banning tenement cigarmaking that is later voided by the courts.
**1886** The AFL is organized, with Gompers as president.
**1889** His first long speaking tour takes him to fifty cities in three months.

## 1893–1916

### Years of Achievement

**1894–95** Lectures and organizes during "sabbatical year" from AFL presidency.
**1895** Visits childhood home in London; travels through Europe.
**1896** Leaves family behind and moves to Indianapolis, the new AFL headquarters; suffers from illness; incurs debts.
**1897** Moves with AFL to Washington, bringing family from New York.
**1899** Death of oldest daughter, Rose.
**1902** Death of son, Abe.
**1906** Daughter Sadie makes vaudeville tour as a singer.

**1893** Succeeds in effort to divorce AFL from any political program.
**1894** Suffers his only defeat for the AFL presidency.
**1895** Reelected AFL president.
**1898** Supports Spanish-American War.
**1901** Campaigns for renewal of Chinese Exclusion Act.
**1907–14** Involved in Buck's Stove & Range case, and barely escapes jail term.
**1908** Backs Bryan for President.
**1916** Strongly supports Allied cause.

## 1917–1924

### The Final Phase

**1918** Death of favorite daughter, Sadie.
**1919** Suffers lasting injuries in auto accident; gradually loses vision.
**1919–23** Prepares his memoirs, assisted by Florence Thorne.
**1920** Death of wife, Sophia.
**1921** Marries Gertrude Neuscheler.
**1924** After being stricken in Mexico City, dies December 13 in San Antonio.

**1918** Meets abroad with other Allied labor leaders in Europe; heads Pan-American Federation of Labor.
**1919** Represents labor on the American delegation at Paris Peace Conference.
**1920** Helps to secure presidential amnesty for Socialists and others jailed under wartime sedition acts.
**1923** Investigates labor conditions in Panama Canal Zone.
**1924** Attends his last AFL convention, in El Paso, and inauguration of new President of Mexico.

| POLITICAL-MILITARY EVENTS IN AMERICA | CULTURAL-ECONOMIC EVENTS IN AMERICA | WORLD EVENTS |
|---|---|---|
| **1850** Compromise of 1850. | **1852** Otis invents first passenger elevator. | **1850** Dickens' *David Copperfield*. |
| **1854** Republican party organized. | **1859** U.S. industrial production equals agricultural production for first time. | **1852–70** Second French Empire under Louis Napoleon. |
| **1861–65** Civil War. | | **1853–56** Crimean War. |
| **1867** Alaska purchased from Russia. | **1866** National Labor Union established. | **1859** Darwin's *Origin of Species*. |
| **1868** Fourteenth Amendment, granting citizenship to Negroes, ratified. | **1867** Invention of hand press for shaping cigars. | **1861** Kingdom of Italy proclaimed. |
| **1869–77** Ulysses S. Grant is President. | **1869** Knights of Labor founded. | **1864** First Communist International organized in London by Karl Marx. |
| **1876** Custer's last stand. | **1873–78** Depression. | **1869** Suez Canal opened. |
| **1877** Federal troops used to put down railroad strikes. | **1876** Mark Twain's *Tom Sawyer*. | **1875** Gilbert and Sullivan begin series of comic operas with *Trial by Jury*. |
| **1879** Hayes vetoes a law restricting Chinese immigration. | **1879** Henry George's *Progress and Poverty*. | **1880** Dostoevski's *The Brothers Karamazov*. |
| **1881** Garfield is assassinated. | | |

| | | |
|---|---|---|
| **1882** Chinese Exclusion Act. | **1882** First Labor Day celebration, in New York City; John L. Sullivan wins heavyweight boxing championship. | **1882** Triple Alliance of Austria, Germany, and Italy established; Koch identifies bacillus that causes tuberculosis. |
| **1883** Pendleton Act is first real step toward a merit-system civil service. | **1883** Metropolitan Opera House opens. | **1883** Fabian Society founded in London. |
| **1884** Suffragettes form Equal Rights party. | **1884** U.S. Bureau of Labor created as a central storehouse of labor statistics. | **1885** Daimler develops internal combustion engine. |
| **1885–1914** Rise in immigration. | **1886** Statue of Liberty dedicated. | **1886** First Irish Home Rule bill. |
| **1886** Haymarket bomb in Chicago. | **1890** Estimated 603,000 children, aged fourteen or younger, at work in U.S. | **1888–1918** Wilhelm II is Kaiser of Germany. |
| **1887** Interstate Commerce Commission established. | **1891–1900** Increasing trend toward consolidation in American industry. | **1889** Japan adopts a constitution. |
| **1890** Sherman Anti-Trust and Silver Purchase Acts passed. | **1892** Homestead strike; John Philip Sousa forms his concert band. | **1891** Pope Leo XIII issues liberal encyclical on labor, *Rerum Novarum*. |
| **1892** Populist party organized on national scale. | | |

| | | |
|---|---|---|
| **1895** Supreme Court declares income tax unconstitutional. | **1893** Ford builds his first auto. | **1893** Verdi's final opera, *Falstaff*. |
| **1898** Spanish-American War; Spain cedes Puerto Rico, Guam, and the Philippines to the U.S. | **1893–97** Panic and depression. | **1895** Invention of the diesel engine; Roentgen discovers X rays. |
| **1901** Socialist Party of America organized. | **1894** AFL formally repudiates socialism; Pullman strike. | **1896** Puccini's *La Bohème*. |
| **1903** Department of Commerce and Labor created. | **1902–12** Era of muckraking journalism. | **1898** Germany begins fleet expansion. |
| **1904–14** Panama Canal constructed. | **1903** Wright brothers' flight. | **1903** Entente Cordiale between France and Britain; Caruso's U.S. debut. |
| **1913** Department of Commerce and Labor split into two departments. | **1908** Supreme Court declares unions subject to antitrust injunctions. | **1905** Workers' revolt brings attempts at reform in Russia. |
| **1913–17** U.S. intervenes in Mexico. | **1909** NAACP founded. | **1907** Anglo-Russian agreement completes Triple Entente. |
| | **1912** Violent textile strikes. | **1912** China becomes a republic. |
| | **1913–16** Mack Sennett begins slapstick school of movie comedy. | **1914–18** World War I. |

| | | |
|---|---|---|
| **1917** America enters World War I. | **1917** First recording of a jazz band. | **1917** Russia's Bolsheviks in power. |
| **1918** Antiwar Socialist leaders imprisoned under sedition acts. | **1917–18** War Industries Board exercises wide powers over U.S. economy. | **1918** Germany deposes Kaiser and declares a republic; Austro-Hungarian Empire is dissolved. |
| **1920** Senate refuses to ratify the Versailles Treaty; Nineteenth Amendment, granting woman suffrage, is ratified. | **1918–19** Influenza epidemic kills more than 500,000 in U.S. alone. | **1919** Mussolini founds Fascist party in Italy. |
| **1920–33** Prohibition of domestic sale of intoxicating beverages. | **1919** Widespread postwar strikes. | **1919–21** Civil war in Russia. |
| **1923** Dawes Plan for Germany's payment of reparations is adopted. | **1919–26** Jack Dempsey is world heavyweight champion. | **1921** Einstein wins Nobel Prize; Irish Free State proclaimed. |
| **1924** Full-scale revelation of scandals of Harding Administration. | **1920–32** Era of setbacks for organized labor. | **1924** Hitler writes *Mein Kampf* in jail; death of Lenin sets off struggle for power in Soviet Union. |
| | **1922–29** Business boom. | |

# ANNOTATED BIBLIOGRAPHY

*The following titles, divided into three major categories, have been selected for their usefulness to the reader.*

## WORKS ABOUT GOMPERS' LIFE

Mandel, Bernard. *Samuel Gompers.* Antioch, 1963.
The only scholarly full-length biography, and the most recent one as well, this book is the product of careful study of Gompers' papers and AFL records and publications. Its detail and documentation make it invaluable for reference; however, it is a rather impersonal account of both Gompers and the labor movement as a whole.

Harvey, Rowland Hill. *Samuel Gompers, Champion of the Toiling Masses.* Stanford, 1935.
This is an older work, not as complete as Mandel's in exploring the issues and controversies surrounding unionism's extraordinary growth, but it does focus more keenly on Gompers and succeeds in giving him dimension.

Thorne, Florence Calvert. *Samuel Gompers—American Statesman.* Philosophical Library, 1957.
Miss Thorne, a close associate of Gompers, has brought together an assortment of his opinions on various topics, all presented more or less reverently, and has interspersed these with strands of her own reminiscences.

*The following specialized studies have pertinence for advanced reading or research on Gompers:*

Reed, Louis S. *The Labor Philosophy of Samuel Gompers.* Columbia, 1930.
A doctoral dissertation, this work attempts to systematize Gompers' thought by centering numerous excerpts from his writings around questions relating to economic and social analysis.

Mandel, Bernard. "Samuel Gompers and the Negro Workers, 1886–1914," *Journal of Negro History*, XL (1955).
Here Dr. Mandel traces in some detail Gompers' "retreat into Jim Crowism," as the AFL and national acceptance of segregation grew simultaneously.

Laslett, John. "Reflections on the Failure of Socialism in the American Federation of Labor," *Mississippi Valley Historical Review*, L (1963–64).
After examining the records of constituent unions within the AFL in which Socialists held power, the author concludes that these unions were not successful in winning benefits for their members until they moved away from "pure" socialism toward "pure and simple" trade unionism.

Yearley, Clifton K., Jr. *Britons in American Labor: A History of the Influence of the United Kingdom Immigrants on American Labor, 1820–1914.* Johns Hopkins, 1957.
A work whose title is self-explanatory, it contains much interesting material on Gompers, as well as on the influence of British trade unionism on AFL policy-making.

Erickson, Charlotte. *American Industry and the European Immigrant, 1860–1885.* Harvard, 1957.
The author carefully sifts fact from fiction in discussing the effects of labor imported under contract, in the years when that practice was legal. The evils of the system were numerous; nevertheless, it did not "dump hordes of unskilled foreigners" onto the labor market, as union spokesmen often charged.

*The following studies of two unions, one in a skilled trade and one in a mass-production industry, significantly illustrate problems of AFL unionism.*

Brody, David. *Steelworkers in America: the Nonunion Era.* Harvard, 1960.
This is a detailed study of the difficulties to be overcome in unionizing the steel industry. Among the many well-nigh insoluble problems were swift technological change, concentration of ownership, and a large immigrant labor force.

Christie, Robert A. *Empire in Wood.* Cornell, 1956.
Concerned with the carpenters' union, one of the AFL's first building blocks, the book explains the expansion of jurisdiction that took place as the carpenters' craft was absorbed into larger industrial processes, and describes how a tough union of skilled workers guarded its "turf."

## GOMPERS' WRITINGS, PUBLISHED AND UNPUBLISHED

Gompers, Samuel. *Seventy Years of Life and Labor: An Autobiography* (2 vols.). Dutton, 1925. Reprinted in one unabridged volume, 1943.
A great quarry that AFL historians mine with caution, Gompers' testament was dictated to assistants when he was in failing health. It is often rambling and at times inaccurate, yet Gompers' personality—warm, combative, egocentric, and life-loving—emerges from it as from few other works. These memoirs are superb for the "feel," if not always for the facts, of Gompers' era.

*Among the several published collections of Gompers' speeches and magazine articles that convey his philosophy in his own words are the following:*

*Labor in Europe and America.* Harper, 1910.

*Labor and the Common Welfare.* Dutton, 1919.

*Labor and the Employer.* Dutton, 1920.

*Out of Their Own Mouths: A Revelation and an Indictment of Sovietism* (with William E. Walling). Dutton, 1921.

*The Manuscript Division, New York Public Library, has a Samuel Gompers Collection containing personal papers, and letters and laudatory messages he received. The Manuscript Division, Library of Congress, has copies of letters from Gompers, along with 350 volumes of AFL copybooks (journals), the earliest of which are handwritten. The*

*National Archives in Washington has copies of letters that Gompers sent to government agencies. The State Historical Society of Wisconsin has a large inventory of Gompers' correspondence, articles, statements, and press clippings.*

## BOOKS ABOUT EVENTS AND PEOPLE CONTEMPORARY WITH GOMPERS

Commons, John R. et al. *History of Labor in the United States 1896–1932* (2 vols.). Macmillan, 1935.
The second half of a four-volume series, these books concern the post-Civil War era and are based on the most careful and "scientific" scrutiny of a wide variety of now-defunct labor periodicals. Both books are heavily detailed, and, though influenced by a strongly Progressive viewpoint, they have never really been surpassed in completeness.

Taft, Philip. *Organized Labor in American History.* Harper, 1964.
By contrast, this is the most recent of a number of one-volume studies, useful for understanding the broad canvas of labor history. Less detailed than Commons, it is also less rich in interesting quotations and biographical data. Its title is refreshingly frank in disclosing what many histories of labor fail to note—that they deal mostly with the *organized* workers.

Taft, Philip. *The A. F. of L. in the Time of Gompers.* Harper, 1957.
This volume (which was followed by another concerned with the AFL after Gompers), in dissecting the inner mechanisms of the Federation, provides a valuable key to the workings of Gompers' mind during the decades of his AFL presidency.

Lorwin, Lewis L., and J. A. Flexner. *The American Federation of Labor: History, Policies, and Prospects.* Brookings, 1933.
Earlier and less thorough than the Taft volumes cited above, this is a good history nonetheless, and less taxing to read.

Rayback, Joseph G. *A History of American Labor.* Macmillan, 1959.
The author maintains that the present cannot be understood without knowledge of the past. Thus the issues affecting labor in the present are examined—and in highly readable fashion— in the light of a history that he traces back to colonial times.

Hoxie, Robert Franklin. *Trade Unionism in the United States.* Russell & Russell, 1966.
Recently updated, Professor Hoxie's book was first published as a compilation of notes and lecture material he developed in 1915–16 when he was teaching at the University of Chicago. It was Dr. Hoxie who urged Florence Thorne, one of his students, to interview Samuel Gompers, and, as a result of the interview, she became part of Gompers' staff.

Stein, Leon. *The Triangle Fire.* Lippincott, 1962.
Events leading up to and including the fire that destroyed the Triangle Waist Company in 1911 and took 146 lives are dramatically recreated here. The book points up the significance of an event which, however disastrous, prompted the creation of safety legislation for factories and gave impetus to organizing workers in the needle trades.

Broehl, Wayne G., Jr. *The Molly Maguires.* Harvard, 1964.
The Irish secret society that existed amid the Pennsylvania coal fields in the 1870's is described in this interesting book.

Kornbluh, Joyce L. *Rebel Voices: An I.W.W. Anthology.* University of Michigan, 1964.
The philosophy of industrial unionism and the growth of the dissident Wobbly organization are expressed through a variety of pictures, songs, poems, essays, and cartoons.

Powderly, Terence V. *The Path I Trod: Autobiography,* Harry J. Carman, Henry David, and Paul N. Guthrie, eds. Columbia, 1940.
This posthumously published autobiography of the onetime Grand Master Workman of the Knights of Labor provides a fascinating glimpse into the mind of Gompers' great antagonist of the 1880's—an idealist, essentially middle class.

Ware, Norman J. *The Labor Movement in the United States, 1860–1895.* Appleton, 1929.
Primarily a history of the Knights of Labor, this work is marked by sharp hostility toward Powderly. Gompers would undoubtedly have approved!

Grob, Gerald N. *Workers and Utopia.* Northwestern, 1961.
This is the best study of the Knights, their supporters, and foes—including many Federationists. Carefully, and without bias, it examines the ideas of those who considered the labor movement a means to achieve a just society in general, and also of those whose aims were more limited.

Quint, Howard H. *The Forging of American Socialism: Origins of the Modern Movement.* University of South Carolina, 1953.
In a good account of the various elements that together made up American socialism, the author discusses many of Gompers' Socialist contemporaries in the labor movement.

Ginger, Raymond. *The Bending Cross: A Biography of Eugene Victor Debs.* Rutgers, 1949.
An extremely well-written biography of the Socialist party's presidential candidate from 1908 through 1920, this book throws much light on the American Left and the working class in the early twentieth century.

Haywood, William D. *Bill Haywood's Book: Autobiography.* International, 1929.
No holds are barred in these memoirs of the contentious and energetic Westerner who headed the Industrial Workers of the World. Though its last pages were probably edited by Communist publishers after Haywood's death in Russia, it is still a vivid document, spirited if not objective.

Brissenden, Paul F. *The I.W.W.: A Study of American Syndicalism.* Columbia, 1920.
A professorial and rather searching study of the Wobblies, it provides less heat and more light than Haywood's book.

Cochran, T. C. and William Miller. *The Age of Enterprise: A Social History of Industrial America.* Macmillan, 1943.
Although old, this is a good overview of the social causes and consequences of the great post-1860 industrial boom, a phe-

nomenon whose accompanying problems have beset the labor movement ever since.

Kirkland, Edward C. *Industry Comes of Age: Business, Labor, and Public Policy, 1860–1897.* Rinehart, 1961.
In analyzing economic developments of the last forty years of the nineteenth century, this is more up to date and sophisticated than the Cochran book. In addition, it devotes two chapters specifically to organized labor.

Diamond, Sigmund, ed. *The Nation Transformed: The Creation of an Industrial Society.* Braziller, 1963.
This is a highly compelling collection of first-hand reactions to the march of industrialism, including some testimony from ordinary workmen, as well as from Samuel Gompers.

Schlesinger, Arthur M. *The Rise of the City, 1878–1898.* Macmillan, 1933.
A classic (though loosely organized) work of social history, it explores the many meanings of the urbanism that made itself felt among large numbers of Americans, including laborers.

Young, George M. *Victorian England: Portrait of an Age.* Oxford, 1953.
Here are some fascinating glimpses of the England, and especially of the London, in which Gompers spent the formative first thirteen years of his life.

Browne, Junius Henri. *The Great Metropolis: A Mirror of New York.* American, 1869.
A veteran newspaperman describes the many sides of life in New York at about the time Gompers arrived and continued his growing-up.

Faulkner, Harold U. *Politics, Reform and Expansion: 1800–1900.* Harper, 1959.
This is an excellent survey of the economic background to the political struggles that culminated in the far-from-gay 1890's, the stormy first decade of the AFL.

Mowry, George E. *The Era of Theodore Roosevelt, 1900–1912.* Harper, 1958.
Mr. Mowry has written a scholarly and valuable study of the political climate of the Progressive period—a climate to which Gompers so shrewdly and sensitively adjusted his own political thermostat.

Link, Arthur S. *Woodrow Wilson and the Progressive Era, 1910–1917.* Harper, 1954.
Like the Mowry work, this is a diligent overview of the conversion to Progressivism, the election, and the domestic achievements of Woodrow Wilson, by all odds the President with whom Gompers felt most in harmony.

Sullivan, Mark. *Over Here, 1914–1918* (Vol. 5 of *Our Times: The United States, 1900–1925*). Scribner's, 1933.
This segment of Sullivan's six-volume work deals with the World War I home front. It is not a scholarly book but a collection of newspaper clippings on every subject from the majestic to the microscopic, and it succeeds brilliantly in evoking the feel of everyday reality half a century ago.

Murray, Robert K. *Red Scare: A Study in National Hysteria, 1919–1920.* University of Minnesota, 1955.
The author has written a disturbing—and good—account of the rise of reaction in post-armistice 1919. He shows how labor's prewar and wartime gains were threatened by an indiscriminate hostility to real and fancied radicalism.

Leuchtenburg, William E. *The Perils of Prosperity, 1914–1932.* University of Chicago, 1958.
Unquestionably the best brief survey of the period it covers, this volume pays requisite attention to the well-known social aspects of the twenties—flaming youth and jazz. It also shows a keen awareness of the subtle economic strains that made Gompers' last years of AFL leadership difficult.

McKay, Kenneth C. *The Progressive Movement of 1924.* Columbia, 1947.
Though far from a prizewinner stylistically, this is a thorough study of the attempt to ally farmers, factory workers, and others for whom "normalcy" was a season of distress.

*The following studies of particular episodes in labor history provide valuable background.*

Bruce, Robert V. *1877: Year of Violence.* Bobbs-Merrill, 1959.
The author provides an exciting tale of the great railroad strikes of 1877, the year the Cigar Makers also had a major strike and the year that Gompers himself became fully committed to the labor movement.

David, Henry. *History of the Haymarket Affair.* Farrar & Rinehart, 1936.
This book is interesting primarily because of the opening chapters, which discuss anarchism in the United States.

McMurry, Donald Le Crone. *The Great Burlington Strike of 1888: A Case History in Labor Relations.* Harvard, 1956.
As the subtitle indicates, this is an investigation undertaken to learn precisely how a labor conflict could develop between a powerful railroad line and a conservative set of railroad brotherhoods. It presents a good illustration of what happens when one digs beneath the slogans of labor conflict and probes the complicated realities.

Gutman, Herbert G. "The Worker's Search for Power: Labor in the Gilded Age" in H. Wayne Morgan, ed., *The Gilded Age: A Reappraisal.* Syracuse, 1963.
In this penetrating essay, Mr. Gutman's contention is that the entire picture of the "struggle" between "labor" and "capital" from 1870 to 1890 is distorted by the customary emphasis on major strikes in urban areas. In smaller and newer industries and towns, the conflict was less dramatic, with fewer heroes and villains.

Lindsey, Almont. *Pullman Strike: The Story of a Unique Experiment and of a Great Labor Upheaval.* University of Chicago, 1942.
The "unique experiment" of the subtitle was the model company town—which failed. As this report shows, a boss-provided utopia was too regimented and too costly to suit railroad carmakers, whose protest grew into a national rail tie-up in which Gompers felt he had to avoid entanglement.

# INDEX

*(\* indicates an illustration; pages 7-88 are in the Biography; pages 89-120 are in the Picture Portfolio; pages 121-229 are in His Own Words.)*

Abbott, Lyman, 186
Actors' Equity Association, *86, 189, 190
Adamson Railway Labor Act, 74
Addams, Jane, *197
　activities of, 194, 195, 197
　ceremonies honoring, 207
Adler, Felix, *185, 186
AFL. See American Federation of Labor
Alien Contract Acts, 178
Amalgamated Association of Iron and Steel Workers, 40, 50
Amalgamated Clothing Workers of America, 63
American Federation of Labor (AFL)
　becomes acceptable to government and business, 57, 75
　and depression of 1893, 51
　earliest years of, 46–50, 148–152, 170–173
　finances of, 44, 47
　first office of, 45, 150
　formation of, 24, 43, 148
　growth of, 44, 46–48, 58, 62, 87, 151, 170–173
　and Hand-in-Hand emblem, 17
　and immigration, 63–64
　intercedes for Mooney, 88
　jurisdictional disputes in, 46
　lends money to needy unions, 172–173
　and Los Angeles *Times* bombing, 68, 215–217
　minutes of executive council meeting, *149
　motto of, 17, *89
　moves office to Indianapolis, 55–56, 181
　and Negro workers, 174–176
　organization and structure of, 43–44, 117, 148, 151
　and politics, 52, 55, 56, 70–74
　presents grievances to Theodore Roosevelt, 70
　and Prohibition, 223
　and racial discrimination, 87
　and racketeering, 86–87
　refuses to join International Federation of Trade Unions, 83
　seal of, *89, 149
　and skilled workers, 66, 87
　strikes, 48, 50
　suffers from fear of radical influence, 85
　supports Wilson in 1916, 74
　transfers headquarters to Washington, D.C., 57, 182
　and unskilled workers, 63–64

Washington headquarters dedicated by Wilson, 57–58, *167
*American Federationist*, *47, 48, 52, 183
　boycott list, 68, 211
　editorials in, 183, 208–209
American Labor Union, 59
　represented in IWW, 64
"American Labor's Position in Peace or in War," 77
American Railway Union, 53
　supports Bryan for president, 56
　*See also* Eugene Debs
anarchists and anarchism, 28, 106, 154, 155
　in Haymarket meeting, 42, 154
Ancient Order of Foresters medal, *114, 115
　pawned by Gompers, 141, 151
Anthony, Susan B., 194
*Arbeiter Zeitung*, 155
Arion Base Ball and Social Club, 127–128
Arthur, Chester A., 163, *164

Baker, Ray Stannard
　describes Gompers in London, 83
Barrymore, Ethel, *189
　caricature by Caruso, *189
　and Gompers, 188–189
　joins actors' strike, 189
Bauer, Joseph, 209
Beecher, Henry Ward, 138, 142
"Benefit Concert" cartoon, *106–*107
Berkman, Alexander, 50
"Between Rounds," *113
Bill of Grievances, 70–71
blast-furnace strike, 202–203
Bloete, Fred, 28
Borland Amendment, 168
boycotts, 68–69, 71, 210–211
Brewery Workers' Union, 215
　and McBride, 180
British Trades Union Congress, 32, 144, 227
　awards medal to Gompers, 115
　exchanges delegates with AFL, 201
Brooklyn, 30
Brooklyn *Eagle* cartoon of Gompers, *76
Brotherhood of Carpenters and Joiners, 42, 48, 156
Brotherhood of Locomotive Firemen, 53
Bryan, William Jennings, 56
　gains Gompers' vote, 162
　and Gompers (cartoon), *162
　presidential candidacy of 1908, 27, 72–73
Buck's Stove & Range case, 68–70, 211–215

Burns, John, *201
Butler, Benjamin, cartoon of, *16
　gets Gompers' vote, 162

Cahan, Abraham, *187
Cannon, Joseph G., *73, 88
　Speaker of the House, 71, 218
Carnegie, Andrew, *160
　and the Homestead strike, 49, 160, 205
　sells steel company to J. P. Morgan, 210
Carpenters and Joiners. See Brotherhood of Carpenters and Joiners
Caruso, Enrico, 111, 188, 189
　caricature of Ethel Barrymore by, *189
　as Don José, *188
　sketch of Gompers, *110, 189
Castle Garden, New York, 92, *93, 98
Catt, Carrie Chapman, 194, *195
Chicago rail strikes, *54–55
child labor, 74, *100, *101, 102, *103, *144
　Gompers on, 195–197
Chinese immigration, 94
　and employment, 109
　riots and violence against, *145
　union pressure against, 145
Chinese Exclusion Act, 145
cigar industry
　Board of Health report on, 133
　Chinese workers in, 176
　factory conditions in, 18, *19, 133–134
　and mechanization, *19, 21–22, 28
　reading aloud in, *20, 134, 136
　strikes, 18–19, 137–141
　tenement conditions in, 21, 35, 36, *100, *101, 133, 143, *144
Cigar Makers' International Union, 18, 21, 23, 29
　benefits to members, 33
　button of, *114, 115
　convention of 1877, 32
　dissident members secede from, 37
　and eight-hour day, 33–34
　introduces union label, 42, 109
　journals of, 48
　Local 15, 28
　Local 144, 28, 29–30, 36–37, 134, 136, 142
　payments to AFL, 47
　political technique of, 35
　and strikes, 29, 33, 138–141
　and tenement cigars, 35–36,

*100, 102, 142–143
　and wage breakthrough, 104–105
Cigar Makers' Progressive Union, 37, 42, 43
cigar mold, 21–22, 28, 100, *101
CIO. See Committee for Industrial Organization
*City of London*, *92
Civil War, 96, 154
　draft riots, 13, *14
Clark, Champ, 72, *218
　career of, 218
Clayton Anti-Trust Act, 74, 85, 212, 218, 219
Clayton, Henry De L., 219
Cleveland, Grover, 36, 163, *165
　advised by Olney, 214
　orders federal troops into rail strike, 54
　presented tenement bill by Theodore Roosevelt, *35
Clothing Workers of America, Amalgamated, 63
coal strikes, 60, 85, 210
Coeur d'Alene miners' strike, 50
collective bargaining, 108
Colorado miners' strike, tent colony in, *66, *67
Committee for Industrial Organization (CIO), 117, 225
Committee on National Defense, 77
Communist Manifesto, 135
Congress of Industrial Organizations (CIO). See Committee for Industrial Organization
"Construction Work in New York," *96–*97
Coolidge, Calvin, 86, *169
　and Gompers, 169–170
Cooper, Peter, 15, 16, *128
　cartoon of, *16
　gets vote of Gompers, 162
Cooper Union, 15, 16, 98, 128
Cox, James B., 162
Crosby, Ernest O., 186
Crystal Palace, London, 90, *91

Dana, Charles, 15, *136
　office cat of, 201
Danbury Hatters' case, 71
Darrow, Clarence, 215–216
Davenport, Homer, 202, 203
　cartoons of Mark Hanna, *202, *203
Davis, John W., 86
Debs, Eugene Victor, *27, 53, *88, 171
　and the American Railway Union (ARU), 53–55
　cartoon of, *53
　and Chicago strike, 54–55

and Gompers, 55, 88
and the IWW, 65
jailed, 55, 81
on labor and Gompers, 26,
  60, 65, 88
on National Civic Federa-
  tion, 60
as orator, 155
presidential candidate, 75
as Socialist leader, 55
De Leon, Daniel, 26–27, 52
Democratic party, 56, 71–73,
  75, 86, 133, 162, 167, 177
Department of Labor, 74, 166
depression, economic
  1873–1879, 20, 22, 136–137,
    *140
  1893, *51, 52, 205
  1920–1921, 84–85
  1930's, 117
Dickinson, Dr. Frances, 194
Doré, Gustave
  engravings of London by,
    *11, *90, *91
draft riots, Civil War, *14
Du Bois, W. E. B., *174
Ducey, Fr. Thomas J., 186
Duncan, James A., 79

Eakins, Thomas, 113
Easley, Ralph M., 204
Edmonston, G., 149
eight-hour workday, 33–34
  for carpenters, 48, 156
  FTLU strike for, 41
  Gompers works for, 22,
    159–160, 163
  made law by Congress, 156
  for railroads, 74
Eighteenth Amendment, 85,
  223
emigrant ships, *92
Ethical Culture Society, 10,
  185
Evarts, William M., 36, *143
Evergood, Philip, 117

Fall, Albert B., 168
Federation of Organized
    Trades and Labor Unions
    (FTLU)
  congresses of, 40, 144–147
  merges with AFL, 43, 228
  minutes of, 114, *115
  strikes for eight-hour day,
    41
Five Points section of East
  Side New York, 98, *99,
  142
Foster, William Z., 63
Frank Leslie's Illustrated
  Weekly, 177
free silver, 56, 210
freedom, Heine quotation on,
  157
freedom of speech
  Gompers' belief in, 69,
    212–215
  injunctions against, 210–
    215
Frey, John P., *221
  accompanies Gompers on
    European mission, 221

on Gompers, 27, 63, 83
on unions and socialism, 27
Frick, Henry Clay, 49, *205
  and the Homestead strike,
    49, 205
FTLU. See Federation of
    Organized Trades and
    Labor Unions
Furuseth, Andrew, *203
  and Gompers, 77, 203
  Gompers' evaluation of, 204

Garfield, James A., 163, *164
garment workers, 62, 63, *102,
  *103, *156, 172
  strike of, 187
Gary, Elbert Henry, *213
Gary, Judge Joseph, 154
George, Henry, *32, *134
  author of Progress and
    Poverty, 21, 134
  in "Benefit Concert" car-
    toon, 106, *107
  and the single tax on land,
    32, 106, 134
  and the Social Reform Club,
    185
Gompersism, 31
Gompers, Abe (son of labor
  leader), 198, 199
Gompers, Alexander (brother
  of labor leader), 122, 150
Gompers, Alexander (son of
  labor leader), 198, 199
  birth of, 141
  in family portrait, *30
Gompers, Bella (sister of
  labor leader), 199
Gompers, Gertrude (second
  wife of labor leader), 17,
  84, *228
  with Gompers, *85
Gompers, Henry (brother of
  labor leader), 122
Gompers, Henry (son of labor
  leader), 198, 199
  in family portrait, *30
  makes cornerstone of AFL
    building, 57
  office boy for AFL, 48, 150
Gompers, Jack (brother of
  labor leader), 122
Gompers, Lewis (brother of
  labor leader), 122
Gompers, May (granddaugh-
  ter of labor leader), 196
Gompers, Rose (daughter of
  labor leader), 150, 199
Gompers, Sadie (daughter of
  labor leader), 199
  death of, 84, 191
  in family portraits, *30,
    *190
  musical career of, 190–191
Gompers, Samuel (grand-
  father of labor leader),
  9–10, 122, 125
Gompers, Samuel (labor
  leader)
  advises Theodore Roosevelt
    on Puerto Rico, 166
  on Advisory Commission
    to 1919 disarmament con-
    ference, 169

and AFL, 46–50, 55–57, 70,
  87, 115, 148–156, 170–173,
  180–181, 200, 226
and Amalgamated Clothing
  Workers, 63
American Legion medal of,
  *114, 115
on the American Railway
  Union, 53
and amnesty for radicals,
  88
and anarchism, 28, 154
apprenticeship of, 11
and Arthur, 163, 164
and attempted assassina-
  tion, 42
attends Cooper Union,
  15–16, 128
attends Jewish Free School,
  10, 124
attends night school, 15–
  16, 124, 128
in audience with George V,
  82
autobiography of, 84, 122;
  excerpts from, 122–126,
  127–152, 153–155, 160–
  174, 176–177, 178–180,
  181–182, 185–191, 193–
  205, 207–208, 210, 211–
  214, 215, 216–219, 221–
  223, 225
awards received by, *114,
  115
becomes involved in labor
  movement, 18–22, 26, 28–
  32, 127, 132–133, 134–136
in "Benefit Concert" car-
  toon, 106, *107
biographies of, 10, 24, 27,
  38, 57, 63, 72, 80
birth of, 9, 122
blacklisted after cigar
  strike, 29, 140–141
on Bolshevism, 222
and boxing, 188, 189
and Bryan, 27, 72–73, *162,
  210
and John Burns, 201
bust of, by Roslyn, *89,
  *227
bust of, by Wheeler, 114,
  *115
buys fiddle, 17, 130
campaigns to admit cigar
  workers to union without
  restriction, 22
campaigns for AFL presi-
  dency in 1895, 180–181
campaigns for McGilli-
  cuddy, 38
and Cannon, Speaker of
  the House, 71–73, 88
on capitalism, 56
cartoons of, *76, *107, *112,
  *162, *218, *225
Caruso's sketch of, *110
character of, 9, 16–17, 31,
  37, 39, 44, 61–63, 69, 78,
  83, 87–88, 111–113, 153–
  154, 180–181, 200, 204,
  210–211
and Chicago rail strike, 55
on child labor, 195–197
childhood of, 9–10, 122–126

children and married life
  of, 16, 17, 29, *30, 44, 45,
  57, 84, 129–130, 141, 150,
  *190, 196, 197–200
and the Chinese, 176–177
cigar brand named for, 109
and the Cigar Makers'
  Union, 18–19, 21–22, 28–
  30, 32–35, 44, 47, 102–103,
  109, 127, 133–134, 136,
  142–143
Cigar Makers' Union but-
  ton of, *114, 115
cigarmaker in New York,
  14, 18, 127, 133–146, 178
on Champ Clark, 218
on Cleveland, 165
and the Coeur d'Alene
  strike, 50
commemorative stamp of,
  *229
on compulsory arbitration,
  180–183
and contempt of court,
  69–70, 212
and Coolidge, 169
and Cooper, 128
Cornell lectures of, 186–187
criticisms of, 26–27, 38–39,
  60, 62, 65, 82–83
and Cuba, 136, 204
and Cuban cigarmakers, 200
and Dana, 200–201
death and burial of, 87, *229
debates Hillquit on socialism, 66–67
and Debs, 55, 88, 155
at dedication of AFL building, 58, *167
denounced by radicals, 62
description of, 38, 39, 58,
  73, 83, 170
early associates of, 26, 28,
  32, 132–133, 135
early unions described by,
  131–133
on economics, 186
as editor, 48
education of, 10–11, 15–16,
  73, 124, 128, 184
on education, 184–186
and the eight-hour day, 22,
  159–160, 163
Elks pin of, *114, 115
emigrates to America,
  12–13, 127
endorses Bryan in 1908, 27,
  72–73
endorses La Follette, 72, 86
estimate of, by:
  Debs, 26
  De Leon, 26–27, 52
  European labor leaders,
    82–83
  Foster, 63
  Frey, 27, 63, 83
  Haywood, 65
and Ethical Culture move-
  ment, 10, 185
European missions of, 76,
  82–83, 207–208, 221–222,
  227
family background, 9–10,
  125–126
first dress suit, 203–204

first vice-president of Cigar
Makers, 44
forces doctor to wife's bedside, 29, 140
and Foresters medal, *114,
141, 151
and free silver, 210
and freedom of speech, 69,
115, 211–215
friendship with actors and
singers, 187–189
and FTLU, 9–10, 40, 43–44,
125–126, 143, 148
funeral honors for, *229
and Furuseth, 203, 204
on Garfield, 163, 164
and George, 134
and Grant, 20, 162–163
and Greeley, 162
and Haig, 221–222
handwriting of, *121, *149,
*151, *171, *196, *199,
*204, *211, *212, *220,
*224
and Harding, 168–169
and Hayes, Max, 27
and Hayes, Rutherford, 163
and Haymarket executions,
153–155
health of, 44, 57, 83, 84, 182,
198, 199, 220, 225
and Homestead strike, 50
home life of labor leader,
61, 197, 199
and immigration, 63–64, 93,
94, 176–180
injured in accidents, 84
at Inter-Allied Labor Conference, 207
and international organized
labor, 76, 189, 207
on IWW, 66
jailed for "disorderly conduct," 141–142
Jewish background of, 9–10,
125–126
joins social and fraternal
organizations, 16, 114,
115, 127–128, 131, 185–186
and Knights of Labor, 25, 39
language study by, 124, 125,
135–136
last words of, 87
Liberty Loan award of,
*114, 115
lobbies to outlaw tenement
work, 35–36, 103
loses presidency of AFL,
55–56
love for America, 13, 17
love of theater and music,
12, 17, 111, 113, 130, 187–
191
and McKinley, 164, 165
and McNamara brothers,
68, 215–217
marriage to Gertrude
Neuscheler, 84, 85, 228
marriage to Sophia Julian,
16, 45, 57, 84, 128–130
Masonic emblems of, *114,
115
medal from National Institute of Social Sciences,
*114, 115

mementos of, *89, *114,
*115
mentors of, 26, 28, 32, 132–
133, 134–136
method of building AFL,
171–173, 200
and Mexican trade-union
movement, 76
militarism of, 77–79,
220–221
at mine strike of 1897, *105
and Morgan, 210
and National Civic Federation, 27, 59–60, 67, 204
negotiates with Mexico, 76
and Negro workers, 173–176
notice of speaking appearance, *170
Odd Fellows badge of, *114,
115
for Oklahoma statehood, 17
on Olney, 214
opposes U.S. overseas
empire, 76
organizational ability of,
209
as organizer for United
Garment Workers, 173–
174
organizes national unions,
172
pacifism of, 76, 220, 224
and Pan-American Federa-
tion of Labor, 83, 87
on panic of 1907, 211
and peace conference at
Paris, 83, 227
and the Pinkerton agency,
154
at Pittsburgh labor con-
gress of 1881, 40, 144–145
place cards for royal luncheons, *224
pleasures of, 12, 17, 57, 58,
111, 113, 129–130, 146,
147, 187–191
and politics, 56, 72, 161–162,
209–210
portrayals of, *7, *71, *79,
*82, *85, *89, *99, *105,
*107, *109, *112, *115,
*127, *162, *167, *170,
*211, *218, *225, *227
portraits with family, *30,
*190
postcard to granddaughter,
*196
poverty of, 14, 44, 45, 61,
140, 149, 150, 152
and Powderly, 38, 39
president of AFL, 44, 46–49,
56, 57, 70, 148, 149–156,
170–173, 225
president of 1883 labor congress, 146
president of FTLU, 40
president of legislative
committee at FTLU con-
gress of 1882, 146
president of Local 144, 29–
30, 136
and Presidents of the
United States, 162–170
prevents swindle of British
labor leader, 201

and prison labor, 114, 115
and Prohibition, 85, 223
reads to fellow cigarmak-
ers, 20, 134, 136
and religion, 10, 17, 126,
185, 194
rides bicycle, *58, 134
in Rome, 83
and Roosevelt (Theodore),
35–36, 61, 103, 165–166
Sarg cartoons of, *112, 113
and second wife. See Gom-
pers, Gertrude
and Sherman Anti-Trust
Act, 212, 217
and skullcap, 10, *127
sociability of, 16, 17, 127–
128, 130–131, 200
and socialism, 26–27, 60, 62,
66–67, 205–208
and Spanish-American War,
76
as speaker and orator, 63,
83, 155, 203–204
speeches of, 78, 83, 87, 153,
156–160, 174–175, 182–183,
184, 203, 214–215, 220–
221, 226–229
and sports, *58, *71, 134
as statesman, 24, 61, 76–77,
82–83, 221–222, 224
and Steffens, 206–208
and Strasser, 28, 31, 34, 35,
37, 47, 133
and streetcar workers, 172
and strikes, 33, 48, 50, 152,
156, 183
and suffragettes, 193, 194
summary of achievements,
88, 223–225
and Taft, 166
Talmudic studies, 10, 125
telegram on Wilson's re-
election, 74
and tenement cigarmaking,
34–35, 100–102, 142–143
and Thorne, Florence, 80
at Tompkins Square meet-
ing, 22
and trade unionism, 145, 153,
157–159, 185
on trusts, 217
union dues book of, *100
union policies of, 31–32
and union racketeers, 86–87
and United Cigarmakers,
133
at the war front, *79, *82
wills one dollar to second
wife, 228
and President Wilson, 73,
74, 82, 167, 227
and womanhood, 57, 191–195
and Woodhull, Victoria, 193
and World War I activities,
61, 76–83
World War I medallions of,
*114, 115
Gompers, Samuel J. (son of
labor leader), 199
birth and childhood, 130, 198
in family portrait, *30
leaves school for work, 45,
198
Gompers, Sara (mother of

labor leader), 10, *12
later years of, 199
Gompers, Solomon (father of
labor leader), 9–10, *12,
14, 122
apprentices son Samuel, 11
emigrates to America, 12–13
later years of, 199
and Negro friend, 12–13
Gompers, Sophia (first wife of
labor leader), 16, *70,
128–130
death, 84
devotion to husband, 57, 70,
140
early hardships, 29, 45, 140–
141, 150–151, 198
in family portraits, *30,
*190
Gompers Cigars, *109
Grant, U. S., *163
and Dana, 136
and Gompers, 20, 162–163
Greeley, Horace, 162
Green, William, *226
Greenback party, 16, 38, 128
Guard, Rosa Lee, 69
guilds, medieval, 109
"Gun Foundry, The," *96–*97
Guy Fawkes Day, *123

Haig, Sir Douglas, 221, *222
Hair Spinners' Union, 212
Hand-in-Hand Society, 17
Hanna, Mark, 60, 165
and blast-furnace strike,
202–203
Harding, Warren G., 85, *168
and Gompers, 168–169
Harris, George, 149
Harvey, Rowland H., 27, 57
Hayes, Max, 27, 65
nominated president of
AFL, 27
Hayes, Rutherford, 104, 143,
*163
Haymarket riot, 41–42, 106,
153–155
execution, *41, 153, 155
Haywood, William "Big Bill"
description of, 64, *182
on Gompers, 64–66
states IWW aims, 65
Hearst, William R., 202
Hebrew trade unions. See
United Hebrew Trades
Heine, Heinrich, quotation
from, on freedom, 157
Henderson, Arthur, *207
Hewitt, Abram S., 103, 106
Hillquit, Morris, *206
career of, 206
debates Gompers on social-
ism, 66–67
Hine, Lewis, photographs of
industry, *102, *103
Holder, Arthur, 219
Holmes, David, British labor
leader, 201
Holt, Hamilton, *184, 186
Homer, Winslow, painting of
mill workers by, 96, *97
Homestead steel strike, *49–
50, 154, 205

horsecar drivers' strike of 1886, *104, 105
Haughton, A. B., engraving of life on an emigrant ship, *92
*How the Other Half Lives*, 100
Howells, William Dean, 186
Hoxie, Robert F., 80
Hull-House, 197

*Illustrated London News*, 124
immigration, 97
    Chinese, 94, 145
    conditions, 12–13, *92, *93, *94–*95
    German, 178
    Italian, 178, 180
    Jewish, 178–179, 187
    literacy tests and quotas, 94
    of unskilled workers, *178
immigration acts, 74, 167–168, 178
*Independent, The*, 184
Indianapolis, 57, 181–182
industrial revolution. *See* technological revolution
industrial unionism, 27, 117, 146, 225
Industrial Workers of the World (IWW), 64–65, 182
    declines after World War I, 65, 87, 182
    denounces military preparedness, 77
    formation of, 59, 64
    harassed in World War I, 81
    marching in 1913, *65
Ingersoll, Robert G., 189
    in cartoon, 106, *107
injunctions, 68–69, 211–215, 218
Inter-Allied Labor Conference, 207
International Federation of Trade Unions, 76, 83
International Labor Commission, 195
International Labor Organization, 83
International Typographical Union, 39–40, 47
International Workingmen's Association (IWA), 25
Iron and Steel Workers, Amalgamated Association of, 40, 50
IWW. *See* Industrial Workers of the World

Jefferson's test of Americanism, 126
Jenks, Jeremiah, 186–187
*Jewish Daily Forward*, 187
Johnson, Andrew, 159
*Journal of the Knights of Labor*, 48
Julian, Sophia. *See* Gompers, Sophia

Keppler, Joseph, *177
    cartoon of priest blessing strikers, *177

cartoon of Uncle Sam as Noah, *94–*95
    founds *Puck*, 94, 177
Kirby, Rollin, cartoon of Prohibition by, *223
Knights of Labor, 24–25, 37–39, 146, *147
    and Cigar Makers' Progressive Union members, 37, 42, 43
    deplores strikes, 25, 39
    driven out of cigar trade, 43
    and eight-hour day, 41
    Gompers' judgment of, 25
    and the Negro, 175
    parade for labor holiday, *131
    and Populist party, 50, 51
    presented ultimatum by craft unions, 42–43
    secret circular of, *37
    supports Bryan for President, 56
Knights of Saint Crispin, 23

Labadie, Jo, 154
labor conditions in nineteenth century, 18–20, 74, 94, *96, *97, *102, *103
    *See also* cigar industry
Labor Day
    becomes holiday, 131
    parades, *120, *131
*Labor in America*, 64
Labor Party, British, 207
La Follette, Robert M., 72, 86
La Follette Seamen's Act, 74
    cartoon of, *74
Lassalle, Ferdinand, 26
Laurrell, Karl Malcolm Ferdinand
    finds job for Gompers, 41
    influence on Gompers, 26, 28, 31, 134–135
    and socialism, 135
League of Nations, 168, 195, 207
Lee, Fitzhugh, governor of Virginia, *175
Lehmann, Lotte, 188
*Leibnitz*, German emigrant ship, 93
Lennon, John, 54
Lewis, John L., *225
    career of, 225
Lexow Committee, 201
Liberty Loan award, *114, 115
Litchman, Charles, 32, *33
Littlefield, Charles, 72
Lloyd, Henry Demarest, 171
Lloyd George, David, 82
Locomotive Firemen, Brotherhood of, 53
Lodge, Henry Cabot, 166
London *Daily News*, description of Gompers in, 83
London in the nineteenth century, *11, *90–*91
    Guy Fawkes Day, *123
    life in, 9, 11–12, 90–91, 122–125
    tobacco warehouse in, *124
Los Angeles *Times*, bombing of, *68, 215

Ludlow, Colo., miners' strike, *66, *67
Lynn, Mass., shoe-factory strike, *25

McBride, John, *180
    advocates compulsory arbitration, 180, 181
    president of AFL, 55, 180
    refuses AFL presidency, 148
*McClure's Magazine*, 208
McCraith, August, 56
McDonnell, J. P., 28, 132
McDowell, Mary, 195
McGillicuddy, Daniel J., 72
McGlynn, Fr. Edward, in cartoon, *106
McGuire, Peter J., 28, *32, 128
    AFL secretary, 32, 149
    disapproves union journals, 48
    influence on Gompers, 31, 132
    president of Carpenters and Joiners, 42
McKinley, William, 56, 164, *165
    caricatured by Davenport, *203
    receives AFL delegation, 59
    and John Sherman, 217
McNamara, James B., and John J., and Los Angeles *Times* bombing, 68, 215–217
McSorley's Old Ale House, *110–*111
"man bites dog," 136
Mandel, Bernard
    biographer of Gompers, 10
    describes Gompers, 38
    on Gompers and politics, 72
    on Rosa Lee Guard, 69
Mann, Tom, British labor leader, 201
Mario, Alexander, 97
Marx, Karl, 25
Meany, George, *118
Melville, Frank, 98
metal workers, 64, 221
mine workers
    Gompers' letter to, *212
    and Green, 226
    and McBride, 180
    obtain funds from AFL, 173
    strikes of, 50, *66, *67, 105
Miners, Western Federation of, 59, 64
Mitchell, John, 59, *159
Mooney, Tom, 88
Morgan, J. P., 186, *210
    and Gary, 213
    and panic of 1907, 211
Morrison, Frank, 10
Most, Johann, 28
Mott, Lucretia, 194

Nast, Thomas, 133
    cartoons by, *16, *193
    drawing of Roosevelt and Cleveland, *35
    labor symbols of, *133

National Association for the Advancement of Colored People (NAACP), 174
National Association of Manufacturers, 67–68
National Civic Federation, 27, 59–60, 67, 159, 163, 204
National Institute of Social Sciences medal, *114, 115
National Labor Union, 23
    demise of, 24, 87
    manifesto of, 25
Negroes and the labor movement, 53, 174–176
Neuscheler, Gertrude Annesley Gleaves
    *See* Gompers, Gertrude
New York, nineteenth century, *8, 9, *13, *15, *16, *96–*97, *98, *99, *172
    cigarmaking in, 18, *19, *20, 35, 36, *100, *101, *144, 200
    draft riots in, 13, *14
    life in, 9, 14–15, 22, *23, *51, *97, *98, 100, 197–198
    parade of workmen in, *34
New York *Daily Graphic*, 140
New York *Journal*, 202
New York *Sun*, 15, 136
    office cat of, 201
Newton, Rev. Heber, in cartoon, *106
NLU. *See* National Labor Union

O'Connell, James, and National Civic Federation, 59
Oglesby, Richard J., governor of Illinois, 155
Oklahoma
    adopts Gompers' clasped-hand symbol as official emblem, 17
    Gompers advocates statehood for, 17
Olney, Richard, *214
    and Chicago rail strike, 54, 214
open-shop campaign
    in 1903, 67–68
    after World War I, 85
Opper, Frederick Burr, labor cartoon by, *106–*107
O'Sullivan, Jack, 182
Otis, Harrison Gray, 215, 216

*Padrones*, 180
Page, Walter Hines, 207–208
panic of 1907, 211
Parker, Judge Alton B., 162
Penrose, Senator Boies, 166
Perkins, George W., 80
*Picket, The*, 48
Pinkerton, Allan, *154
Pinkerton guards, *49, 154
Pittsburgh national labor congress, 40, 144–145, 226–228
Populist party, 50–51, 57
Porto Rico (old spelling)
    *See* Puerto Rico
Powderly, Terence V., 38, *146

238

in "Benefit Concert" cartoon, *106
cartoon of, *39
and Gompers, 38–39
McGuire on, 48
and Negroes, 175
and strikes, 38, 39, 41
with Virginia's governor and Negro delegate, *175
Printing-House Square, *13
prison labor, 102
Gompers' award from national committee on, *114, 115
"private eye," origin of phrase, 154
*Progress and Poverty*, 21, 134
Progressive party, 86
progressivism, era of, 75
Prohibition, 85, 223
cartoon of, *223
*Puck*, 94, 106
cartoon of Knights of Labor, *147
cartoon of priest blessing strikers, *177
Puerto Rico, 166
Pullman strike, 53, *105
becomes a wider strike, 54
and Grover Cleveland, 165

**Q**ueen Victoria Badge, *114, 115

**R**ailroad strikes
in 1877, 20, *21, *104, 137, *138
in 1894, *54–55, *105
railway unions. *See* American Railway Union; Brotherhood of Locomotive Firemen; United Brotherhood of Railway Employes
Rainsford, W. S., *186, 210
Reconstruction, end of, 32, 163
Reno brothers and the Pinkerton agency, 154
Republic Steel strike of 1937, *116–*117
Republican party, 71–73, 75, 85–86, 133, 162–163, 177
Reuther, Walter, *118
Riis, Jacob A., *185
author of *How the Other Half Lives*, 100
describes tenement cigarmaking, 144
member of Social Reform Club, 186
and Theodore Roosevelt, 185
Robins, Lucy, 10
friendship with Gompers, 88
on Gompers' home life, 45, 57
on the Hand-in-Hand Society and its symbol, 17
Roosevelt, Franklin Delano, third term of, 225
Roosevelt, Theodore, *35, *166
and Addams, Jane, 197
candidate for mayor of New York, 106
and coal strike, 60

editorial, "Murder Is Murder," 216
and Gompers, 35–36, 61, 103, 165–166
and Powderly, 38
presented Bill of Grievances by AFL, 70–71
and Progressive ticket, 75
and Rainsford, 186
and Riis, 185
and tenements, 35, 36, 100
Roslyn, Louis, bust of Gompers, *89, *227
Russell, Lillian, *113

**S**t. George's Church, 186, 210
*Samuel Gompers: American Statesman*, 10
Sarg, Tony, cartoons of Gompers, *112, 113
scabs
at Homestead and Coeur d'Alene strikes, 49–50
use of the word, 18, 37, 132
Schimkowitz, Samuel, 37
Schwab, Justus, 28
Scott, Marsden, 78
Seamen's Act, 74, 203
cartoon of, *74
"Seeking Work," *117
*Seventy Years of Life and Labor*, 84, 122. *See also* Gompers, Samuel, autobiography, excerpts from
Sexton, James, British labor leader, 201
*Shame of the Cities, The*, 208
Sherman Anti-Trust Act, 68, 217
in Danbury Hatters' case, 71
Gompers' battle against, 212, 217
Sherman, John, *217
Sherman Silver Purchase Act, 217
shoe-factory strike, Lynn, Mass., *25
Sloan, John, works by, 62, 110–111
Social Democratic Party of North America, 26
socialism and Socialists, 25–27
denounce military preparedness, 77
discredited during World War I, 82
and Gompers, 26–27, 55, 60, 66–67
Hillquit, 66–67, *206
and the IWW, 64, 65
view of World War I, 79
*See also* Debs, Eugene
Socialist Labor Party, 26
Socialist Trade and Labor Alliance, 59
Social Reform Club, 185–186
Sovereign, James R., 56
Speyer, Karl, 28
Spies, August, *155
Spitalfields, London, 9
Stanton, Elizabeth Cady, 193, *194
Starr, Ellen, 197

steel strikes, *49, 50, 60, 85, *116–*117, 202–203, 213
Steffens, Lincoln, *208
clashes with Gompers, 206–207
Stephens, Uriah, 24, 32, *33
Stowe, Harriet Beecher, 193
Strasser, Adolph, *33
and Gompers, 28, 31, 34, 35, 37, 133
and railroad strike of 1877, 138
and socialism, 32
streetcar workers' union, 172
strikebreakers. *See* scabs
strikes, 18–19
Actors' Equity, *86
arbitration of, 118, *119
balloting for, 118, *119
of blast-furnace workers, 202–203
Boston police, 169
British dock strike, 201
Buck's Stove & Range Company, 68, 70
Carpenters and Joiners, 48
cartoon of, *177
in cigar industry, 18–19, 29, 137–140
coal, 60, 85, 210
of Colorado miners, *66, *67
deplored by National Labor Union and Knights of Labor, 25
federal troops used in, 138, 165
in garment industry, 187
Homestead, *49–50
of horsecar drivers, *104, 105
of miners at Coeur d'Alene, 50
present-day importance of, 120
Pullman, 53–54
railroad, in 1877, 20, *21, *104, 137, *138
railroad, in 1894, *54–55
Republic Steel, *116–*117
shoe factory, *25
steel, *49–50, 60, 85, *117, 202–203, 213
textile, *191
violence in Chicago, *43
of West Virginia miners, 105
wildcat, 33
women's, *191
suffragettes, *29, *192, *193, *194, *195
*See also* woman suffrage
sweatshops, *52, *102
*See also* cigar industry
Swinton, John, 28, 38, 48
Sylvis, William H., 23–25

**T**aft, William H., 72, 73, *166
Teapot Dome scandal, 168
technological revolution, 20–22, 90–91, 96–97, 120
in cigar industry, *19, 21–22
in London, 90–91
tenement workshop legislation federal, 103

state, 34–36, 103, 143
"Ten Philosophers, The," 28
Terry, Ellen, *110, 111
textile mills
child labor in, 102, *103
strike of women in, 191
Thorne, Florence
assists with Gompers' autobiography, 223
author of book on Gompers, 10
on Gompers and human relations, 63
on Gompers and socialism, 26
on Gompers as statesman, 24
meets and becomes assistant to Gompers, 80
on National Civic Federation, 60
Tillett, Ben, British labor leader, *58, 201
Tobin, Daniel J., 78
Tombs, the, 141, 142
Tompkins Square meeting, 22, *23
trade unionism, 31, 66, 109, 132, 144–145, 153, 182, 193, 226
Train, George Francis, 28
Triangle Waist Company fire, cartoon on, *62
Tweed, William M. ("Boss"), 15, 133
Typographical Union. *See* International Typographical Union

**U**MW. *See* United Mine Workers
*Union Advocate*, 48, *89
union-busting drives, 67–68
union label, 32, *108, 109
battle of the, 42
union membership
benefits and fees, 33
card, *108
Union Square workmen's parade, *34
unions in America, early history of, 23
United Brotherhood of Railway Employes, 64
United Cigarmakers, 133
United Garment Workers, 62
obtains funds from AFL, 172
United Hebrew Trades, 63, 126, 178–179
United Metal Workers, 64
United Mine Workers, 105
Gompers' letter to, 212
and Green, 226
and McBride, 180
obtains funds from AFL, 173
United States Steel Corporation, 210
United Workers of America, 26

**V**an Cleave, James, 68
Versailles Treaty, 83
Victoria, Queen, 90–91

Wages, 173
  minimum for women, 192–193
  in nineteenth century, 20–21
War Committee on Labor, 80
Washington, Booker T., 174
Washington, D.C., 57–58, 182, 190–191, 199, 217
Washington Disarmament Conference, 169
*Wealth Against Commonwealth,* 171
Weaver, James B., 162
Weber, Max, painting by, *117
Weir, John Ferguson, painting by, *96–*97
West Virginia miners' strike of 1897, 105

Western Federation of Miners, 59, 64
Western Labor Union, 59
Wheeler, Kathleen, bust of Gompers by, 114, *115
White, Henry, 72
Williams, Senator John, 81
Wilson, Francis, 189, 190
Wilson, William B., 74
  at AFL headquarters dedication, *167
Wilson, Woodrow
  and Clayton Anti-Trust Act, 219
  dedicates AFL building, 57, *167
  and Department of Labor, 74
  and labor, 73–74, 79, 160

and Gompers, 73, 76, 81, 82, 162, *167
and Henderson, 207
and immigration acts, 74, 167
refuses to pardon radicals, 88
speaks at AFL convention, 79, 81–82
Wobblies. *See* Industrial Workers of the World
woman suffrage, 29, 192–195
Woman's International League for Peace and Freedom, 197
Woman's Peace Party, 195
women in industry, *77
  strike of, 191
  wages and hours of, 192–193

Women's Trade Union League, 194–195
Woodhull, Victoria, 193
  acquainted with Gompers, 28
  attempting to vote, *29
  caricatured by Nast, *193
  speaking to House committee, *192
World War I
  labor in, 78–83
  posters, *81
  women's part in, *77
Wright, Judge Daniel T., 69

*Yarmulke,* 63, *127

*Ziegfeld Follies girls,* *58–*59

# PICTURE CREDITS